GROUP WORK

The new edition of *Group Work* adds a focus on diversity and the use of self in group work, an area too often neglected in professional training but essential to meeting current competence standards set by the Council on Social Work Education. As in previous editions, students and professors will find thoughtful analyses of complicated value dilemmas and specific techniques for use in a diverse range of settings, including confrontations and situations where humor is appropriate. Complete with more games and exercises, an updated discussion of values and ethics, and an expanded skills section, *Group Work* also contains excerpts and discussions of case studies that can be applied to students' own experiences and will serve as a valuable reference for years to come.

Sondra Brandler, DSW, associate professor and former director of the BASW program at the College of Staten Island, City University of New York. Formerly executive director of the Jay Senior Citizens Center, she is the author of various articles on aging, pedagogy, and social work with groups and has worked in many settings, primarily in the field of aging.

Camille P. Roman, LCSW, is in private practice in New York City and is a clinical consultant to Calvary Hospital and Hospice in New York City. For many years she was an adjunct associate professor at the Hunter College School of Social Work of the City University of New York and has also worked as clinical supervisor and director of training at the South Beach Psychiatric Center, Bensonhurst Clinic.

GROUP WORK

Skills and Strategies for Effective Interventions

3rd Edition

Sondra Brandler and Camille P. Roman

 Routledge
Taylor & Francis Group

NEW YORK AND LONDON

Third edition published 2016
by Routledge
711 Third Avenue, New York, NY 10017

and by Routledge
27 Church Road, Hove, East Sussex, BN3 2FA

Routledge is an imprint of the Taylor & Francis Group, an informa business

First edition published by Haworth Press 1991

Second edition published by Routledge 1999

Library of Congress Cataloging-in-Publication Data
    Brandler, Sondra.
    Group work: skills and strategies for effective interventions/by
    Sondra Brandler and Camille P. Roman.—3rd Edition.
        pages cm
    Includes bibliographical references and index.
    1. Social group work. I. Roman, Camille P. II. Title.
    HV45.B69 2015
    361.4—dc23
    2014049092

ISBN: 978-1-138-79057-5 (hbk)
ISBN: 978-1-138-79058-2 (pbk)
ISBN: 978-1-315-76411-5 (ebk)

Typeset in Classic Garamond and Myriad
by Florence Production Ltd, Stoodleigh, Devon, UK

Printed and bound in the United States of America by Publishers Graphics,
LLC on sustainably sourced paper.

None of our parents is alive today to see this edition of our book come to fruition, but in a strange way, each has contributed to this text by instilling in us sensitivity to others, the capacity for joy and humor, tenderness and appreciation of simplicity, strength and courage to confront challenges and pain, and the ability to listen compassionately. These qualities, we believe, are essential in helping others to reach their potential, and we are grateful for their examples:

Joe (Noito) and Josephine
Ralph and Bernice

CONTENTS

PREFACE

Our group work text is now in its third edition but our basic premises and format remain the same as in earlier editions, reflecting a philosophical point of view that demands an eclectic approach to groups, borrowing heavily from various models, and fully within social group work tradition. We know that the group is a powerful instrument, that group members have the capacity to help each other, and that a worker, to be effective, must respect difference and individuality while reinforcing shared concerns and common bonds. In general, as with both of our previous editions, the importance of the creative use and exploration of self is central to the text.

In our third edition, we have focused our attention more specifically on understanding how diversity among the populations we serve has an impact on the process of achieving group goals. To this end, we have included an entirely new chapter in this edition solely dealing with diversity and the use of self, recognizing the special challenges to the worker in serving groups in which the members are diverse. We have also introduced new vignettes and analyses in several chapters of the text which address emerging populations dealing particularly with oppression. Throughout the book, we have focused on the questions and comments raised by students in the course of our teaching and have tried to discuss these matters by including whatever they expressed interest in or found helpful in the earlier editions in an expanded form in this edition. As a result of the students' and our colleagues' feedback over the years, we have also expanded sections in our skills and programming glossary. Additionally, we have updated our references with the recognition that older and classical entries may have continuing value to the current understandings of today's students and with the awareness that more recent materials enrich and inform our knowledge base.

Considerable controversy still exists in the field as to the distinction between therapy groups and traditional group work. Without getting into an elaborate discussion of these issues, we would like to share our thinking about them once more. Whether a group has gathered to provide tenant rights or to work on resolving feelings after a loss, the worker needs to be actively and skillfully involved to assure that members work cooperatively and effectively toward meeting their goals. As we continue to view it, every group, regardless of purpose and content, has therapeutic value and demands clinical skills. We have tried to present a range of experiences in this text that both touch on a variety of settings and populations and, despite their differences, address some very similar issues in improving communication and in facilitating change.

Once again, we would like to thank the many individuals who contributed to this book. In a general way, we owe our greatest thanks to our colleagues, clients, and students, whose struggles in working in groups resulted in our learning and our ability, in turn, to teach others. Workers risked sharing their most intimate and often difficult processes to allow us to share these with you, the reader. We offer an array of real-life process vignettes that, although abbreviated or edited, appear essentially as they occurred. Nothing has been fabricated. Of course, all identities have been disguised to preserve confidentiality.

Much appreciation goes to those whose records are included here (listed alphabetically): Anne Abbott, Dwayne Britton, Mark Bronnenberg, James Cacopardo, Lin Campbell, Lizette Corman, Tina Del Purgatorio, Barbara Fanning, Joseph Garrambone, Michael Gast, Winston George, Susan Goodman, Joan Granucci-Lesser, Ann Lemerise, Jacqueline Levine, Kevin Mahony, Carol Manning, Jun Matsuyoshi, Erik Mercer, Lynn Polasky, Karen Remey, Mort Scharfman, Andrew Schoenfeld, Barbara Segreto, Jody Shatkin, Scott Smith, Naomi Soulet, Rebecca Steinfeld, Bruce Sussman, Dorothy Van De Stouwe, and Julie Walsh. We are fortunate to have many others who contributed material that, though not included, enriched our thinking; we thank them as well.

We continue to be grateful for the support and encouragement of our colleagues. Our special thanks to Dr. George Getzel and Dr. Robert Salmon, both formerly at The Hunter College School of Social Work, who, throughout our professional lives, have made themselves available for consultation and provided friendship, guidance, and laughter. We miss the company and the exchange of ideas provided to us by Dr. Roselle Kurland, whose untimely death cut short a prominent career of important contributions to our profession. Thanks also to Dr. Lacey Sloan of the College of Staten Island who encouraged the pursuit of a third edition of this book to meet the needs of both undergraduate and future MSW students.

No endeavor like this could be accomplished without the consistent and loving support of our friends and families. The dedication of our book is to our parents, for it is their spirit which has motivated our choice of profession and sustains us even though they are no longer with us in body. Our life partners, Jacob and James, continue to be our most ardent supporters; there are no words that adequately express our feelings of love and gratitude.

1   INTRODUCTION

Unless the person feels that he belongs somewhere, unless his life has some
meaning and direction, he would feel like a particle of dust and be
overcome by his individual insignificance. He would not be able to relate
himself to any system which would give meaning and direction to his life,
he would be filled with doubt and his doubt eventually would paralyze
his ability to act—that is to live.

Erich Fromm
Escape from Freedom (1941)

People are, by their very nature, relational beings. From one's earliest contacts
reaching out beyond mother to the extended family and to the other children
in the sandbox, one seeks the approval, the support, the feedback, the
companionship, and the communion with others. It seems ironic, therefore,
that it took practical considerations—the need for providing services
simultaneously to many, the wave of European immigrants in the early 1900s,
and the numbers of soldiers returning shell-shocked from the world wars
(Konopka, 1963)—to provide the impetus for treating people in groups.
Working with groups is a natural place from which to begin understanding
individuals.

This book views group work both as an enormously useful tool in treating
pathology and as a means of reaching people struggling with the normal life
issues of growing up, getting along with others, sharing, working, dealing with
partners, adjusting to economic and health changes, and growing older and
facing death. Settings for group practice are consequently as varied as the needs
and difficulties faced by people. Throughout this book we address concerns
of work with various populations and agencies while emphasizing that,
although themes and needs may differ, certain fundamental approaches and
principles remain the same.

Every interaction between people contains multiple levels of meaning;
communications must be understood symbolically as well as literally. We
suggest that both latent and manifest content always exist. There are thoughts
never expressed—some of which are not yet known to the person thinking
them—thoughts only alluded to and expressed in seemingly unrelated ways,

and thoughts expressed freely and openly. One responsibility of the group worker is to help unravel what is actually meant from what is said, thereby assisting the freer expression of feelings and the ability to hear others. In this sense, the group worker is a cross between a detective and a puzzle solver. We also contend that the group situation, even more so than the one-to-one, stirs transference and countertransference issues, the likes of which shall be explored later. Both ideas, that latent and manifest content always exist and that transference and countertransference are reflected in all human contacts, are central to our understanding of group process and fundamental to the way we approach the analyses that follow.

The history of group work development has been traced and discussed at length by others, and our purpose here is not to state again what has been presented elsewhere more than adequately (Konopka, 1963). Rather, we would share with you thoughts about why groups develop, what needs they serve, and why they are effective.

Humans are social animals, concerned primarily with survival and secondarily with a need to belong with others of their kind. Belonging to a group actually seems to assist in meeting the primary need of survival. Early humans provided a host of evidence to testify to the necessity for group-tribe survival. As in some other species, the individual's survival is often dependent on the group.

Isolation is a condition humans do not choose. If forced to experience isolation for long periods of time during developmental years, individuals suffer severe social and psychological impairment. Early studies of primates confirm that separation from the group results in problems in functioning. The need to survive and the need to belong are powerful drives that, because of the human's uniquely and highly developed brain, can be gratified through many complex routes. The special capacity for learning, which distinguishes humankind from other animals, is stimulated by an environment in which there is a rich group life. From the primary family group to various peer groups, the human infant learns from every facet of the complex society into which he or she is born. Societal and cultural forces influence all aspects of one's personality development and continue to do so until the moment of one's death.

Identity formation, validation of self, acceptance, support, and effective communication are necessary for human survival. How to meet those needs is learned initially through the primary group (family) and continually reinforced or changed through other significant secondary groups (peer groups). The effectiveness of meeting these needs determines the quality of an individual's life. Therefore, the group modality becomes an effective secondary societal force in developing the ability to negotiate need gratification more effectively, both within the individual and between the individual and his or her cultural environment.

What, then, is a group? Let us conceive for a moment of the group as an entity, a separate living being, a being with its own personality composed of many separate and unique parts, each part contributing to the whole. Similar to the personality of a person, it is multifaceted. It has a total personality all its own and distinct from any other; yet it is composed of various personality characteristics. It includes a dependent part, an obsessive part, an aggressive part, and others. In a group, the separate members (each a complete universe within himself or herself) are representative of the various personality characteristics that compose the total person/group.

The process of group interaction reflects the conflicting components within the complex structures that struggle against each other toward some resolution. In this process, there is, one hopes, movement to enhance growth and survival.

As the group members interact with, challenge, push, and stretch each other and their leader, they temper and modulate some parts, bolster others, create anew, and cast aside. Ultimately, they foster a healthier "whole." As the individual's inner psychic struggle must resolve conflicting feelings before psychic health can be achieved, so, too, the group's inner psychic struggle, as played out through its members' interaction, moves toward resolution of conflicting feelings. Thus the group as a whole begins at a primitive level of functioning and ends at a higher level, thereby increasing its chances for survival and improving the quality of that survival.

The parallel between the individual and the group helps to conceptualize the "movement" dynamic we talk about when we refer to "group process." The process is the psychic energy that moves the group, the force of the interaction, the latent dynamic that underlies the manifest content, the "unconscious" of the group. Indeed, as any group worker will testify, that energy is a force with which to be reckoned. The power of an individual's unconscious drives has challenged and terrified many a worker, but that force multiplied six to ten times is awesome. Any group leader has felt it to be similar to riding a tiger, unable to stay on and afraid to get off.

Yet, that force has the greatest capacity for creativeness. It is a million bouncing atoms that need to be harnessed, directed, and channeled in order to create a healthy explosion of life. A group in the midst of creative force resembles no other experience. From each member, strength is gained, ideas stretched, and risks taken and applauded. It is a rich culture in which new and healthy organisms grow and develop.

What composes this "rich culture"? How does the group help its members? What are these growth-producing factors? If we are more able to identify and successfully isolate them, perhaps we can help to recreate them. Our purpose is to provide a group environment that enables growth factors to exist and flourish.

The growth factors can be reduced to a few major concepts related to mutual aid and support, cohesiveness, catharsis, and mastery. These terms, which will be used repeatedly throughout our later discussion, are briefly defined here.

Mutual Aid

The mutual aid and support process supports open expression of feeling and sharing of information relevant to the purpose of the group (Shulman, 1979). Sharing ideas and experiences fosters an atmosphere in which many positive changes may occur. First, there is a sense of validation, of belonging, of universality of experience and feeling: he, too, is unable to handle his adolescent son; she, too, feels alone and abandoned. The realization that others experience and feel the same (or similarly) helps reduce the sense of alienation and loss suffered during crisis. Thus, the member not only feels entitled to the full range of emotion but is then helped to move beyond mere feeling to a more objective understanding and, ultimately, a resolution. Sharing feelings provides a reality-testing base where members' ideas are accepted, confronted, and challenged by others. Through feedback, other group members offer possible alternative responses to various situations. That reciprocity is encouraged and strengthened by the worker. The group is a place for taking "safe risks" in a safe environment and playing out new and different parts of oneself.

Most of the behaviors exhibited in the group are reflections of the way one interacts outside of the group. For example, a passive member might not be able to allow himself to express his rage over being abused, whereas another group member is better able to express her rage but less able to be passive. In the group, each can model the alternate pattern for the other. The ability of the group to "hear" different responses acts as an accepting environment for the more angry response, thereby enabling the more passive member to be angry and survive while allowing the angry member to experience the acceptance of a passive response. Also of importance is the opportunity for an angry person to experience, from a safe distance, how anger is felt by other people. Similarly, in observing other passive people, the passive individual can sense the group's reaction to passivity. Each participant now has permission to feel and witness the other side of herself or himself. As data are exchanged, ideas shared, and alternate responses and feelings experienced, challenged, confronted, and accepted, the individual's experience of an issue is expanded and enlarged in every respect. The person has grown to see multiple aspects of the issue and is less locked into historical responses.

Through this process of support, advice, and validation, the individual has been given to and, equally important, has given to others. The result is an increase in self-esteem and an ability to see oneself as having something valuable to give. This reciprocity occurs even when a group member is in the midst of feeling empty or worthless. Additionally, the person has experienced a specific struggle as part of being human. Judgment of oneself becomes less harsh when one is not punitively criticized by one's "significant others." Last, members see that they are not alone in what they feel and that no matter how great the loss, the self is maintained as well as the connection to others.

Group Cohesion

Mutual aid and support is heightened as the group becomes a tighter and more intimate entity. This joining together and bonding of group members is called group cohesiveness. The more the group works together toward its common needs and goals, while still satisfying the needs of its individual members, the more effective it will be. The collective strength and mastery of the group members are then harnessed for a greater good. Again, the need for cohesiveness in group treatment is not so different from the task of integrating the parts of the self in individual treatment to propel the whole forward. Group cohesiveness, in that sense, may be equated with group ego strength.

Catharsis

The social worker engaged in work with individuals knows the importance of giving the client an opportunity to express feelings, some of which may be buried within. The mere disclosure of certain previously unexpressed thoughts often provides relief for the individual. The cleansing or purging of emotions (the catharsis) can take place with the group just as it occurs in individual treatment. In the group, however, one member's ability to come to grips with a particularly painful issue may stimulate others to deal with their own struggles. The contagion can be helpful in exposing and draining the poisons.

Mastery

In general, the group experience is a learning experience. Mastery of social skills in the group carries over into other areas of individuals' lives, teaching group members to cope and to increase control over aspects of their functioning. The acquisition of specific concrete skills also enhances functioning. A cooking-for-one group of newly widowed older men, for example, teaches nutrition and food preparation and, as a result, concretely aids in the adjustment from married to widowed life. Programs can be designed to meet emotional, social, and physical needs of clients.

Acting as a societal force, the group helps to shape the individual's experience in a way that is uniquely growth-producing. No amount of individual work can supply the same complexity of impact. Perhaps the major growth factor of the formally structured group is that it is a microcosm of society. With proper leadership, it is a healthy society, a healthy family. The group allows enactment of every life drama, providing a growth opportunity through accepting and nurturing while challenging and confronting. The emphasis must be on the individual's uniqueness and right to be separate without being isolated from the nurturing group. The code of the group is to provide for the growth of the whole as well as the growth of each part. The worker hopes each part of the group will eventually mature beyond the whole and make a healthy separation (termination). Here, too, the group parallels the role of the psychically healthy family, which provides a rich, nurturing environment. This environment allows family members to develop in their own ways, contribute to the quality of family life, and eventually separate from it to begin their own units.

Models

Social work has often found its gurus in its sister professions of psychology and psychiatry. Social group work, however, is strongly imbued with its own tradition, which originated in the settlement house movement and extended to schools, hospitals, rehabilitative settings, mental health clinics, institutions, and various community programs. Certain core concepts derived from this tradition are noted throughout social group work literature and are utilized as guideposts in our discussions.

Group theory often refers to models for conducting groups: the reciprocal or contractual model (Schwartz, 1971), the remedial or rehabilitative model (Vinter, 1967), and the psychosocial model (Northen, 1988). Loosely defined, the reciprocal model rests on the idea that group members are equal in terms of the group's work, the contract is reached by mutual decision, and the worker regards himself or herself as a facilitator rather than as a group "leader." The worker in such a group assists the democratic process and encourages mutual aid. The goals and structure of the group are set by the members within the limitations imposed by the agency. The assumption is that the worker has the knowledge to help the group explore issues touched on by members but should be nondirective in his or her approach, allowing the group its own growth and power. Most importantly, the group contract and group norms continuously evolve during the process and are not predetermined by the worker. The reciprocal model has, at times, been referred to as a democratic model.

The rehabilitative or remedial model suggests that the worker is in a somewhat superior position to group members whose social skills are impaired or not fully developed. This model might be used, for example, in a skills of daily living group for retarded children or a group for schizophrenics. Using this model, the worker instructs, exercises considerable authority, models behavior for group members, and creates an atmosphere which motivates individual growth. The group participants are regarded as clients rather than members. Although an attempt is made to involve clients in decisions regarding goals, structure, and direction for the group, the expectation is that the professional will actively guide the group. The rehabilitative model, as its name suggests, is strongly allied with structured learning and can be viewed as an educational model.

The psychosocial model for group work uses intrapsychic methodologies in treatment and consequently relies heavily on reflection and insight development. This model is used primarily in work with long-term groups. Over time, recurring themes and relationships between group members become the focus for discussion. While psychotherapy groups are included in this model, the model is not restricted to these but includes various support, maintenance, and prevention groups. The worker in this sort of group, as in the remedial group, has special authority, power, and control. The worker is responsible for norm setting and stresses the need for self-disclosure and confidentiality. The boundaries separating these three models are artificial indeed, for in real practice we use aspects of each. Nevertheless, for theoretical considerations and for orienting the student, the distinctions have some usefulness.

Group Phases

Another valuable way to examine group structure is to visualize the group as an organism moving through several life stages to achieve growth. The first of these is generally called the beginning or contracting phase; the second, the middle or work phase; and the third, the ending or termination phase. The group process parallels the life process in several ways. First, as in life, the group begins with tentative explorations of the environment, its demands, its rewards, and its expectations. Essentially, this is an orientation phase. Next, the group passes into the work phase in which norms are refined and struggled with, and goals are established, and some are achieved. This is the adaptation phase. In the third and final stage, a more sophisticated and complete mastery of survival skills takes place. This is the final acceptance of self in relation to norms. It prepares the way for separation with individuation, the termination phase.

Each session of each group also has a beginning, middle, and end phase in which a particular theme emerges. A single session may then be thought of as a complete cycle. Each group session plays out a theme that fits into a larger theme with which the group may struggle over time. This can be thought of in terms of the way each moment fits into a day, each day contributes to the week, each week to the month, and so on. Even a single session can have a profound impact on the whole of group life. Our book, as a matter of convenience and direction, is divided into sections focusing on these three phases.

In each section, we select processes illustrating the phase and its dynamics, concentrating on each group's special characteristics that differentiate it from other groups experiencing the same phase. With a recognition of the peculiar needs of populations and the differences in styles and techniques of workers, we analyze each piece of the process. Aside from identifying the dynamics, we suggest alternative approaches and examine the possible ramifications of each.

Techniques

Throughout the book, readers will be introduced to vignettes that pose particular group practice issues and suggest ways in which workers address the concerns of their groups. In all groups, the broad goals are generally the same:

to help group members to speak with each other honestly, to enhance the fluency of meaningful communication, to problem-solve and to find mutual aid and support in that process, and to develop insight. Various techniques assist in achieving these goals. All of the techniques need to be applied within the larger context of professional ethics, which will be discussed in greater detail in Chapter 2, Value Dilemmas in Group Practice.

We believe that workers, in reading the processes and analyses of others, find a sort of methodology for tapping into their own natural resources and creativity. One of the most difficult aspects of working with groups is asking oneself the appropriate questions concerning why one did or did not intervene in a particular encounter and what were the unconscious motivations determining one's behavior. We will use these processes to address some of these questions.

Throughout the process analyses presented, we discuss interventions and alternate approaches used by workers in a variety of settings. Certain worker skills can be used in all groups and aid communication, focus the work of the group, and eventually help achieve the group goals. We review some of the specific skills and summarize others. We list skills in particular categories, although no skill can really be characterized as applying to a single category or group phase.

Communication Skills

Skills to Aid in Mutual Understanding

1. *Clarifying*—Are you saying . . .?
2. *Clarifying with urgency*—No, no, it's really important we understand . . .
3. *Rephrasing*—So what you're saying is . . .
4. *Framing*—I think the larger issue this group has identified is . . .
5. *Widening the frame*—So you're saying you're having problems communicating with your wife, let's widen that to possible communication problems with others in your life . . .
6. *Focusing*—Wait a minute. We seem to be losing what we were talking about.
7. *Reflecting*—It sounds as if you're saying . . .
8. *Reality testing*—What are other people hearing Sally say?
9. *Confronting*—Every time we talk about parents, Joe, you change the topic.
10. *Redirecting*—We seem to be getting away from what we were talking about.
11. *Interpreting*—It seems that the group is saying . . .
12. *Setting limits*—We're not allowed to hit each other here . . .
13. *Exploration*—Could you tell us more about that?

14. *Worker taking responsibility*—I apologize, I meant something different.

Affective Skills

1. *Reaching for and exploring feelings*—How has the week been for you?
2. *Reaching for feedback*—What are others in the group feeling about this?
3. *Identifying resistance*—I think it's hard for us to talk about this.
4. *Staying with the resistance*—I know it is difficult, but let's try to talk about this a little bit longer.
5. *Identifying nonverbal cues*—I noticed that we're all very quiet today.
6. *Connecting behavior to feelings*—Whenever we talk about . . .
7. *Validation of feelings*—It must be very rough for you.
8. *Scanning* (worker looks at individual members during the group interaction), a part of active listening.
9. *Listening, identifying conflict and feelings*—It seems people want to tell Joe something but are having difficulty.
10. *Confronting affect*—I wonder what's so funny.
11. *Identifying specific feelings*—You seem very sad.
12. *Active listening*—A group member expresses her anger at her father. The worker responds, "So you're saying you're angry with him."
13. *Staying with the feeling and sustaining it*—I know this is very difficult, but let's try to explore it a little more. So you're really sad.
14. *Translating the message*—I think that what George is trying to tell you is that he is very angry with this group . . .
15. *Lending support*—We're really sorry you have to go through this . . .
16. *Use of nonverbal cues*—raising an eyebrow to indicate disbelief without interrupting verbally.
17. *Conscious provocation*—Oh, really, you never get angry?
18. *Separation of thought from action*—It's okay for you to want to hit him but you can't hit him.

Cohesion-Building and Contractual Skills

1. *Limit setting*—People need to come on time.
2. *Making connections*—What John is saying is a lot like what you're saying, Sally.
3. *Reaching for commonality*—I guess we can all relate to that.
4. *Recognition of difference*—That sounds similar, except . . .
5. *Summarizing*—So, today we talked about several things . . .
6. *Bridging*—It sounds as if you're saying something like what we spoke about last week.

7. *Using words of inclusion*—"We" are saying "our group" feels . . .
8. *Establishing structure*—So, we will be meeting every Tuesday at 4:00?
9. *Establishing purpose and goals*—I think we've decided we're here to . . .
10. *Clarification of needs*—So, we've agreed you want to get X, Y, and Z out of this group?
11. *Definition of roles*—My job will be to keep things safe in here, and you will take responsibility for bringing up the issues that are important to you.
12. *Reaching for consensus*—Are we all in agreement that . . .?
13. *Identifying process*—The group seems quiet whenever the subject of the group's summer break comes up.
14. *Making the problem a group issue*—It seems this is not only Ida's problem, but the group's problem as well.
15. *Mobilizing the group as a therapeutic agent*—How can we help Dahlia with this problem?
16. *Holding the group responsible for sharing information*—Is there anyone who has any additional information that needs to be shared?
17. *Making a member a part of the group*—Alice, we haven't heard from you. What do you think?

Problem-Solving Skills

1. *Identifying need for a decision and assisting implementation*—We need to figure out how we will get to the museum. Any ideas?
2. *Clarifying*—The issues on the table seem to be . . .
3. *Suggesting alternatives*—We might try . . .
4. *Asking for feedback*—What do others think?
5. *Focusing*—Can we get back to business?
6. *Demand for work*—We have to address this problem.
7. *Partializing and prioritizing*—What's the most important part of this problem, the thing we should focus on?
8. *Mediating*—Let's see if we can't look at both sides.
9. *Negotiating*—Do you think you could agree to . . .?
10. *Identifying areas for work*—It sounds like we need to struggle some more with Brian's leaving the group.
11. *Confronting the problem*—Like it or not, the reality is . . .

Admittedly, this little exercise in listing skills and examples is limited. Workers must find their own language for communicating with their groups. To be open, receptive, creative, and comfortable with your own style is surely the most useful skill.

References

Konopka, G. *Social Group Work: A Helping Process.* Englewood Cliffs, NJ: Prentice-Hall, Inc., 1963, pp. 1–22.

Northen, H. *Social Work with Groups*, 2nd ed. New York: Columbia University Press, 1988.

Schwartz, W. "Social Group Work: The Interactionist Approach." In *the Encyclopedia of Social Work.* New York: NASW, 1971, pp. 1252–1263.

Shulman, L. *The Skills of Helping Individuals and Groups.* Itasca, IL: The Peacock Press, 1979.

Vinter, R., Ed. *Readings in Group Work Practice.* Ann Arbor, MI: Campus Publishers, 1967.

2 VALUE DILEMMAS IN GROUP PRACTICE

> Everything had changed suddenly—the tone, the moral climate; you didn't know what to think, whom to listen to. As if all your life you had been led by the hand like a small child and suddenly you were on your own, you had to learn to walk by yourself. There was no one around, neither family nor people whose judgement you respected. At such a time you felt the need of committing yourself to something absolute—life or truth or beauty—of being ruled by it in place of the man-made rules that had been discarded. You needed to surrender to some such ultimate purpose more fully, more unreservedly than you had ever done in the old familiar peaceful days, in the old life that was now abolished and gone for good.
>
> Boris Pasternak
> *Dr. Zhivago* (1957)

While the general social work literature devotes many discussions to the importance of dealing with value dilemmas in regard to work with individuals, relatively little of that literature focuses on value dilemmas as they relate to group practice. Respect for the dignity, autonomy, and confidentiality of individual clients is complicated when groups form, revealing a heterogeneity of opinions, cultures, and prejudices. People joined together also may exercise considerably more power than individuals alone, and interactions among group members may be volatile and contrary to the values intended either by the worker or the agency. The violation of ethical principles held dear by the profession, a lack of respect for democratic process, a discriminatory or racist policy by group members, or a breach of confidentiality is often not within the control of workers, and these transgressions by group members often pose important value dilemmas for workers. The following scenarios, as the other vignettes in this text, are drawn from actual practice experience with groups in the field, and they illustrate several of the value conflicts inherent in understanding working with groups.

Matters of Confidentiality

A psychotherapy group for young women who have difficulty in intimate relationships has been meeting for many months and has been discussing the members' most personal problems. An often-discussed cardinal rule for this group is that it should maintain confidentiality. Jessica, a vocal and active member of the group, had a housewarming party to celebrate her move to a new apartment; excited with her plans, she invited to the festivities the other group members, who accepted readily. During the next session of the group, they speak about the party. All agree the party was very beautiful, but they met other friends of Jessica, who greeted them with remarks such as, "Anna, how wonderful to meet you. Jessica has told us so much about you!" As the group members perceive it, the outsiders clearly know about what has been shared in confidence in the group.

In most cases in which individuals receive assistance from social workers, it is fairly easy for the worker to maintain confidentiality. In groups, however, maintenance of trust is more complicated because many people have to be relied upon to keep confidences. Although Jessica would surely have been appalled to learn that others in the group had shared her most intimate thoughts with outsiders, she was oblivious, at least on a conscious level, of the impact her talking about the group with friends would have on the ability of the group to continue to share painful or difficult material. Once confidentiality has been violated, trust may be impossible to regain.

Workers need to consider various approaches to avoid this situation or to deal with its aftermath. The first step in achieving confidentiality is to develop an initial contract that emphasizes the framework in which the group will proceed. In the contract, the group members learn what is expected of them and what they should expect from the worker. Members also learn in the contracting period the ways in which the work will be conducted. In the group situation described above, the contract was clearly and repeatedly explored throughout the beginning and middle phases of the group, but nevertheless, confidentiality was violated.

Because the discussion of confidentiality and of the process of the group had been established early, the group had a mechanism for dealing with this issue. The group understood that it needed to discuss the issue and that it was appropriate to explore Jessica's underlying motivation in inviting the group to her home and discussing group members with outsiders. Another aspect of this process involved a discussion of the group's motivation for socializing outside of the group, another violation of the group's already established code of behavior. In short, situations arise in which group members breach confidences, but these breaches always should be explored fully with the goal of providing insight and reaffirming a trusting atmosphere.

Joe has been working with a group of adolescent boys in an after-school program. One afternoon, Billy, a fifteen-year-old group member, asks to speak in confidence to Joe about something. Joe agrees to see Billy. Billy tells Joe that another group member, Rick, has been threatening to get a certain girl alone in the rest room at school and get "revenge on her" for disrespecting him in front of his buddies. Billy says that he is going to warn the girl anonymously. He wants Joe to know about this circumstance but asks Joe to avoid discussing this matter in the group.

In the case of a group matter shared in an informal individual meeting between worker and group member, it is generally the worker's responsibility to urge that the issue be raised in the group session. If the group is to be effective, the group worker needs to respect group process as a way to resolve issues. Also when a group member shares information privately, something is amiss in the functioning of the group that has made the member believe that individual sharing is safer or more helpful. As much as is possible, the worker should encourage the matter to be brought back to the group. Ultimately, the worker must take responsibility for helping in the sharing process should the group member willingly open up the discussion in the group.

The exceptions to this rule might occur when raising an issue will pose a physical threat to the group member or others. The key matter in the case of Joe and Billy concerns the reason for Billy not wanting this information shared with the group. Is it simply his concern that he will be perceived as a tattler, or is it his legitimate belief that sharing this information will place him in physical jeopardy? Since this group is dealing with adolescent boys rather than adults, the worker has a special obligation to alert various authorities of a threat of violence. This too should be a part of the initial contracting in which it is made clear that the only violation of confidentiality by the worker will occur if someone is in physical danger. When group members are informed that situations in which someone is in physical peril will be reported, sharing these matters, even under the guise of confidentiality, is actually a request for the worker's assistance.

Sandy has been seeing a worker, Barbara, in individual sessions and in a women's group conducted in a mental health clinic. After several months of treatment, Sandy tells the worker, during the individual meeting, about an early ongoing sexual experience she had with her stepfather while she was growing up, an experience that she believes has permanently destroyed her ability to sustain relationships with men. Sandy indicates that discussing this with Barbara has been terribly painful and that she surely is not ready to share this with the group. Barbara, who has worked with a number of the women individually, knows that at least two other women in the group (and perhaps others) have histories of childhood sexual abuse and that none of the group members seems willing to mention this matter at all in the group.

The confidentiality required for building relationships in individual treatment settings is occasionally breached inadvertently when the same clients are seen in groups. The worker may simply forget where the comments were first shared. Some suggest that it is not recommended for the same individual to work with the client both individually and in groups for this reason. In the situation presented here, however, Barbara may be feeling that the clinical advantages of Sandy sharing her secret with the group, and ideally receiving the support and mutual aid of other group members, may outweigh the disadvantage in breaking with confidentiality.

This assumption usually is incorrect. It may be possible, however, for the worker to raise the general discussion of historically abusive sexual encounters and their relation to the management of current relationships. Once a group member raises the issue in the group, even offhandedly, the worker may use various skills to focus on the material and solicit more personal sharing. The worker may employ various exploratory skills including asking for clarification, asking group members about other experiences, partializing, requesting feedback from members, or interpreting silences. The worker should not specifically address the member who has shared information in individual meetings but keep the focus on the general group discussion. It is likely that Sandy, and perhaps some of the other women in this example, would be able to share secrets in the group once the worker has made such discussion acceptable.

Individual versus Individual and Individual versus Group

Eva and Amelia are two members of an issues-for-aging group in a day care program for seniors. The group members know each other from various aspects of the center program, and these two members are identified by the workers as rivals for the attention of the staff. Both are extremely lonely and have problematic relationships with their sons. Two of Amelia's adult children have died; she has one remaining. Eva has an only child, a bachelor son, who seems very dutiful in visiting and doing chores for her but who is emotionally distant.

During one group session, Amelia pours her heart out to the group, noting that her son is going through a divorce and that her daughter-in-law and teenage granddaughter will have nothing to do with her, not responding to her gifts, letters, or phone calls. Her son is also rarely in touch. Throughout this description of her plight, Amelia is sobbing uncontrollably. Eva interrupts the process by telling Amelia to quit the crying, whatever has happened to Amelia is deserved because she is a constant whiner and surely a terrible mother. Eva adds that she is tired of listening to the stories of Amelia's "wonderful, perfect husband, who died twenty years ago but who Amelia is still crying about." Eva is in a rage. Amelia is hysterical.

Although workers are unlikely to be purposefully cruel in addressing group members about painful feelings, no worker has or should have control over the expressions, however mean, of group members. The first impulse for many workers in situations like the one between Amelia and Eva is to offer protection and comfort to the person being verbally assaulted. They may also be inclined to discipline the perceived abuser with a lecture on how the group members must not be hurtful to each other. But the first thing the worker must do is to check her natural impulse to protect a member in pain. To protect Amelia might even feed into the rivalry between Eva and Amelia.

Also the suggestion that the matter is only between Eva, Amelia, and the worker denies the importance of the other group members who are also involved. It would be best for the worker to acknowledge the role of the group in addressing this exchange. The worker needs to enlist the group as a therapeutic agent. In fact, in almost every group discussion in which the worker may be unsure of how to proceed, it is helpful for her to ask the group for feedback: "I wonder what people in this group feel about what is going on here between Eva and Amelia?" Often in these situations, the attack may hold an element of truth. Perhaps Amelia is always caught up in her past losses to the extent that her self-involvement prevents her from enjoying present relationships; her depressive qualities may push people away from her. The worker needs to explore this phenomenon as a real possibility with the group, because she recognizes that Amelia is probably not the only one in the group who has experienced multiple past losses that cause difficulties in current relationships.

So too the worker must be aware that Eva's assaulting behavior, also a dysfunctional defense in terms of improving key relationships, is a reflection of the way in which she responds to perceived injustice. After soliciting responses from the group about their feelings concerning the dispute, the worker may find the group totally in support of one position or the other. In such cases, it is important for the worker to help the group explore the issues from other perspectives: "It seems everybody is in agreement. I wonder if anybody has ever felt differently." In general, it is always helpful to move a personal attack between two members back into the group context, universalizing the discussion, recognizing the curative powers of the group, and avoiding the "casework in a group" syndrome.

A socialization group of approximately a dozen members has been meeting in a psychiatric day program. One goal for the group is to plan leisure time social activities for the weekend when the group members, most of whom live alone, have little structured time and are most vulnerable to periods of depression. Most of this planning is done with minimal guidance from staff to maximize feelings of capability for group members who often feel inadequate and powerless. The participation of the group members in the planning process is regarded by staff as therapeutic and is consequently encouraged.

Rosalind and Elliott, two of the group members who are most sophisticated and high functioning, have become remarkably self-sufficient in suggesting and implementing some of the group activities. This leadership role has benefited them and has even sparked a friendship between them. During one group session, they come in with plans they made for an outing to a Broadway theater performance. Rosalind and Elliott have even ordered tickets at a discount through a special connection Elliott has with his cousin who is a theatrical manager. Although Elliott and Rosalind both have the financial support of their families and are able to participate in the program, at least half of the members of the group cannot afford to attend a Broadway show even at a discounted price.

The worker in this group is in a peculiar bind between the needs of one segment of the group and another. On the one hand, the encouragement of independence and taking control has resulted in exactly what the worker desired, Elliott and Rosalind taking charge. On the other hand, the choice of a Broadway show as the weekend activity excludes several group members who also need to participate. The worker must acknowledge the dilemma this group is facing and encourage it to problem solve as a group so that this matter can be resolved. It is also necessary to plan to avoid these difficulties in the future.

Providing a supportive non-blaming atmosphere for Elliott and Rosalind, so they are acknowledged for their considerable accomplishments, is essential to begin to achieve any resolution. Perhaps the group may also be encouraged to find a practical solution that will necessitate group cooperation and solidify the group's sense of unity and mutuality, such as the entire group organizing a bake sale to raise funds to subsidize those in the group who cannot afford the tickets. Whatever the solution to the matter, the importance of the group members' full participation in the process cannot be overestimated.

Group versus Agency

For approximately six months, John has been a valued member of a sobriety group in an alcohol treatment center. He has been doing extremely well and has served as a role model to others in the program. In the past few weeks, he has had a series of personal problems culminating with the loss of his job. The agency policy requires all clients to pay a fee for service (the amount determined on a sliding scale) as part of making a sincere commitment to the therapeutic process. John says that he is unable to pay at this time, and the agency has indicated that he will be dropped from the program. The other group members are enraged by this policy and are openly considering withholding their own fees in support of John.

The goals for this group are for all members to feel empowered to take control over their lives and to eliminate making impulsive self-destructive choices. The fact that they have bonded in support of one of their members is positive. Treatment groups for substance abuse rely heavily on the importance of mutual aid and a feeling among the members of being in a place where others have a shared understanding of the issues. The cohesiveness displayed in this group contributes to the therapeutic atmosphere and is itself a curative factor. Their proposed solution, however, is problematic because it has the potential to defeat the group purpose to seek and sustain treatment. If they refuse to pay fees, they may be dropped from the program. Although it may seem unreasonable to the group members for the agency to insist on collecting a fee for service, even from John who is now unemployed, charging a fee is a therapeutic decision based on an acknowledgment by the agency of the importance for clients to make a commitment to treatment. This commitment is vital to the therapeutic process.

The worker needs to support the members' connection to each other, while helping them to explore all the possible alternatives, including withholding fees, and the implications. Suppose the group members wish to encourage John to remain in the group by assisting him temporarily to pay his fee. John would then feel supported and be able to continue treatment. A possible negative implication of this plan is that it will further foster John's dependency rather than encourage him to seek other ways to meet his responsibility for his own treatment. It also might perpetuate the negative behaviors associated with the caretaker's role in codependent relationships, often characteristic of the alcoholic personality.

Alternate approaches for the group to use its positive feelings for John include exploring the realities of his ability to pay his fees and encouraging him to seek other means to earn the needed funds. While this may be helpful to both John and the group, it may also leave him feeling accused or rejected. In that instance, the therapeutic skills of the worker need to be directed to provide a safe and supportive atmosphere.

If the group needs to act as the advocate for John, as they seem to be suggesting by their consideration of withholding fees, they may explore other alternatives. The group needs to be helped to recognize means, other than direct confrontation, to achieve its goal of allowing John to stay. Rather than offering solutions, the worker should solicit from the members their suggestions for approaching the problem, a process that will further empower them and help toward a resolution of the problem. Perhaps they wish to write a group letter to the agency or send a representative to the administration or invite an administrator to their meeting to discuss the matter.

Whatever the approach, the worker must keep in mind her role and the therapeutic purpose of this group. A worker may easily fall into the trap of either arriving at some resolution of the issues herself or advocating with the agency on behalf of John or the group. Both of these approaches are natural responses to the cry of the group to be taken care of by the good mother and saved from destruction by the bad mother, the agency. As tempting as it is to take on the good-mother role, it is not in the best interests of the group to give it what it appears to want rather than what is beneficial to the group's development. To approach the agency on the members' behalf is to infantilize them and foster the dependency that is part of their difficulties. Whenever a worker feels the pull to play the part of savior, a cautionary alarm should sound.

Evan has been working with a tenants' group in a public housing development. The group is funded through a locally sponsored community development agency with strong political ties to the mayor's office. Over the years, the group has become known as activist, often taking on unpopular points of view and advocating for controversial public housing policies. Their current elected leadership is among the most politically militant and has openly expressed hostile feelings toward the mayor and his policies. The mayor is currently planning a campaign stop in the community to explain his point of view and the tenants' group has voted to stage a civil disobedience protest, which will involve blocking several streets during the time of his visit. Evan has been asked by his employers to dissuade the group from this sort of demonstration and generally to cool the public rhetoric.

When groups challenge their funding sources, they need to be aware of the possible consequences of their actions in regard to the ongoing provision of resources and must weigh the importance of their current activities against their future group goals. Evan is in a difficult situation as well, for support of the group's activities may ultimately endanger his job. In some sense, this is a personal moral dilemma complicated by practical considerations. Both as community organizer and as group worker, Evan must be sensitive to the implications of the group's actions and must guide them to an understanding of the long-range issues. He cannot control the actions of members, but just as he might do in any clinical setting, he needs to solicit responses, maintain objectivity, explore the alternatives, and help the group to understand the possible ramifications of whatever action they elect to take. Ideally, their exploration of and knowledge about the implications of their actions will empower them to achieve their goals.

Unlike a group in a treatment situation, in which it may be essential for the group members to maintain their connection to the agency in order to achieve their therapeutic purpose, this group may be able to stand on its own, independent of the agency and the worker. The group obviously has already developed a fairly strong independent leadership from within and may form its own coalitions or splinter groups to do its work as it sees fit. This process may involve Evan or not, as both they and Evan choose.

Groups as Reflective of Democratic Process

Liz has been working with a parenting group affiliated with a day care center for the children of hospital employees. The program is open to all employees including physicians, nurses, social workers, aides and orderlies, maintenance workers, and clerical personnel. The hospital staff is extraordinarily heterogeneous in terms of race, culture, socioeconomic status, and level of education. As a result, extremely divergent opinions often are expressed, particularly in relation to values and approaches to parenting. In a discussion of establishing discipline with children, two West Indian members of the group indicate their strong feelings that children need physical punishment to eradicate misbehavior and to toughen them for meeting a harsh world. Others in the group become infuriated and will not permit these two women to speak, identifying those points of view as unacceptable and totally invalid in any discussion. The discussion erupts into a shouting match, and the two women, drowned out by the others, eventually leave the group early.

The most difficult chore for the worker to manage in this situation is maintaining an objective appreciation of the values expressed by others, even when these may be entirely contrary to her own. Also, in all groups, an atmosphere allowing freedom of expression is essential to basic functioning. A process that forces group members to leave the room because they are not allowed to be heard damages the possibility that anyone can express a divergent opinion. Consequently, no one will feel safe talking. Since the purpose of any group is to promote growth through an open exchange of ideas, a group in which ideas are unexpressed is self-defeating.

In Liz's group, the child-rearing philosophy of the women is not shared by other group members. Clearly, if anyone had admitted to committing child abuse, the worker would have been forced to report the matter to authorities, but in an open discussion of differences in child-rearing philosophy, the obligation for reporting is not at issue. Rather what is important is how this group will be able to continue toward its goals if group members are denied permission to express themselves. It is essential for workers in groups with a high degree of intensity in interactions to prevent the group from reaching an explosive point in which the shouting, cursing, and physical contacts are obstacles to the work of the group. In general, when the worker, through her own personal barometer, perceives that communication is endangered, she should rapidly introduce intervention skills to slow things down to a level where discussion can be processed. These skills may include clarifying, reformulating, insisting that members speak one at a time, verbalizing, interpreting, and focusing. In all groups, the worker must above all maintain her commitment to the democratic process.

Donna has been working with a union group whose leadership has been elected by the general union membership. These leaders have a decidedly dictatorial managerial style. No minority opinion is allowed in the discussion. Committee votes concerning union matters are generally conducted by voice vote or a show of hands rather than by secret ballot, and pressure is nearly always exerted on the committee membership to vote in keeping with the demands of the leadership. In a recent, relatively close, vote regarding strategy in planning a strike, the union leaders called the vote before all interested parties could voice their objections to the proposed action. When Donna attempted to intercede, she was told that the group would conduct business as it saw fit.

Clearly it is problematic for Donna to remain in a neutral position while democratic process is abandoned. The very core of group process is respect for minority and majority positions and the free exchange of ideas and opinions. As it stands in this group, neither democratic process nor freedom of expression is tolerated. The worker is faced with the dilemma of trying to negotiate with the elected representatives of the union who are not abiding by their own constitution. The worker may feel tempted to give up trying to move this group in a more democratic direction, and in fact, she may be unable to achieve the desired results.

Nevertheless, some possible approaches will remove the obstacles to better group functioning. The key is helping those in power to feel powerful without denying the rights of others. Ideally, those in power can be enlisted in the process of making positive change. To begin with, the worker should join with the indigenous group leadership and share her observations about the group process, without any suggestion of blame, which might alienate them. This sharing should engage the leadership by appealing to them as a source of a solution to a problem that, the worker acknowledges, they may already have noticed themselves. By meeting with the subgroup, the worker validates their importance.

The group dynamics are likely to be quite different in the small group. As a subgroup in the large group, they usually need to be more unified, but in the small group, they may have more room for individual expression. Often, some voices within the subgroup are not heard when the larger group is in session. In the more intimate meeting with just the power elite, those who are more open and perhaps more moderate may be freer to express themselves. The worker may start the process by asking some general questions: "What do you think about how this group makes decisions?" "Does everyone feel that they are fully heard?" These questions assume that the power subgroup values the democratic process, which may or may not be the case. Enlisting members in a positive way sometimes breaks defenses and helps those in the group who wish to be allied with a more democratic position to come forward.

The worker may also, even with little support for free expression, use a more pragmatic approach with the leadership: "What are your goals?" "Does it feel important for a group strategizing about a strike to assure a cohesive stand in which all members favor the positions the union takes?" "If so, might it not be helpful to air divergent opinions before the issues reach the general union membership?" "Perhaps the cause of the union is better served by more discussion among all committee members before decisions are made?" No worker should immediately desert the process, whatever the case, but rather should explore various avenues for improving group interaction.

Positions of Professionals Dealing with Ethical Issues Expressed in Groups

Craig and Paul are members of a group in an outpatient mental health clinic. Craig is a large man who wears cowboy boots and an imposing ten-gallon hat. He swaggers when he walks, and he speaks in a loud aggressive tone, creating an atmosphere in which others are fearful about expressing themselves. Paul is quite the opposite, easygoing, pleasant, and rarely combative. He is generally well liked by his peers. Periodically, Craig is known to pontificate on a subject, to distract the focus away from a matter he is unwilling to address. At these times he goes into political or philosophical diatribes, often raising his voice in a threatening manner. On one such occasion, he begins to talk about the decline of morality and the "faggots" who are taking over the media. Unknown to the other group members, Paul is gay. The group makes no move to counter Craig's vituperative comments.

Whether or not the worker is aware that Paul is gay, the issue of maintaining a safe environment for all group members is vital to groups. Also important is the notion that group members have the right to speak out, even when their comments are offensive. As a result of these two sometimes contradictory group values, the skills of workers are sorely taxed in sessions such as the one with Paul and Craig. The issue concerns Craig's manner in dealing with his fears and his anger management. His expressions are intimidating to others, and his bravado is a defense against feeling out of control—feelings other group members likely share. A goal for the worker is to get everyone to recognize the commonality of fears and defenses and to move away from the focus on name calling, which is a form of displaced aggression.

The worker can try to reframe Craig's comments and then ask for feedback from the group: "So, Craig, you're saying that this kind of change makes you angry. What are others feeling?" This approach accomplishes two things. First, in the reframing, the comment dilutes the intensity of the anger, thereby making it safer to discuss. Second, this approach removes the attention from Craig to involve the group and to identify the issue as the province of the whole group and as one that invites discussion of members' responses to Craig's affect as well as to the content of his remarks.

If Craig's comments had been directed at Paul with the knowledge of group members that Paul was gay, the use of the word "faggot" might have a quite different meaning. Craig's language then might be perceived by all as an assault that would mandate a more direct intervention by the worker. This might include addressing Paul about how the reference made him feel and extending this question to other group members as well. Such a comment probably would necessitate a review of the contractual obligations of group members regarding acceptable expressions of anger that would not include name calling or similar verbal assaults. In any case, the role of the worker is to help Craig and the group move to an exploration of feelings that underlie behavior and that are an obstacle to functioning.

Patricia, an African-American social worker, is providing four sessions of in-service training on the psychosocial aspects of patient care for a group of home health aides who work with homebound elderly. The group members are black and Latina women, many of whom have been working in the field for several years. In the course of the discussion, the group members begin to talk about their experiences with patients who were openly racist and treated them badly. One woman, Angela, tells the group about being accused of stealing because she carried a bag (of her own change of clothes) out of the patient's apartment. Another, Claudette, notes how one patient who constantly criticized her cooking called her a *melanzana* (Italian for "eggplant" and a vulgar slang term for blacks). Mary tells the horrible tale of how she was kept in the patient's room with a vicious guard dog at the door to prevent her from stealing household items. When Mary needed to use the bathroom, she had to call the patient's family member, who was on the floor above, to temporarily remove the dog. As they trade stories, the women become more and more animated and enraged at what has occurred in the course of their work. Soon their language becomes peppered with derogatory remarks about other races and ethnicities, with vulgar slang terms for various groups, and with talk of revenge on clients who are abusive to them.

It is certainly easy for a worker to ally with group members when they speak of the mistreatment they experience as a result of racism and prejudice. Although this is an educational rather than a therapeutic group, it is important for the group members to express their feelings about abusive situations. In addition to the therapeutic aspects of sharing with others in "the same boat," not discussing these issues would be an obstacle to the training process. Learning to understand abusive behavior or learning tools to respond to it would be essential for these homecare workers to manage their assignments effectively. The difficulty for the worker in the scenario described comes when the group members move to using prejudicial language about other groups and suggest that they will find ways to seek revenge.

Although the worker must validate the sense of outrage felt by the members, she also must help them see that seeking revenge is counterproductive. The acting-out of vengeful feelings no doubt will endanger their employment, but the tactful verbal expression of their dissatisfaction with the ways in which they are treated may yield more understanding and a change in behavior on the part of the abusive patient. For both the home health aide and the patient, feelings must be separated from actions.

The purpose of the training group for the aides is to provide them with the skills needed to accomplish their work with their patients. These skills include helping the patients to be more receptive to medical treatment and therapy, assisting the patients to accept help with household tasks and personal care, managing with interested relatives of patients, and developing a pleasant sociable relationship with the patients, including persons of various cultures different from their own. For these goals to be achieved, the aide and patient must establish a relationship characterized by mutual respect and acceptance, which is not always possible but certainly is a goal.

Exploring various avenues to achieve this goal is a necessary part of the worker's intervention with the training group. Throughout the sessions, the worker should talk with the group about various approaches to problematic situations, perhaps utilizing role playing and psychodrama techniques as a means to help group members experience what their patients may be feeling. These activities also allow the aides to test out various approaches in dealing with troublesome patients. During the role playing, group members are helped to diffuse some of their rage and channel their energies into creative problem-solving activities.

One must recognize that even with the best of approaches, some aides will still find themselves in untenable situations in which they experience abuse and mistreatment from their patients or the families of patients. The group worker is responsible for helping the aides to be assertive on their own behalf so that when they have exhausted their repertoire of problem-solving techniques, they can solicit help from involved family members or the agency. As a final alternative, aides need to be aware that the agency usually will be supportive of a change in assignment.

A senior citizens' center current events group meets regularly with a social worker, Julia, to discuss issues in the news. Nearly every week, the discussion drifts away from the original topic—a news article suggested for discussion by the membership—toward some issue related to crime, the changes in the neighborhood, and the arrival of "unacceptable" new third world immigrants and minority group members in their communities. They blame the decay in their neighborhoods on these newcomers, who, several group members say, have no morals, are dirty, live off the dole, are irresponsible parents, and have destroyed the city.

When clients express their prejudices in individual sessions, most workers are comfortable addressing the underlying issues and exploring feelings. When this discussion occurs in a group, however, workers have a tendency to shrink from the discussion and ignore the expressions or to enter the discussion by "teaching" the group about the evils of whatever "ism" they are supporting, guiding the group members down the right moral road. Unfortunately, the response of this group to the changes they have experienced is a racist, hateful, angry, biased one. All of the ethical principles of the social work profession—notions of social justice, democracy, protection of populations-at-risk, the dignity of all people, support for basic human rights—are offended by the comments made by the group members and by their almost obsessive quality of reciting these statements repeatedly during nearly every session.

Although no worker should support positions so contrary to what are understood as core professional values, workers also need to be sensitive to the issues for this group. Members are elderly persons experiencing enormous losses in their lives, including but not limited to the loss of their familiar surroundings, their sense of community, their friends and neighbors, their physical well-being, and their informal support networks. The expression of vicious prejudices by group members, although offensive, really concerns the loss of the familiar, the loss of communities as they used to be and of the key people who inhabited them. An approach that addresses the needs of the group members by focusing on what it is like for them in this new world, which directs the exploration of feelings on how difficult it may be for them to adjust to changing times, and which acknowledges their contributions and the values they still cherish, is more helpful than one merely condemning the expression of racist thoughts. Additionally, the discussion of powerful memories regarding their own experiences or those of their parents in coming to America may help them to recognize some connection with the current newcomers.

It is also likely, though not always the case, that several members in the group do not have bad feelings about other races and nationalities. It is often difficult for such people to assert themselves in situations in which a loud, overpowering subgroup makes insulting remarks. The worker here might also encourage the expression of positive thoughts and experiences in the changing neighborhood that some group members may wish to share with the group. Whatever the case, support for a rational exchange among members who have different points of view certainly will be more helpful than a lecture from the worker about the golden rule.

Conclusion

The issues related to values in groups are complicated ones, and many alternative approaches address these. The worker must recognize that definitive solutions to any value dilemmas rarely exist, but rather, a process should incorporate the group and recognize its phase and its dynamics to come to some conclusions. The primary value, in which every worker must be invested, is the respect for the process and for the group's ability to grapple with the issues.

In every group experience is the potential for growth and change. In every ending is the seed of a beginning:

> Unseen buds, infinite, hidden well,
> Under the snow and ice, under the darkness, in every square or cubic inch,
> Germinal, exquisite, in delicate lace, microscopic, unborn
> Like babes in wombs, latent, folded, compact, sleeping;
> Billions of billions, and trillions of trillions of them waiting,
> (On earth and in the sea—the universe—the stars there in the heavens,)
> Urging slowly, surely forward, forming endless,
> And waiting ever more, forever more behind.

Walt Whitman
"Unseen Buds"
From *Leaves of Grass*

3 MANIFEST AND LATENT CONTENT

The table was a large one, but the three were all crowded together at one corner of it. "No room! No room!" they cried out when they saw Alice coming. "There's plenty of room!" said Alice indignantly, and she sat down in a large arm-chair at one end of the table.

"Have some wine," the March Hare said in an encouraging tone. Alice looked all round the table, but there was nothing on it but tea. "I don't see any wine," she remarked.

"There isn't any," said the March Hare.

"Then it wasn't very civil of you to offer it," said Alice angrily.

"It wasn't very civil of you to sit down without being invited," said the March Hare.

"I didn't know it was your table," said Alice: "it's laid for a great many more than three."

"Your hair wants cutting," said the Hatter. He had been looking at Alice for some time with great curiosity, and this was his first speech.

"You should learn not to make personal remarks," Alice said with some severity: "It's very rude."

The Hatter opened his eyes very wide on hearing this; but all he said was, "Why is a raven like a writing-desk?"

Come, we shall have some fun now! thought Alice. "I'm glad they've begun asking riddles—I believe I can guess that," she added aloud.

"Do you mean that you think you can find out the answer to it?" said the March Hare.

"Exactly so," said Alice.

"Then you should say what you mean," the March Hare went on.

"I do," Alice hastily replied; "at least—at least I mean what I say—that's the same thing, you know."

"Not the same thing a bit!" said the Hatter. "Why, you might just as well say that 'I see what I eat' is the same thing as 'I eat what I see'!"

"You might just as well say," added the March Hare, "that 'I like what I get' is the same thing as 'I get what I like'!"

"You might just as well say," added the Dormouse, which seemed to be talking in its sleep, "that 'I breathe when I sleep' is the same thing as 'I sleep when I breathe'!"

"It is the same thing with you," said the Hatter, and here the conversation dropped, and the party sat silent for a minute, while Alice thought over all she could remember about ravens and writing-desks, which wasn't much.

The Hatter was the first to break the silence. "What day of the month is it?" he said, turning to Alice: he had taken his watch out of his pocket, and was looking at it uneasily, shaking it every now and then, and holding it to his ear.

Alice considered a little, and then said, "The fourth."

"Two days wrong!" sighed the Hatter. "I told you butter wouldn't suit the works!" he added, looking angrily at the March Hare.

"It was the best butter," the March Hare angrily replied.

"Yes, but some crumbs must have got in as well," the Hatter grumbled: "you shouldn't have put it in with the breadknife."

The March Hare took the watch and looked at it gloomily: then he dipped it into his cup of tea, and looked at it again: but he could think of nothing better to say than his first remark, "It was the best butter, you know."

Alice had been looking over his shoulder with some curiosity. "What a funny watch!" she remarked. "It tells the day of the month and doesn't tell what o'clock it is!"

"Why should it?" muttered the Hatter. "Does your watch tell you what year it is?"

"Of course not," Alice replied very readily: "but that's because it stays the same year for such a long time together."

"Which is just the case with mine," said the Hatter.

Alice felt dreadfully puzzled. The Hatter's remark seemed to her to have no sort of meaning in it, and yet it was certainly English. "I don't quite understand you," she said, as politely as she could.

"The Dormouse is asleep again," said the Hatter, and he poured a little hot tea upon its nose.

The Dormouse shook its head impatiently, and said, without opening its eyes, "Of course, of course: just what I was going to remark myself."

"Have you guessed the riddle yet?" the Hatter said, turning to Alice again.

"No, I give it up," Alice replied. "What's the answer?"

"I haven't the slightest idea," said the Hatter.

"Nor I," said the March Hare.

Alice sighed wearily. "I think you might do something better with the time," she said, "than wasting it in asking riddles that have no answers."

Lewis Carroll
Alice's Adventures in Wonderland (1865)

The notion that unconscious motivations underlie all human encounters is a basic principle of psychotherapy and a cornerstone of individual treatment.

In groups, too, another level of meaning exists below the surface. What is initially apparent is not necessarily what is really going on; what is seen and heard may be a symbolic way of saying something else or something more. Every comment, even if taken at face value, can have a myriad of meanings. The interpretation of what is really meant and its relation to what is said are as varied as every speaker and every listener. A person may remark that another person is wearing an attractive sweater. The wearer may read the comment as, "I wish that were my sweater," or "I'd like to know you better," or "You turn me on," or "You usually look so unfashionable, how come you look so nice today?" or even "I want something from you." The speaker may believe he or she wants to communicate one idea but, through body language, tone, and word choice, actually communicates something else.

The failure to communicate an accurate message may lie in unconscious motivations. These motivations lead to communicating thoughts not consciously intended or to selective hearing, also the result of unconscious feelings, by those addressed. In groups, communication is complicated by the many different speakers and respondents and the baggage brought by each to the group setting. The fact that we deal with numerous people at the same time makes transferences and countertransferences more complex.

Chapter 1 explained that the group has its own personality derived from the individual personalities of its members interacting as each struggles with conflicting feelings. The group is greater than the sum of its parts because a seemingly infinite number of interrelationships exist among the members, creating different wholes. The group maintains both a group consciousness (a shared understanding motivated by latent dynamics) and many individual consciousnesses, each with its own latent qualities.

The nature of the latent material is strongly influenced by the needs of the group members and the group phase. An interesting example of how phase and population issues come together may be seen in a group of pregnant teenagers and teen mothers who are in a program to earn high school equivalency degrees and develop job skills. The group is approaching termination, and the members have decided to do something special for their worker. They choose to take her out of the agency and buy beer and pizza for themselves and for her. Several of the adolescents are minors, and all of them have been cautioned against using alcohol during pregnancy. The fact that many of the girls in the program have had difficulties related to substance abuse complicates matters further.

By threatening to celebrate with beer just as they approach the end of their program, the teens seem to express their continuing need for the program and the worker. Beer drinking in this group is a form of regressive behavior, and regression is often typical of groups during termination. Also, for the teens, the beer symbolizes their adult status: they can use beer if they desire it, and no one can stop them. Their rebelliousness and acting-out of ambivalences about growing up reflect on those adolescent issues concerning loss, separation, and individuation just as the termination phase concerns itself with loss, separation, and individuation.

The group worker's most difficult task is to uncover the latent issues of the group personality and individual members' personalities to propel the group forward toward resolving conflict and maximizing mutual work leading to growth. The process of reaching for latent content involves a new kind of listening, new in its capacity for hearing what is left unsaid and for ferreting out the connections between what occurs on the surface and what may be happening below. For example, a senior group created to talk about the psychology of aging slipped into a seemingly tangential conversation about a television program that several had viewed the night before featuring Milton Berle. At first, the worker thought the group was losing its focus and that it was appropriate for her to help the group return to its purpose. The worker was not exploring the relationship between Berle, a performer whose heyday was some thirty to forty years earlier, and the group members. "Look at Berle," someone was saying, "at his age and still going strong." "He looks older, but he's still funny, successful." Others in the group were sharing memories of Berle's old skits, memories that their children and grandchildren might not be able to share with them. The discussion of Milton Berle was evidently a metaphor for a discussion about the issues of aging.

Use of Self: The Worker's Role as Authority

What we have said so far about latent content concerns the group and its members without regard to the unconscious or latent factors that motivate the worker. The worker, after all, is no more a tabula rasa than are the group members. Ideally, what keeps the worker on track is the conscious way in which she or he constantly monitors personal reactions and listens for feedback. The goals of the group should have been developed after reviewing the needs of the population, the clients' expressed goals for the group experience, and the needs and goals of the agency (see Chapter 7). Each session, the worker contemplates general and specific goals to assist the group.

Determinations about areas for work are connected to the worker's knowledge about the goals for the group in any particular session as well as over the lifetime of the group. The worker may not set up the group agenda to deal with what she or he deems important but will rather listen for the content, which reveals what is important to the group goals, and to personal knowledge of the population. If certain areas key to the needs of the population seem to be addressed only peripherally or avoided altogether, the worker may infer that some resistance is present. Some of this may be accentuated by the worker's own difficulty with the material.

A worker in a mastectomy group, for example, knows that issues concerning body image and sexuality need to be explored if the overall goal of the group (adjustment to the crisis of a breast amputation) is to be achieved. In early group meetings, these issues are unlikely to be addressed; resistance to such discussion is probable. Such matters involve intimate self-disclosure and are difficult for many people to talk about, particularly in a beginning phase.

Although these issues may continue to be unaddressed, they are present, part of the latent material, and are probably problematic on some level. The reasons these or other issues remain submerged may have to do not only with their delicacy but with the message the worker gives that she or he, too, finds the discussion uncomfortable; when sexuality is mentioned in an offhand way, she or he squirms, moves the content elsewhere, picks up on another issue. The latent message the worker communicates threatens the ability of the group to explore painful issues.

Clues to latent content are found throughout each session. Body language, an unexplained feeling of tension in the room, sadness, anger, a tone that seems inappropriate to affect, affect that seems inappropriate to content, a repeated avoidance of emotionally charged material, and many intangibles alert the worker to another level of meaning. Although workers can never be certain what is going on, they need to be sensitive to their own feelings, willing to pursue those about which they are unclear. Workers may ask directly about the feeling they are experiencing or a pattern they are observing: "Everybody seems so quiet today. What's going on?" Or the worker may offer a tentative interpretation: "It seems every time people start to talk about how scared they feel, someone changes the topic. I wonder what that's about . . .?" Group members may continue to claim that nothing special is happening. Perhaps they are not ready to confront troubling subjects; perhaps they are still unaware of other things they are feeling. Ongoing querying, exploring, and striving to understand the symbolic ways in which communication is proceeding all help the group to reach its goals. If the worker models a method of meaningful exploration, group members learn how to participate in the process.

We have developed a useful tool to help the worker identify latent content in any particular session (Roman, 1980, unpublished). By charting certain variables, the worker can make some educated guesses about what is going on and easily connect them with his or her knowledge about the population and the phase. The chart (Table 3.1) also demands that the worker acknowledge personal feelings in the process, which is necessary for a clearer understanding of his or her interventions or difficulty in intervening.

Table 3.1 Identifying Latent Content

Worker's Feelings	Members' Feelings	Population Dynamics	Group Phase Issues	Manifest Content	Latent Themes/ issues

In order to use the chart, the worker simply documents what is observed about the session and what is known about the population and the phase issues. At first, this documentation is mainly record keeping. Then come the preliminary analyses as the worker evaluates and assesses patterns apparent in the chart. As time goes on, however, the charts from several sessions provide an almost graphic accounting of the group's movement. The chart, because of its brevity, is unlike a process recording and is not as elaborate as a record of service (a recording tool discussed later in this chapter). Instead, it is a quick, nonconflictual guide to identify latent content. To illustrate the use of the chart, we have drawn from a short process excerpt of a multifamily group for parents of psychiatric patients seen in a community mental health clinic. The group is led by two workers. One has been with the group since its inception three years ago and the second, a student worker, has been with the group for only two meetings. The process is recorded by the student, Amanda:

Mrs. R: Both of my daughters seem quite accepting of Jack and try to help him. Maybe that's because they're both social workers and have more patience with him than I do.

Mrs. B: That's really interesting. Do you think they became social workers because of him?

Mrs. R: No, they were doing social work before he got sick, so I don't think that he had anything to do with that. But they do get a lot of satisfaction out of helping people. That's really what they're into.

Mrs. B: But I would think your background would have something to do with the reasons for wanting a job like that. Don't they ask those kinds of things when you apply for social work?

Co-worker: Yes, Amanda could attest to that. You have to write an essay about it as part of the application process.

Amanda: Yes, they want to know about your background, why you're interested in going into the field, and things like that.

Mrs. B: I knew someone whose son went to XYZ School of Social Work, and after he was done with the training, they told him that he shouldn't be a social worker since he was in it for the wrong reasons (looking directly at the student). Could that be true? Could someone do all the training and everything and then be told he had the wrong motivations? They said he was there more to help himself than to help others.

The following chart of this small vignette (Table 3.2) is immediately valuable. By reading the chart, the worker can see the emergence of several themes. Clients are mistrustful, wary, and suspicious (column 2). They question issues about the backgrounds and motivations of social workers and their ability to help (column 5). The worker is feeling uncomfortable, aware on some level that the conversation is not so general but is rather directed at her as a newcomer. She fears rejection (column 1) and notes that there is an angry tone (column 2) even in a seemingly casual discussion (column 5). The testing common to beginnings (column 4) appears to occur here. Unable to feel in control of their lives because of the unpredictability of their children's illnesses (column 3), the parents are asking whether the worker can be in control, knows what to do, and most importantly, whether she cares (column 5). The dependency on the worker, an issue in beginnings (column 4), is particularly charged for this population, who must deal with the unnatural dependency of their adult children (column 3). The presence of a new worker forces the group back to a beginning phase (column 4), which parallels the members' feelings about being unable to move forward with their lives (column 3). Once the worker has identified patterns and interrelationships among the columns of her chart, she can (with some confidence) begin to choose areas for focus, addressing issues from whatever arena in which she feels most comfortable.

Table 3.2 Emergence of Themes

Worker's Feelings	Members' Feelings	Population Dynamics	Group Phase Issues	Manifest Content	Latent Themes/ issues
Fear of rejection	Misunderstood	Stigmatized	Beginnings —trust	Talking about siblings' feelings re: identified patient	
Startled	Suspicious, mistrustful	Feeling out of control			
Uncomfortable	Wary	Feeling helpless	Approach-avoidance	Social workers' qualifications, ability to help, and motivations	
Conflicted	Angry	Feeling unable to move forward with their lives due to the dependence of their adult children	Unclear expectations		
		Feeling guilty	Dependence on leader		(see text)

Tuning in to Nonverbal Cues

When working with clients who have difficulty in verbalizing feelings, the worker must be more attuned than usual to nonverbal messages. The next process excerpt deals with nonverbal cues and the worker's attempt to decipher the coded communications in a job-training group for multihandicapped, blind, mentally retarded adults. A worker in such a group must actively solicit participation, and because of clients' limitations, be quite concrete and clear in every explanation or question.

The worker enters the room and is told by the teacher that the group, upset about something, has been agitated all morning, with much yelling, movement, and confusion. One group member, Laurie, is particularly frenzied, running about, yelling, crying, and laughing—a pattern she has manifested before when she was anxious or worried. The other group members, although seated, are also quite restless. They rock and gesture as they await the beginning of the group session. Billy is making faces. John is playing with his pants leg. Alicia and George are both rocking vigorously, begging Laurie to be quiet. Michael seems to be in a daze. While telling Laurie to stop the noise, Alicia and George try to console her and find out what is wrong.

The first phase, when a worker readies herself or himself to move into the group as a helping person, is the tuning-in phase. Tuning-in is essential to the task of uncovering latent content. Over time, workers familiarize themselves with the characteristic behavior of clients, with the ways the group usually expresses itself and responds to stress. Then they compare the current situation with what has been seen before. Workers need to concentrate on making themselves more receptive to verbal and nonverbal clues and must integrate their general knowledge about the population and its needs with their specific knowledge about their clients. At this session, the worker already knows about Laurie's response to anxiety-provoking situations and that Laurie will continue to act out nonverbally if she is not confronted with whatever is bothering her:

> *Worker*:   Something is wrong. Everyone seems very nervous to me.
> *Alicia*:   Laurie's crying is making everyone nervous.
> *Worker*:   I don't think that's the only thing. Maybe we need to talk. Why are you crying, Laurie?
> *Laurie*:   I just feel like it!
> *Worker*:   I don't think that's the reason.
> *George*:   That's not why you're crying. That's no reason.

By saying that she thinks something is wrong, that everyone seems nervous, the worker helps the group to begin by recognizing their behavior and opening this area for discussion. The suggestion that they need to talk relates directly to the contractual understanding that this group is for discussing feelings. Because of the members' limitations in expressing themselves, the worker must actively identify the problem and reach for feelings.

Worker: (She has heard that Laurie's caseworker is about to go on an extended vacation and knows that this is potentially problematic for Laurie.) Laurie, sometimes people we like go away, and this makes us feel sad, and maybe that has something to do with your feeling sad. Laurie, are you feeling sad because someone is going away?

Laurie: (calming down) Ms. Stone is going away.

Alicia: Ms. Stone is going for a vacation in Europe.

Worker: (to the group) How do you feel when someone you like goes away?

John: I feel sad.

The group and worker partialize the problem, moving from an abstract concept of going away to the specific circumstances of Ms. Stone's leaving. The worker focuses for a moment on Laurie but then generalizes to the whole group and their concerns about "going away." The worker has seen that Laurie is in distress but recognizes that the larger group has also been upset. With the worker's help, the members start to share ideas and feelings, support each other, and work together on what "going away" means. The notion of going away and disappearing seems particularly problematic to this group who, as blind, mentally retarded people, are missing cues about their environment that other people have:

Worker: Are there different kinds of going away? Some people go away on vacation and come back, as Ms. Stone plans to do.

Alicia: I'm going away on a vacation to Puerto Rico.

George: Steve went on a vacation, and he'll be coming back. Everyone is going away for a good time.

John: Parents can die and go away, and you have to go away.

Alicia: To a state school like Kingston, where they don't have any clothes, and you have to eat bad food.

George: Michael, you've been there; you know.

Michael: (Michael had spent more than twenty years in the institution, a distinction he wears as a sort of badge of honor in this group.) We had fishcakes there and ice cream and cake, but they hit you with sticks and straps, and you have to wear a nightgown and sit on the floor.

Worker: Going away to Kingston is a different kind of going away from going away on vacation, the way Ms. Stone is doing. We know lots of people who have gone away, but there are different kinds of going away. Sometimes it makes us feel sad.

Billy: I feel sad when someone goes away.

Alicia: I feel sad when someone passes away.

Worker: Yes, it feels sad. (a brief silence)

What was initially a group struggling to communicate has become a group expressing itself around painful and confusing areas. It is not surprising that the group was so agitated at the beginning of the session, since the loss of Ms. Stone to her vacation was so mixed up with other profound losses: deaths of parents, institutionalizations, friends disappearing from the program, and graduations to nowhere. The worker tries to clarify and concretize by reaching for more information:

Worker:	But some people go away for good reasons. Can you think of the people we know who have gone away? Laurie, do you know anyone who has gone away?
Laurie:	Danny. (Danny had been riding to the program in the same van to which Laurie is assigned. He was removed from the car without any explanation.)
Worker:	Danny is in this building in the workshop.
Laurie:	I don't know where he is, upstairs or downstairs.
George:	Ronnie went away.
Alicia:	Stan went away, too.
Worker:	Does anybody know where all these people have gone?
George:	When people graduate, they might get thrown out of the program like Stan.
John, Michael, and George:	Stan didn't cooperate, so he had to go away.
Worker:	Stan did go away, but he is probably in his home or participating in another program.
George:	Ronnie graduated.
Michael:	I hope I can graduate right away.
Worker:	Why would you like that, Michael?
Michael:	I just like to graduate like Ronnie.
Worker:	Where does everybody think Ronnie is now?
George:	(after several of the group members give confused accounts of Ronnie's whereabouts) I think Ronnie works in another program in this building.
Worker:	Maybe we could take a tour of the building next week so that we can find out about the other programs, and most important, so that we can find out where our friends have gone. Would you like to do that? (The group members respond with enthusiasm.)

The worker finally recognizes the need for this population to have a concrete way of understanding "going away" by planning for the group to tour the building the following week. By their enthusiasm, the group members seem to acknowledge the value of the tour to gain mastery over their fears and a clearer understanding of what some of the "going away" means.

Acting out Feelings

Sometimes the symbolic ways in which people communicate are not so hard to uncover and are plain to both group members and the worker. The latent message in the following vignette is a source of rueful amusement for all concerned. The exchange takes place in an inpatient psychiatric ward in which some patient self-government is encouraged as part of the treatment plan. Patients participating in the operation of the unit feel as if they have some control over what is happening to them, and this participation is thought to be therapeutic. In response to a patient's request, a patients' committee has been formed to draft a booklet of unit-life rules. The group is now meeting for a reading of the newly developed rules:

Worker:	Number one, patients should not bother other patients' visitors for cigarettes.
Mr. T:	(raising his hand) Mr. Green, I don't feel good. Can I be excused? (Without waiting for a response, he darts out of the room.)
Worker:	Number two, kissing and other forms of sexual behavior are not permitted on the unit. (Miss G. and Mr. R. jump up from their seats and start to leave.)
Worker:	Where are you going? Miss G? Mr. R?
Miss G:	To the bathroom. I feel sick. I can't wait.
Worker:	Number three, patients should respect the property of other patients and should not take things from the rooms of others. (Mr. B. begins to fake symptoms and hobbles off to his room, twisting his face into grotesque shapes.)
Group members:	(general laughter)
Mr. V:	What's going on here?
Worker:	That's a good question, Mr. V. Does anyone have any ideas?
Group members:	(laughter again and then quiet)
Miss L:	Well, Mr. B steals all the time (the others murmur assent), and Mr. T drove my boyfriend crazy for cigarettes when he visited me.
Worker:	So there seems to be a connection between the rules you've drawn up and some folks' difficulty in listening to them read aloud? (a general roar of laughter)
Mr. V:	Yeah, boy! It looks like all the rule breakers split.

It seems that, by their actions, the members of this group are saying that they need to leave in response to rules they have already been breaking. More significantly, by leaving they are, in effect, challenging the authority of the group. The group does not have the power to hold them in the meeting room. Nor does it have the power to enforce its rules. Exiting the room before the end of the group is part of the testing process and a way of separating oneself from the group, its sanctions, or its mandates.

Following a Theme

A useful way to identify latent content and encourage it to surface so that it does not become an obstacle to work and growth is to study important group themes that develop over time. Issues that repeat themselves in different sessions, sometimes in disguised forms, are issues that are important to the members. The skilled worker learns to be sensitive to timing, not necessarily addressing problematic material in early sessions before worker and member trust each other but filing those issues for future consideration at a more appropriate time. Key concerns for a particular population are likely to show up, although sometimes in a veiled manner, repeatedly throughout the lifetime of the group.

A valuable tool in educating oneself to listen for latent content is the record of service (Schwartz and Zalba, 1972). This method of process recording focuses on a particular group problem or issue over time. By writing the analysis, the worker attempts to identify skills or rubrics used in the course of the process. The next practice excerpt uses the record of service format to follow a group of eleven- to thirteen-year-old boys over a period of approximately one month. Four sessions are excerpted, as they pertain to the issue under consideration. The female worker, who reviews the record and her thoughts in this piece, has been working for a short time with the group and the co-leader, Craig.

Throughout the piece, what stands out most framatically is the worker's continued listening to, identifying of, and partializing of the problems and feelings that are verbally and nonverbally expressed by the members. The worker helps the members to engage around its issues but reframes the discussion in a manner that dilutes its intensity. By using correct terminology for sexual activities and body parts, the worker permits a more normal discussion of charged emotions. For this population, sexuality is associated with hostile feelings toward women, and control and dominance themes. In a nonpunitive manner, the worker accepts their form of expression and helps them to clarify some of the confusing things they are experiencing:

12/28—It was during a discussion about riding the train that Richard spoke of a book he had found on the train. The boys, apparently aware of the book already, said, "Show her the book." They argued back and forth and decided not to show me the book. I said it seemed they were wanting to tell me something but couldn't (listening, identifying conflict and feelings). I wondered why (attempting to help them identify the problem). Lawrence said, "Now, it's not right to talk about it in front of a woman." I said I wondered what they thought would happen if they did (partializing). They said nothing, but it wasn't right to talk about it, and they wouldn't. I said I guessed they didn't know me too well yet, but that they would learn, in time, that we could talk about anything at all in the group. That was the purpose (identifying feelings, accepting feelings, talking to the source of feelings, contracting). I let it go at this point in part because I did not want to force the matter and in part because of my own uneasiness at the time. But the boys were fast to pick it up the next week.

1/4—We were planning a bowling trip and the boys questioned whether or not I, because I was a woman, could bowl. The conversation went to why they felt women were inept at sports and then to what makes a man. One boy mentioned men growing hair. The others began to laugh. I said I wondered what the joke was (confronting the affect). Lawrence said, "They're crazy." Craig suggested that the boys tell us what was funny. They said, "No, you know; you tell her." Craig said they were afraid. I said it seemed they wanted me to know, but they couldn't tell me, so they wanted Craig to talk for them (listening, identifying feeling and process, pointing out conflictual feelings, identifying a problem). Craig told me, and then the boys insisted he tell me about the book. He did, and the boys asked me if I was embarrassed. I wondered if they thought I should be. They said, "Yeah, what he said." Craig suggested that they had feelings about talking about sex to women. They said yes. It was for men to talk about, not women. I asked why that was (seeking clarification). Each one began to discuss it in terms of sex being an act for men, women being passive. I continued to clarify messages, confront more directly, and help the children identify their concerns.

Time was up after this. As usual, the boys brought it up at the end of each meeting. The boys were still hesitant to speak openly about sex, but there was definitely a need for information to clarify their ideas and feelings about sex.

1/18—After a very active meeting and the introduction of a new member, two boys lingered asking what we (Craig and I) did in the office after they left. I said I wondered why they hadn't brought this up in the group and had waited till afterward (confronting their actions). Lawrence wanted to know if we dated. I told him this was something we could talk about next week in the group (setting limits, identifying problems of resistance, making the problem a group issue). He sat on the third-floor bannister, threatening to "jump to his death" if I didn't tell him if Craig and I kissed in the office afterward. I put my coat on, ignoring his threat, and said, "Next week in the group, guys, we'll talk about it" (sticking with feelings, confronting the problem).

1/24—The next session, the boys said they were angry because we didn't answer their question. Since the other boys were unaware of what had happened, I suggested they tell them (focusing, holding the group responsible for sharing information). They wouldn't, but after a good deal of group pressure, they did. They asked Craig, "Do you like her?" I said it seemed the question was very important to them (listening, reaching for feelings). "Yes, we want to know what you do in the office after we leave." I said they really seemed concerned about this and wondered whether they really weren't asking something else. Thomas said, "What do men and women do when they're alone behind a locked door?" Richard said, "Yeah, if they're naked." Lawrence said, "We're talking about sex." "Yes, you're talking about the sexual relationship between men and women," I said (identifying the issue). "Yeah," they yelled and began joking around. We commented on their feelings about talking about this.

They quieted down and asked us to tell them everything. I said it seemed that they were asking us to lecture them, and I wondered why they didn't want to participate (identifying the problem, reaching for clarification, sticking with the issue). After a short discussion on their thinking that "you don't talk about this stuff with a woman," Thomas said, "What's the answer? You didn't answer us." I said, "Okay, what do you think happens between a man and a woman?" Lawrence mumbled, "Fucking." I said, "You think sexual intercourse—that's another name for fucking or screwing—happens when a man and woman are alone?" (reframing, partializing, translating messages) "Yeah," they said. The others disagreed. "First you play with a woman," they said, using a variety of slang terms. Craig and I repeated what they said, using different terminology—breast, vagina, penis—in place of slang. They quieted down and began asking some serious questions: "Where did a baby come from? How did it come out? How was it really made?" We threw the questions back out to the group, helping to clarify, explaining labor pains, sperm, ejaculation, etc. The discussion covered everything from sexual stimulation to birth deformities. I suggested some pictures on fetal development for next week. They agreed eagerly. Several meetings passed before they brought up the subject again. They were more comfortable and less anxious about discussing it and the pictures.

Growing by Respecting the Message of the Group

Sometimes, as noted earlier, the issues for a population parallel the phase issues in a particular session. In work with many disenfranchised populations or in work with involuntary clients, the general issues concerning trust are exaggerated. Parenting groups conducted by agencies that are also responsible for removing neglected or abused children from families are likely to have members uneasy about self-disclosure; sharing is simply a potential danger. Groups working with battered women or with the batterers themselves take more time than other groups might to develop the intimacy necessary for reaching goals. A good deal of the work that has to be done with such groups focuses on overcoming the suspicion, mistrust, and concerns about confidentiality.

The next piece chronicles a series of worker errors in understanding the latent material regarding trust and responding appropriately to it. The excerpt then highlights the worker's attempts to recover from her mistakes and move toward a recognition of the group issues. The members of the support group for welfare mothers, each with at least one child under the age of six, are preparing for general education and employment training. The worker has been with the group for approximately two months.

Prior to the sessions under examination here, the worker had been approached by two staff members who had asked permission to join the group as observers. One of the staff members, Harriet, would be conducting a series of workshops for the group and wanted to get a sense of the group and to hear about their interests.

> 11/15—*Worker*:   Would you mind having two people observe the group today?
>
> *Group members*:   No. We don't mind.
>
> *Harriet*:   How do you feel about health and nutrition? (silence) Birth control? (silence) Domestic violence? (silence, some members shrug, some nod their heads)
>
> *Worker*:   Would you like to continue last week's discussion on parenting? (silence) I want to try something a little different today. I realize everyone is tired from sitting for several hours. Let's do a short relaxation and meditation exercise. I want you to imagine that you are lying on a beach somewhere with the sun shining overhead. There are some birds flying overhead, too. When they fly over, all your negative thoughts fly away with the birds. (after the exercise) Does anyone care to share any feelings or thoughts you might have had during the exercise? (silence)
>
> *Maria*:   When you said there were birds flying overhead, I imagined they were seagulls, and I hoped they wouldn't shit on my head. (laughter) I just wanted to put in a little humor. (There is more silence, and the worker tries to move into another topic.)
>
> *Worker*:   Shall we talk about getting along with co-workers? (more silence) You are all so quiet today. You don't seem to want to talk about any subject I mention. What do you want to talk about?
>
> *Lottie*:   Why don't you discuss good study habits? That's what everybody else does. (The group continues in a half-hearted discussion of the topic for the rest of the hour.)

The moment she introduced the guest observers, the worker lost her group. They express their anger with the intruders by refusing to participate, but the worker responds only to the issue of content, never recognizing the mood in the room or the circumstances contributing to the feelings. She takes at face value the expressed agreement to allow the guests, when in fact, the group members feel that they have no choice about accepting visitors and do not really agree to it. The worker might have given notice or allowed for discussion during the prior week, but instead she puts the group members in the awkward position of refusing guests who are already present.

The worker continues to try to motivate the group after their repeated silences, finally deciding that a relaxation technique may help dispel the lethargy. Again, she fails to hear the response: the birds in her exercise are transformed, in Maria's words, into seagulls whose droppings fall on Maria's head. This is the ultimate symbolic expression of anger, the seagulls (intruders) dumping on the group members. Maria is telling the worker that this process is demeaning her. Still, the worker is deaf to the message. The following week, the worker listens more effectively and begins to work with the previously unexpressed material:

11/22—*Worker*: I think we need to talk about the group. When I come in here, you all seem to be very tired. When I try to do exercises to wake you up, you don't seem to want to do them. Last week, every topic I initiated met with silence. I feel like I'm pulling teeth to get you to say anything, and that's not what this group is all about. How do you feel about this group?

Maria: I like it.

Peggy: When I was in the group last spring, everyone was close, and we tried to support each other, and it was really good.

Worker: So what's happening now?

Ginny: How are we going to say anything if it's not confidential?

Worker: What do you mean? I thought we discussed how everything stays in the room?

Ginny: Sometimes it doesn't.

Worker: What do you mean?

Ginny: Something was said in the group last spring, and the group worker told the caseworker who came down on this person's case.

Lily: One time I even had a caseworker call me at home and accuse me of something I didn't even do.

Maria: It's like being betrayed.

Peggy: You get suspicious of every worker.

Ginny: We don't want anyone sitting in on our group.

Worker: But I asked you last week if it would be all right if Harriet sat in, and you said yes.

Ginny and others:	What were we supposed to say, no?
Worker:	Yes. You are supposed to say no, and I would have respected your wishes.
Group:	Well, from now on, we don't want any observers!
Worker:	Okay, but my supervisor has to observe me some time during the season.
Group:	Okay, but no one else.

The worker's openness in addressing her own feelings and reactions to the previous session and her honest exploration of the group members' feelings yield a real response. Concerns about confidentiality and trust finally surface and can be discussed. The potential for meaningful work exists only after the latent content is uncovered.

Clarifying Communication

In certain groups, reaching for latent content involves interpreting communications between members to assure that speaker and listener understand the message in the same way. The following vignette, which is taken from a group session for persons with head injuries, demonstrates one way in which a worker can help clarify communication among members:

Ken:	Everything I try to do is more difficult now.
Mollie:	I find things more enjoyable now because I don't have to do them (speaks about preparing a dinner for friends). Now that things are harder, they're more challenging, and so I enjoy them more.
Robert:	It's not like they were easy before. It's just that you took them for granted.
Mollie:	Exactly, like walking.
Ken:	Like walking, that's true . . .
Mollie:	(wistfully) I used to walk and run and cook and do everything.
Ken:	Listen, I used to kick my leg all the way up in the air . . . but now . . .
Mollie:	Ken, I used not to be able to move my legs either, but now I can. You must keep the faith and keep trying. You can do it.
Ken:	I understand. I understand.
Mollie:	It's one thing saying it, and another thing doing it. (As she speaks, Ken looks away from her and hangs his head.)
Worker:	Ken, do you hear what Mollie's saying to you?
Ken:	Well, she's saying that I don't, sort of like, I don't . . . have the faith.
Worker:	What does that mean to you?

Ken:	Like I'm not trying hard enough.
Worker:	And what do you think?
Ken:	Believe me, Mollie, I try.

Symbolic Expression

In the course of work with groups, one finds numerous examples of symbolic ways to express difficult feelings. Symbolism is more likely to be present when the pain is incapacitating. It acts as a defensive posture by helping some of the difficulty to be expressed, if only in a cloaked fashion. In some ways, there is a strong parallel between the symbolic expression of pain in groups and the manner in which difficult feelings are addressed in dreams. We have chosen a few powerful examples of such symbolic communication in groups.

A farewell party, including refreshments and entertainment, was conducted by a co-worker and a group for a long-term worker in a psychiatric residence. One severely regressed hebephrenic man, who rarely talked, was particularly distressed by the loss of the worker. Rising to his feet and standing in the middle of the room, directly in front of the honoree, he started to sing "Stormy Weather" with almost no affect.

The song suggests that the sun has disappeared with the absence of the singer's loved one and now there is perpetual rain. There is no doubt about the nature of the message from client to worker.

A young singles' support group was discussing the plans of one member, Claire, to attend her sister's wedding. Attending the wedding was problematic for Claire, because she had recently broken away from the family and established her own different lifestyle. She viewed her return to her parents' home with much trepidation:

Claire:	I better dress warm. It's cold back in Montreal. (to the worker) You have such rich long hair. Mine is falling out. Maybe you could give me some.
Nancy:	You want her to cut it?
Claire:	No, just give it to me for a loan to get me through the wedding.

Claire expressed her need to hold on to the worker's hair (a sort of transitional object) as she moved from her not fully secure new life to the potentially consuming old life of her primary family. She literally wanted to take a piece of the worker and the group with her to help keep her warm and safe in the threatening emotional climate to which she was returning. Following this revelation, a discussion of the underlying meaning helped the client to meet the challenge of maintaining her newly discovered identity in her old environment.

A single parents' group was meeting close to the Christmas holidays and raising issues about the difficulties of celebrating given their life circumstances.

The father of Joan, one woman in the group, had died some years ago. As she reported it, he was the only one in her family who had really enjoyed the holiday and made it bright for everyone else. Joan had never fully expressed her grief, and she had difficulties sharing any emotions about her losses or about other issues in the group. For many weeks, group and worker struggled to help Joan express herself, but she was unable to do so. At this session, as she was leaving, Joan revealed a bottle of Liquid Plumber which she had been carrying with her, saying, "Damn sink's clogged! Lousy plumbing, but I'm not giving up. If this doesn't work, I'll try plunging."

The worker seized upon the interpretation that Joan, like her sink, was clogged up, but with feelings that were blocking the works. The group, too, heard the message that, despite their difficulties in reaching Joan, she did not want them to abandon her. The following session the discussion resumed and led to Joan's unburdening her pain. Tears finally flowed and brought welcome relief.

Sometimes an entire group meeting is similar to an extended metaphor in which some hard-to-talk about subject serves as a latent theme throughout. The latent content may manifest itself repeatedly with various symbolic representations. The group worker's awareness of the theme's importance for the group allows her to recognize its reappearance and to continue to explore its meaning. When further discussion is necessary, the group will continue to provide the clues and the worker must stay with them, helping the group members to focus, clarify, and struggle with the issues.

For example, in a psychiatric day treatment center, chronically mentally ill people attend a variety of social, recreational, and therapy groups as part of their long-term treatment. Goals for these groups center around keeping participants as functional as possible so that they can continue living in the community without hospitalization. Day treatment attempts to create a therapeutic milieu in which every activity is designed to make participants feel more normal, cope better with stressors, and learn to manage as independently as possible within the limitations of their illnesses. It is not uncommon, in such settings, to have clients act out feelings in a destructive manner rather than address them and deal with them. So, it is particularly vital to the success of the program to look at behavior and connect it with feelings. When exacerbated during termination, the intensity of the dependency, loss, and separation and individuation issues for this population creates a potentially lethal situation.

The Hunger Artist

In the following excerpt, group members of a social club in a day treatment center have been meeting with co-therapists, both of whom will be leaving the agency in the near future. One worker's departure is imminent; the co-worker who is working with the group during this session will be leaving the group in a few months. As the worker enters, the group members are seated in the meeting room. They begin to complain that nobody has ordered food for them. The worker suggests that group members collect money and that somebody go out to make the purchases for the group. After considerable bickering among the members, the worker comments that members seem to be saying that no one is taking care of them. Paul hushes the others in an almost conspiratorial fashion, and he, Rodney, and Judith go out to buy the food. On their return, Judith and Vinnie grab the food and start wolfing it down:

Paul:	Look at them! Look at them! Look at them! (laughing almost hysterically and being joined by Iris and Richie)
Rodney:	You know it's not funny to laugh at them. They might be on medication or something. Paul, you know what it's like when you're sick. You wanna stuff yourself. You can't never eat enough. You shouldn't laugh at them that way. They might be sick, and if you laugh at them, that'll make them feel bad. (Paul quieted down.)
Worker:	Food is something that makes us feel better. Are you saying, Rodney, that we shouldn't laugh at people who are trying to fill up with something that will make them feel better?
Rodney:	You shouldn't laugh at them. I remember what it was like to be sick. You eat and eat.
Paul:	Yeah, but they stuff themselves, and then we don't get a chance to get anything.
Worker:	You mean, what will we have left to make us feel good? It's like they get all the good feelings, the nurturing, before us.
Rodney:	It's like my cat. Whenever he sees food, he gets happy. Just the sight of food makes him happy. You get happy from eating sugar things. It makes you relax.
Worker:	It's like putting something sweet inside of you. (to Paul) Sometimes we laugh at something because we're scared. Like here, maybe Judith and Vinnie will get all the food— the thing that makes us feel good—before you get a chance to.

This discussion of food and never having enough is a theme which recurs throughout the meeting. Each time it appears, it is loosely connected with the impending loss of the worker, reviving the dependency issues. Group members sense that they are being abandoned and that no one will be left to care for them. The inappropriate hysterical laughter and the accompanying scapegoating of Vinnie and Judith alert the worker to the intensity of the feeling. Vinnie and Judith are identified as sick; it's their problem, not ours. The other members separate themselves from those who must eat ravenously to be insulated against the pain.

The ultimate fear is that nothing will be left when Vinnie and Judith are through. There will be no comfort. Continual reference is made to the void, the emptiness within, the hunger, which will remain after the worker's departure. As the process excerpt continues, a different energy is in the room. The talk is louder than usual, the restlessness constant. The worker again tries to make the connection between the feelings about the expected changes in the group and the members' nervous activity. Some group members appear frightened by the discussion and respond accordingly:

Judith:	Let's change the subject. It's gonna kill us talking about this.
Richie:	If Ellie leaves, I'll die. Who will I talk to?
Worker:	It's like Ellie is a part of us, but if she leaves, you won't die. You'll just miss her, but you'll still have the memory inside you. You'll still have what she gave you.
Iris:	Yeah, that part will still be there.
Richie:	Is the agency closing? Is it closing?
Worker:	No. The agency will stay open. Just Ellie is leaving.

Again, the worker tries to clarify and reassure, but the issue is still difficult and is expressed symbolically several times more. A reading of a single paragraph from the short story, "The Hunger Artist," stimulates Shirley to lie down on the couch, lift her shirt, and begin rubbing her stomach. The other group members again begin to laugh uproariously. As before, Rodney is disturbed by the laughter and begins to speak about how serious the story and the notion about going hungry is to him. The discussion flows naturally into talk about parents. Feeding, starving, pain, mothering, and Ellie become intertwined:

Worker:	I think in a way we can all relate to the pain, but I get the feeling we're laughing because something hurts inside.
Rodney:	Yeah, it's like when my parents . . . I don't got a mother and father who take care of me. I know what it's like to starve.

The poignancy of Rodney's remark, and the threat of starvation now that the worker (the group's mother) is leaving, is felt by all. The session continues, moving from the symbolic to the real and back. The worker must seek the appropriate balance by gently making the connections, encouraging the expression, and separating truth from fiction: the worker is leaving, the group members will not die from talking about it, they will not die from her leaving, the agency is not closing, people can feel sad without falling apart, crying will not kill you, and so forth. Some of the discussion becomes confusing, and the worker must focus repeatedly, but finally he succeeds in helping the group to open up around the difficult issues. No doubt this discussion will extend over many sessions and will remain partially unresolved. For this population, however, an important crossroads has been reached; this group has talked about loss and has survived.

Reference

Schwartz, W. and Zalba, S., Eds. *The Practice of Group Work.* New York: Columbia University Press, 1972.

4   IN THE BEGINNING

When you see a strange cat in a weird looking hat, there is no need to lose your composure. Just keep him in view—he will soon grow on you, all you need is a bit more exposure.

Lewis Carroll
Alice's Adventures in Wonderland (1865)

The Members' Issues

The first phase of group development is generally termed "beginnings." In many ways, this early phase parallels ideal early individual development. Beginnings have been likened to infancy, a stage in which the baby learns to trust both himself and his environment (Erikson, 1963). During this phase, the infant learns that father and mother are dependable and still love the infant, even when they must be absent. The idea that the infant can risk certain expressive behaviors and still be rewarded with nurturing is reinforced during this stage as well. As babies advance, they reach out to the environment in general and to significant others in particular, expanding their horizons and feeling safe because the beginning was secure. If there is an early environment of nurturing, consistency, safety, and low frustration, children develop an ability to risk and thereby extend their pools of initial nurturance and learning. Early on, babies also begin to understand the structures under which their families operate and the symbolic exchanges among family members.

In a social group work relationship, the worker also must help create an atmosphere that allows for safe expression of intimate private feelings. Trust, nurturing, consistency, safety, and low frustration must be provided here to facilitate risk taking and promote growth.

The beginnings of all groups are characterized by some degree of fearfulness for members, with a higher incidence of concern in groups in which self-disclosure is anticipated. The degree of fearfulness also depends on the members' level of functioning and the members' familiarity with group participation in the past. After all, how can I, a group member, know what will be expected of me in this group, what can be gained from the experience, who these other people are, and how they are going to receive me? The group may be a terrifying place in which I am open to attack. I feel vulnerable, anxious, and unsure of myself and others. Consequently, I am cautious, testing and choosing what I say carefully. I talk little, waiting for the leader and other members to clue me in on the norms of the group and what is okay to say and what is not. Or I talk nonstop about the weather and sports and keep the conversation safely light, in my own control, and nonthreatening.

In general, I am like a stranger in a foreign land, unfamiliar with the language, anxious about the unknown, and without signposts. I struggle to determine the local customs and then question what will happen to me should I try them. Worst of all is the fear that my mistakes in this potentially dangerous arena will have larger consequences in my entire life, that my remarks here will not be held in confidence. As a result of all of these concerns, I maintain a position of constant vigilance, always providing myself with an opportunity for retreat and maintaining some distance from these strangers.

At the same time I am wary of this new group experience, I yearn for it. The chance to share with people, to feel a sense of belonging and acceptance, to talk with others who can understand the things that matter most to me, and to accomplish some purpose, pull me toward the group.

The issues raised by any group member about tuning-in, engagement, and beginning contracting are the same regardless of group structure, methodology, purpose, or composition. During the beginning phase, group members experience, to a greater or lesser degree, classical approach/avoidance conflicts (Garland, Kolodny, and Jones, 1975), wanting to share, explore, belong, and be close with others yet fearing vulnerability, hurt, and rejection.

The Worker's Role: Use of Self and Issues of Authority

Just as group members approach the group with some ambivalence and trepidation, the worker may have some anxiety about the experience. With beginning workers in beginning phases, this anxiety manifests itself in two extreme stances. On the one hand, workers tend to involve themselves in every interaction, being directive and controlling. Workers believe, on some level, that to allow the group process to evolve without maintaining control invites chaos and the overthrow of the worker. To bind up their own anxiety, workers hold the reins tightly and direct the group. Workers in this state allow the group to move only where they feel safe, areas usually related to concrete issues. They try to keep the discussion light and lively, entertaining and nonthreatening not only for group members but also for themselves.

This may express itself in an over involvement with rules governing some group activity (for instance, how many minutes should be used by each member during introductions or what specific questions should be asked). Attention to details rather than latent content protects the worker by creating a distance between the group and any material it needs to discuss that may be stressful for the worker as well as group participants. The group, also needing to feel safe, comfortably colludes with the worker to limit the arena available for discussion.

On the other hand, some workers defend against the terror they feel by withdrawing entirely. These workers allow their groups to go their own ways, proceeding in an unfocused, wandering style not directed toward the group's goals. The worker hopes that if he or she does not make waves, everyone will remain safe. Again, group members collude with the worker to stay away from what is believed to be a dangerous and perhaps self-revealing discussion. Members of this group have no guidelines to assess what is appropriate, helpful, or necessary to raise in the context of the group. Neither are they helped to understand what they can achieve as a group. If they have had no prior formal group experience, they need some education about how to use their group to accomplish individual and collective purposes. In this sense, the retreating worker fails to facilitate the work of the group.

Another issue for workers in beginnings and throughout the course of the group concerns the exerting of authority and the assumption of a professional role. Many social workers are uncomfortable with a role of authority, preferring what appears to be a more egalitarian position. Yet the worker is responsible, when the group is in a formative stage, to introduce the group members to the initial purpose of the group and its structure and to maintain a safe beginning atmosphere by taking charge of the contractual phase. When the group first assembles, the worker may direct them to take their seats, call the meeting to order, and greet the members individually and collectively, thereby informally establishing her or his role. With certain populations, this initial process may be even more directive, and the worker may need to be more active in controlling certain behaviors. Examples include restricting physical acting-out with populations with impulse control problems; enforcing agency rules or mandates, such as no one can participate in a group while inebriated; or reporting involuntary clients who fail to attend meetings or who are in violation of the law, such as child abusers.

Workers must perform these important tasks as the authority in the group, but personal identity issues create countertransferential responses and often complicate notions about this professional role. Workers may feel that they are not entitled to set limits on people who are struggling with concrete or psychic boundaries. They may be overwhelmed by the enormity of the problems group members are facing and believe that their own personal experiences do not prepare them adequately to help in certain situations.

All workers need to feel accepted, but some have unresolved conflicts that drive this need for acceptance into an inability to exercise control or authority. Consequently, a worker may avoid limiting a monopolizing group member, may allow an adolescent to break agency rules, or may fail to challenge the group to work for fear of being rejected. For some young workers, still struggling with their own unresolved conflicts regarding authority, identification with adolescent group members is a powerful inhibitor to taking control, which often results in workers' unconscious support of inappropriate behavior. In some sense, the adolescents end up acting out the workers' unresolved issues.

An interesting illustration of some of the issues relating to authority concerns the relationship between an exceedingly gifted young worker and his elderly clients. Nathaniel, who is twenty-five years old, has been struggling with issues concerning his authority in working with a senior citizens' music appreciation group. As strange as it may seem, Nathaniel seems to be regarded by the group as the authority on everything, despite the fact that he is relatively young and inexperienced and appears even younger and more fragile than his actual age. In the beginning, Nathaniel is quite concerned that he will be unable to provide any sense of control or direction for the group.

The group's purpose is to use music to give group members enjoyment and a focus for sharing their memories. Each time Nathaniel comes to the group session, he asks the group members what sort of music they would like to hear, and they reply that whatever Nathaniel likes is fine with them. "What is your choice, Beethoven, Glenn Miller, Gershwin?" Nathaniel asks. They respond, "Whatever you like, Nathaniel." "Beethoven?" "Okay!" "Glenn Miller?" "Okay!" "Gershwin?" "Okay!" Group members remain docile and cooperative and refuse to make a decision.

Nathaniel knows that the power he feels in the group is a result of the disempowerment of the elderly group members rather than his own worthiness. He comes to the group the next session and spreads the six hundred or so record albums from the center's collection on the floor in the middle of a circle of chairs. When the group assembles, Nathaniel asks the members once again what they would like to hear and refuses to make any selection himself. Nothing proceeds until a group member finally makes a choice. In a few weeks, group members are coming to every session with suggestions for musical selections and even with their own albums or those borrowed from the library. Unlike many young workers, Nathaniel was able to overcome his own needs for power and recognize the needs of his clients.

Most workers, even those with a great deal of experience, face uncertainty in beginning. This is true in the beginning phase of the group and for the start of each individual session in the life of the group. Just as group members have mixed feelings, the worker also experiences great anticipation and hope for the group along with the initial concerns and fears (see fear of groups syndrome in Shulman, 1979). In some sense, both the worker and the group members approach and avoid at the same time.

Role of the Worker: Beginning Tasks and Issues for the Group

The worker's responsibility is to use the beginning phase to help establish guidelines, structures, goals, and purposes, and to assert the worker's own role in facilitating the achievement of those goals. The group's beginning phase is characterized by the creation of norms and values, the development of structure and goals, and the establishment of patterns of communication. These activities relate to "contracting." In the beginning, the worker assists in the contracting tasks by stimulating the work of the group and providing clarification and some structure. Early on, the group needs to know that its work will be conducted in a secure environment that nurtures and promotes growth. Developing a trusting atmosphere also becomes the task of the worker, who must maintain a delicate balance between adequate exploration of beginning themes and overexposure of vulnerabilities.

Although the ultimate goal of the group is empowerment and individuation from the worker, in the beginning phase, the group needs to be dependent upon the worker. Sometimes, this need arises from a feeling of powerlessness on the part of group members who come to the group experience, and especially to the worker, for answers to life problems. The worker may easily be convinced to feel omnipotent. The desire of the worker to be a savior or an all-nurturing mother arises from the mutual needs of the worker and the group. It takes time for group members to conceive of the group experience as the means to reach solutions. For some beginning workers, it also takes time for them to have confidence in the group process. The worker must be active in this stage, always guarding against becoming overly controlling and providing some magical answers, offering instead a means to help the group work through the questions.

The struggles of group members and workers to meet the demands and stresses of beginnings are illustrated by examples from every sort of setting. We have selected a few such examples to clarify some of what has already been discussed.

Contracting: Formal versus Informal

The following excerpt is taken from a first meeting of a leadership training group. The group members were formerly involved in a self-help group for divorced Catholic women titled the "Starting Over" group. Starting Over had grown unexpectedly large and had to be subdivided into smaller groups, which necessitated the training of many lay leaders. A local psychiatric facility was commissioned to provide training by its community education team. Although group members knew each other from participation in the large group, the group worker was meeting the group members for the first time. The group begins with some informal exchanges and greetings among members. The worker says hello, states her name, and invites group members to be seated wherever they want.

> *Worker:*   I would like to introduce myself more formally now. My name is Mary DeVito. I'm a psychiatric social worker at the community mental health center, which is where you are now. As part of our community consultation and educational work, we provide all kinds of group treatment and training for different community organizations, schools, and so forth.

How this all came about was when Father John, who we work very closely with through the Golden Age Club, contacted us for some assistance around developing the group you have going—"Starting Over," right?—for some assistance around leadership. He explained that it had grown rapidly into a large group and people were more interested in having a smaller group experience where they could talk and share, and he asked us to come down as some kind of leader to see if we can get some kind of a small group experience going. My interest and involvement in the community is to develop leadership from within the ranks, so to speak, where there are people who are already part of the group, to try to develop leaders from that core who can then take on the running of discussions in the group themselves and not involve a whole bunch of outside people who do not belong there. So that is my feeling, my commitment to the work that I do in the community, developing various kinds of support groups, self-help groups, leadership groups, and things of that sort. That's why me and that's what I'm doing here. As for any questions of training or background in this area, I will share with you that I've been doing training and running groups both therapeutic in the clinic as well as teaching, consultation, and support groups; that's my area of work. I've gotten my training at New York University in psychiatric social work in individual and group as well. So, that's the experience and background I bring, and interest as well. This is something I'm excited about because I'm committed to it, and it's always exciting to do. So, that's who I am, and having said that, I'd like to ask each of you, even though you know each other [for the purposes of this group you don't, because it's starting new], to introduce yourself. Say anything you'd like to share with the group, as I have done, including only one thing, and that's why you wanted to be here. So whoever would like to begin, please do so.

Group: (a long silence)

The group worker begins the session with some review of how the group came to be and what has brought its members together. She notes their common interests, their history, and the contact between the two agencies. She is contracting with the group, setting goals almost immediately, and utilizing classical skills: reaching for reciprocity by asking to "share with the group, as I have done, why you wanted to be here" and reiterating what the agency sees as the contract for the group, "to provide training in leadership." Most importantly, she acknowledges that her agency has been invited to address the problems in maintaining the self-help program. This part of the introduction sets the common purpose and a link with an already trusted friend, the priest. To make a connection of this sort is not usually possible in groups, but the worker demonstrates her skill by using her knowledge of the special relationship with an ally of the self-help project. The use of the formal presentation as a kickoff to what will develop later into a less formal interaction seems central to developing trust in this group. The worker lists her credentials and makes clear what she sees as her intent. She places herself in the position of trainer as opposed to group member and directs the next part of the meeting by assigning a question to be addressed in the members' introductions. These interventions begin to separate the worker's role from that of group members. By distancing herself in this way, the worker models the kind of distancing group members need to emulate when they become leaders of their own groups. By enumerating her qualifications, the worker establishes herself as an authority. This also gives group members a feeling of safety and trust in her ability. This formal presentation of self is particularly useful in groups whose population needs clear boundaries: this group, whose members are in the process of redefining their roles (moving from member to leader), and groups of emotionally dysfunctional clients in which the psychic boundaries are poorly defined.

In the process excerpt, the leader's discussion of her "commitment," "interest," and "excitement" about working with groups sets a somewhat less formal tone and allows for engagement even in the midst of the formal presentation. In effect, the worker is saying that she likes being with the group. She communicates her genuine desire to do this work, to be helpful to the group members, and to assist achievement of the group goals.

This worker's approach is only one in a repertoire of styles for beginnings that might be used to achieve the same purposes through the introduction of the worker and how she uses herself. In some groups, the worker merely states her name and defines the purpose of the group from her own and the agency's perspective. In other groups, only the briefest introduction and statement of purpose is followed by the worker's reflection on the mood in the room and the difficulties in beginnings. Other workers immediately try to elicit client reactions to attending the group and what each client's objectives are in participating.

The listing of professional credentials might, in some groups, distance the members in a way not conducive to the development of trust. The formality may be misinterpreted as superiority and may set up an atmosphere of challenge and testing rather than one of trust and sharing. The worker's task in beginnings is to respond to challenge and testing as they occur but to avoid initiating confrontation until greater cohesiveness and bonding occur among group members. The worker's knowledge of the population should guide her as to how formally to present herself. The setting and, importantly, the needs of the clients govern the level of formality.

In a hospital setting, some patients may be more at ease with a credentialed worker in her white lab coat because she represents protection, authority, and knowledge—someone with the clout necessary to negotiate, advocate, and provide answers. Other patients, alienated from the treatment team and distrustful of the sterile, unfamiliar, and unresponsive medical atmosphere, may need the warmth, informality, and friendliness of the worker who does not wear a uniform of others in the facility.

In short, the formal presentation of the self is most effective in any of the following situations:

1. lack of clarity about roles (as in the training group presented here);
2. poor psychic boundaries and a special need for structure and consistency (as in many inpatient psychiatric settings);
3. clients who are frightened, dependent, and in need of more control and less ambiguity (as in large, complex bureaucracies—a hospital, for example).

The informal presentation might be most effective in any of the following situations:

1. a need for the worker to be viewed as less authoritarian and more real (as in work with an adolescent group);
2. groups in which, despite the pull for dependency, the worker wishes to foster independence and autonomy (as in work in a senior citizens' center);
3. training situations where trainees are threatened by the status issues symbolized by the trainer (as in groups led by social workers to train police about mental health issues).

In all groups, regardless of whether her presentation is formal or informal, the worker must understand how to integrate her personal and professional self. For example, when she identifies tension in the room, she arrives at this idea by tuning in to her own internal responses. She first asks herself, "What am I feeling?" Once this is clear to her, she asks, "What is stimulating this feeling, and what does it have to do with where the group is at this moment?" Finally she asks, "How can I best use this feeling to help the group accomplish its goals?"

When the worker considers telling the group about some aspect of her own life, the process should be the same. She should ask herself (in order): "What am I feeling?" "What is stimulating me to want to share this information?" "What does it have to do with where the group is at this moment?" "How, if at all, should I use the disclosure of this personal information to help the group accomplish its goals?" What must be made clear is that the professional use of self is different from the mere exposure of self. The professional use of self is the conscious and appropriate use of the worker's personal experiences and feelings to enhance the viability of the group. Under all conditions, the needs of the client and the needs of the group take precedence over the needs of the worker. The worker must constantly struggle to monitor all her interventions with an awareness of her own internal responses.

In the leadership training group process, the worker chooses to provide her group with certain information about herself and how she is feeling about coming to the group. Although she tells the group what school she attended, she says nothing about her marital status, a fact that would surely have an impact on this group of divorced Catholic women. The worker addresses her "enthusiasm" but delays mentioning her own trepidation about beginnings. Later, she also acknowledges these feelings as a means to reach for group members' feelings. Thus, she shares personal data and feelings only after she has monitored the group's response to her initial introduction. A long silence follows the conclusion of her contracting effort, which suggests that more is needed to engage the group members.

The worker has another advantage here: the fact that she is culturally connected to them and consequently sensitive to their cultural issues and values. She knows the meaning of the Church, the power of the priest, the role of women in the Church and in the family, and the attitude of the Church toward divorce. Yet, she must be wary of her knowledge and its potential for closing off differences, because she may be assuming factors rather than exploring their existence. In her, the members recognize their commonalities— a gesture, shared laughter, a way of expressing herself—which are revealed as the process unfolds. This is not to say that a worker of different background could not be aware of cultural patterns and connect to this group, but the trust apparently develops more quickly in this group because of the similarities between worker and clients and because of her skill in using them.

The worker goes one step further to join with the group by noting that the group wants to avoid contact with "a whole bunch of outside people who do not belong there." On the surface, the alliance appears to be an expression which reinforces the empowerment of group members (we can draw leaders from our "own ranks"). If we look further, however, we might conjecture that the worker needs to identify herself as an "insider." This need may be an expression of countertransferential issues for this worker. She is ethnically similar to her clients and comes from the same economic and social class they do. For her, what has changed is that she is no longer one of them, having achieved educational and professional status. One could suggest that the very formal nature of the worker's introduction is an unconscious attempt to create separateness from the group members while use of "outsider" is an unconscious attempt to remain part of the group and the past it represents for her. A worker's desire to be different from and yet part of the group is a common countertransferential struggle when working with clients who share a worker's background.

The length of the worker's introductory speech may also be a manifesta-tion of this same countertransferential issue. By talking for a time, the worker creates a distance between herself and the group members; the river of words acts as a protective barrier. The long introduction may also reflect the worker's style and the way in which she manages her own anxiety about beginnings. As noted earlier, the worker, as well as the members, experiences anxiety related to expectations, performance, and newness, which influence the desire to be more directive and controlling.

Engagement

Engagement, the process in which the worker assists the group members to feel safe and welcome to share difficult feelings and thoughts and to return to future sessions, is a key element in beginnings. In the previous piece, the worker allows for considerable freedom for group members to decide what they see as their needs and goals, but in other groups, particular structures, rules, and directives prevail and the worker, particularly in early meetings, is more active and authoritative. Eric, a student intern, has been assigned to work with a newly formed truancy group in an elementary school. The five eleven-year-olds (three girls and two boys) in this group have been selected to participate because they have been identified as having attendance and lateness issues throughout the previous term. The children know each other from their classes together, but Eric has not met with them previously. The following exchange takes place in the first session of the group after some of the group rules from a formal agency group contract have already been read.

Eric:	Okay, I will move on. So those were the general rules of the group. I have another list here with some informal rules that I think, if we followed, would allow for us all to have a good time here in the eight weeks we are going to spend together. Does anyone want to read the first one?
Alice:	You can read it. I like when you read it to us. (The worker reads the first slide on the computer screen. When the second slide comes up, Tommy raises his hand.)
Tommy:	Can I read it?
Nikki:	(mumbles something under her breath)
Eric:	(looking at Nikki) Did you want to say something?
Nikki:	Yes. You didn't ask him to read the screen. So I don't know why he is always trying to be extra.
Tommy:	I'm not trying to be extra. I'm funny. (Nikki rolls her eyes.)
Eric:	This is the third time that you have said you were funny but it seems like Nikki is having some sort of problem with that. What's going on?
Tommy:	I don't know what her problem is. She's always trying to put me down. (Tommy is smiling and not making eye contact with the worker.)

Nikki: No one is trying to put you down. Mr. Norton, you don't understand. He is like this all the time. In class, calling out, interrupting people. Always doing the most. And it's annoying. I'm trying to follow the rules and let him be. But I just can't.

Eric: Tommy, did you know that Nikki felt that way?

Alice: I feel this way too. What about you (looks to Jasmine)?

Jasmine: Yeah, me too. But I don't say too much.

Alice: She is kinda shy.

Eric: Well this is a space where you can say how you feel. I think your voice (looking at Jasmine) is important in this group. Tommy, did you know the girls felt like this?

Tommy: No, well kinda, not really. I like being funny. Being funny is my thing.

Alice: But no one thinks you're funny except for you and Kyle.

Kyle: He is my friend, so . . . I don't know.

Nikki: I just think it's so corny for him to act like that and this is the first time we are meeting. Like we all know each other and the two of them used to be in the same class. But none of us know you. And you can't even get a chance to speak. Every time you start talking, here comes Tommy trying to be funny. It gets so old. It happened all day long, in every single class.

Eric: Let me make sure I have this right. Tommy, you said earlier that you felt like Nikki was always putting you down. And Nikki, you seem to get frustrated with Tommy's jokes (both parties nod their heads), so how can we move forward to make this group a place where the both of you are a little more comfortable? (a couple of moments of silence).

Kyle: Maybe Tommy cannot make so many jokes all of the time. Then Nikki wouldn't have anything bad to say to him.

Eric: Oh, so I just want to make sure what you said. Maybe if Tommy tried to not make jokes so often, then Nikki can make sure she doesn't put him down. Is that correct?

Kyle: Yeah.

Eric: So what do the two of you think about that?

Tommy: I can do that. I don't have to make all the jokes (whispers "just some of them").

Nikki: I can definitely not make all of those comments. I just want to come here and have fun. And look we had to waste so much time that we didn't even get to do the activity yet.

Alice: Yeah, what is the activity? What kinds of things will we be doing here? I like coming here. I can tell already. But what are we going to be doing?

Eric: Well I don't think we wasted time. We had to go over the rules and get that out of the way before we can start and look, we already came to an agreement! That's really big. And as far as the activities, the activities are going to change each week . . . The activities are so that we can come up with ways to hopefully help each other. Others will be for other reasons, but they all are going to be fun and have some purpose. I think your time is very valuable so I want to make sure it's spent in the best way possible, while having fun of course. But sorry I got a little off track. We are going to start with activities that will help with attendance. But after that what we do is going to be based on what you guys want to do and are interested in.

Eric has at least two tasks he hopes to achieve in his work in engaging the children. First he must assure the group that he is on their side, an "okay" guy who is there to support and respect them and different from the teachers that, earlier in the meeting, the youngsters have identified as being a source of their difficulties with their attendance. He must persuade the group members that the group also can be a "fun" experience ("if the group follows its rules"), so that they will want to come back and participate. Second, Eric must establish his authority to maintain the group as purposeful, to make certain that what they are doing in the group is helpful in understanding themselves, leading to cooperating with each other to problem-solve, and, hopefully, resulting in reduced truancy and tardiness. Above all, Eric needs to show that he can be "trusted" to make this group setting a safe place in which to share sometimes painful and difficult feelings, some of which are, no doubt, influencing their attendance behavior. Additionally, since these children do not have a history of compliance with attendance in school, one might speculate that there will be difficulties in promoting group attendance unless there is a strong motivation which sets the group experience as extremely positive and worth returning for. The fact that the group members know each other already and have had somewhat rocky relationships prior to this session makes the situation even more complicated.

The excerpt begins with Eric's offer to have a group member volunteer to read. This suggestion conveys a message that this group belongs to everyone and is not dictated by the worker. What follows is Nikki expressing her annoyance at Tommy's clowning and interruptions. Eric could easily tell Nikki just to ignore Tommy or to stop making such a fuss about nothing, but instead he listens to her complaints and gives Tommy some feedback about what is being said—"This is the third time that you have said you were funny but it seems like Nikki is having some sort of problem with that. What's going on?" When Tommy responds with "she's always putting me down," Eric again takes a nonjudgmental stance and queries Tommy about whether he knew about how Nikki was feeling. The other girls are now able to tell Tommy that they too are bothered by his behavior, and he, in turn is able to share his upset about being "put down" by them.

The frankness of the exchange suggests the climate that has already been established here, one in which group members can speak freely, even Jasmine, who has been described by Alice as a "shy" person. Eric once again reminds the group about the contract—"This is a space where you can say how you feel. (Looking at Jasmine) I think your voice is important in this group." Eric is making it clear that everyone is included. This constant reinforcement of the contract and its recognition that everyone is encouraged to speak and be heard is repeated throughout the piece. Erik also does not neglect Tommy's opinion and feelings. He wants to be certain that Tommy too is included in any decision about how they will all continue as a group and asks Nikki and Tommy, "how can we move forward to make the group a place where the *both* of you are a little more comfortable?" Remarkably, Kyle now is able to come up with a proposal that Eric, clarifying, reframes and presents to the members: Tommy will try to joke less and Nikki will try not to "put him down." Nikki and Tommy both agree to these terms.

What is extraordinary about this process is the way in which the worker engages the youngsters as maturing adults and their ability to meet his expectations that all participants are entitled to express themselves honestly, that no one is to be shamed or blamed for his/her limitations, and that everyone deserves to be respected. Alice comments enthusiastically, "I like coming here. I can tell already." When everyone does come to an agreement after their dispute, Eric too is delighted and supports their achievement—". . . and look we already came to an agreement! That's really big." He also comments that he thinks that their time is valuable and will not waste it. One wonders whether these children have ever experienced any other adult who considers their time as important. Without doubt, he communicates that he genuinely likes them and is certain that they can accomplish their goals together.

Trusting and Testing

The establishment of trust is the most crucial factor in a group's development. It is the basis for all of that to follow. As demonstrated in the previous piece, trust creates the sense of safety that "holds" the group as it struggles towards becoming a cohesive unit. When the worker is clear about contract, boundaries, goals, and roles, there is beginning definition of the amorphous grouping. Acceptance, authenticity (on the part of the worker), and timing give further clarity to what is being formed. The predictability of procedure, the strength and clarity of structure, provide a sense of trust that leads to a feeling of safety that enables members to risk. It is not an easy task for the worker to establish trust nor is it quickly resolved. It takes time, keen observation, and effective intervention. Testing of the leader's character, intent, and skill starts early and is often in disguised messages. The leader's skill is in identifying and addressing those "coded" messages, whether they are passively delivered or aggressively confrontational. To establish trust in the beginning phase can be even more challenging for the worker when there are clear differences between the worker and the clients, such as gender, race, and ethnicity.

The following example is taken from a Lesbian, Gay, Bisexual, Transgender (LGBT) community center for gay men who are newly diagnosed as HIV positive. The purpose of the group is to help members deal with their anxiety and fear and to begin to integrate a positive HIV diagnosis into their lives. This meeting is the second session of a short-term, closed support group. The group is co-led by a male facilitator from last cycle's group and a new female MSW student who replaced last cycle's co-facilitator, who was also female. Half of the members present were returning from last cycle's group. The group had not yet dealt with the loss of the previous co-facilitator. The following interaction takes place during the last few minutes of the group.

Steve: I really hope we'll be able to get over the hurdle of last cycle's group and be able to talk about sex, because that's what got us here.

Jeremy: But there's a woman in the group (said in jest).

Student worker: Jeremy, you're bringing up an important concern.

Jeremy: I'm just joking. (Other members chuckle.)

Student worker: Yeah, I get that was a joke, but I'm wondering if there is any truth behind the comment. What's it like to have a woman as the facilitator?

Jeremy: You don't want to hear about anal sex . . . (other members chuckle).

Pete: She's a social work intern. She needs to learn to hear this . . .

Steve: For me, it's a cultural thing. I was raised not to talk about sex in front of women. I mean maybe I would in front of a very close girlfriend, but it's not just something I was raised to do . . . It's just something you can't really understand . . .

Student worker: Steve, concerns about me not being able to understand because I'm a woman sound very similar to concerns that have been raised about people who are negative not understanding what you're going through as someone who's positive.

Steve: Well, yeah, I guess.

Sam: (to the group) I had just assumed she was positive and gay and that's why she was facilitating—I guess I was wrong.

It is important to note that the discussion initiated by Steve is introduced in the last few minutes of the group. Commonly referred to as the "doorknob" effect, it is the act of raising an important issue when there is little or no time left to explore fully. This behavior thereby prevents a discussion before there is a sense of safety or sufficient trust in the group's ability to "survive" difficult interaction. Steve's comment is a reference to the "unfinished" business in the last group's cycle and of a particular level of difficulty involving the discussion of sexual behavior. He expresses his hope that this current group can be different and accomplish his desired goal. This comment is Steve's contribution to establishing contract. It is also his way of bridging the past group with the current group. He is indirectly identifying a theme concerning loss that has not yet been addressed—in either group. The loss of old leaders, regret about how the time was or was not spent, is a powerful latent theme in this population. Perhaps the power of this topic was too threatening to bring up earlier in this session when there was more time to explore.

What follows is a shift from contract (expression of goals, expectations, and norms) to the issue of the members' discomfort in relating to a female worker (trust). The testing of the new worker becomes the focus. Can she tolerate their openness? Is she comfortable with the sexual discussion (anal sex)? Is she experienced (she's an intern) and what is her sexual identity? Who is she, can she handle us, and are we safe with her? These questions are all direct and indirect expression of testing to establish trust. How the worker responds to the members' comments will set the tone for safety in the group.

Initially the worker identifies Jeremy's comment as a legitimate issue, "Jeremy, you're bringing up an important concern." She is not afraid to address the issue directly. Jeremy retreats to the safety of denial but she pursues. She invites them to look directly at the issue. He, perhaps feeling she can handle the topic, pushes on in more explicit terms, "You don't want to hear about anal sex." The group members chuckle, recognizing a level of potential discomfort—a challenge to the worker. Clearly it is a concern for them all. The worker allows space for the laughter and for other comments regarding their struggle with trusting. She is being open, accepting, and authentic. She is able to connect their concerns, of who she is, to trusting. She reframes the sex issue to an issue about "trust" of others who are different from them and who may not understand their concerns. She is, by staying with difficult material, allowing them to test her without her reacting defensively. The worker is also identifying the subtle latent theme of trust by saying in effect that she is all right with this, able to handle them, and solid. This message provides for a sense of safety. Perhaps it may be safe to risk here. These subtle exchanges between the worker and the members constitute the work of contracting.

At this point, the worker makes a decision not to pursue the potentially painful and intimate discussion of experiencing themselves as toxic to and different from others. Such discussion, if occurring before trust has developed between them, may lead to flight from the group and a heightened awareness of exposure and vulnerability. Rather the worker may elect to identify the issues as topics of discussion for future sessions.

Casework versus Groupwork

The following piece, unlike the material analyzed earlier, is immediately identifiable as problematic. The experience of an enthusiastic but inexperienced beginning worker, it illustrates some of the difficulties present in many beginnings. The excerpt is drawn from the third session of a group meeting in a day center program for chronic adult psychiatric patients. They live in a variety of settings and come to the program for recreation and the development of social skills. This particular group was designed as a forum for discussion and planning of leisure time activities.

Worker:	Hi, everybody. How's everyone doing this afternoon?
Mike:	Okay, Susan.
Rose:	Fine, fine.
Joel:	Good.
Worker:	How about you, George?
George:	Okay.
Worker:	And how about you, Joe? How are you feeling today?
Joe:	Fine, Susan.
Worker:	Well, I'm glad to see all of you here. What are people planning for the weekend?
Rose:	Bazaar. At the church. There's going to be games—like Atlantic City. And bingo.
Worker:	So, you're planning to go to a bazaar this weekend.
Rosie:	Where is that being held?
Rose:	Coney Island.
Roy:	I'm going to a church board meeting. At St. Gabriel's . . . (Roy speaks on in an extremely disconnected fashion and is often incomprehensible. He tends to go on and on and to interrupt other people unless some limits are put on his behavior.)
Worker:	Thank you for sharing that with us, Roy. How about you, Mark? What are you planning?
Mark:	Not much. Not much.
Worker:	I thought I heard you mention earlier today that you were going to visit your family?
Mark:	Yeah, yeah.
Worker:	Is anybody else planning to visit with friends or family this weekend?
Jane:	I'm going to visit my boyfriend in Philadelphia.
Worker:	You're going to visit your boyfriend? How are you feeling about that, Jane?
Jane:	Good. It only costs nineteen dollars.
Worker:	That sounds reasonable. What about the rest of you guys? What are you thinking about doing this weekend?

When she reviewed this material, the worker identified her goals in the session as twofold: calling the attention of the group to common themes and engaging them in problem solving. Her attempt is in line with some of the expectations for a beginning group: the need to draw clients together (cohesion) and the desire for engagement around common purposes (a task-oriented planning for leisure time)—in this case complicated by members' dysfunctional coping skills. Up to this point in the process record, however, neither of the worker's goals is more than slightly realized. Rather than encouraging interaction among the members, the worker interrogates each member in a dyadic relationship within the group meeting. Each member waits in turn to receive the questions of the worker and then responds by addressing her, "Okay, Susan." None of the members are talking to each other. We recognize both the need for her to be more active in the beginning stage and the special dependent and limited quality of this population in social interaction. It still appears, however, that the worker is overly controlling, further limiting the possibilities for expanded interaction.

The worker models or teaches a norm that does not foster a group approach but rather a casework approach. At this point, no one in the group has any notion about its "groupness" or its value in the therapeutic process. The worker's intervention does not lead the group in the direction of finding out. As it stands, the group might be able to draw up an agenda for weekend activities, accomplishing an immediate goal, but the group's true goal or purpose (to enhance independent functioning and increase socialization skills) will not be achieved unless the worker can risk lessening control.

When she asks, "What are people planning for the weekend?" the open-ended nature of the question invites engagement. Instead of focusing on this engagement by responding, "Oh, that sounds interesting. Has anyone else been to a bazaar? What was it like?" thereby reaching for commonalities, the worker cuts off further interaction by focusing on the concrete aspect of the client's response (where this particular bazaar is located). A little later in the process, the worker again responds to a member's comment about being with family or friends for the weekend by asking whether others will be with friends or family. When Jane says that she will be with her boyfriend, the worker makes no connection between Jane and the previous speaker, but instead jumps into a short discussion with Jane.

One could hypothesize about some of the issues governing the worker's difficulties in this session. Inexperienced workers in psychiatric settings often struggle initially with their fears about what they believe to be the potentially explosive nature of their patients. It is not unusual, therefore, to have that fear translated into the worker's controlling behavior. In some ways, any population draws upon the worker's fear about that aspect of herself, which that population represents. For instance, a worker with the elderly may experience fears about her own aging (of dependency and loss); or a worker with an adolescent group may react to her own unresolved adolescent issues (of rebellion and identity). In work with a psychiatric population, the worker may experience fears of her own primitive thoughts and loss of control. This discussion is admittedly conjectural, but the points raised here often have a bearing on work with groups.

Aside from many countertransferential issues that may be present, this worker's difficulties probably partially stem from her anxiety about beginnings. The worker seems to see herself as having sole responsibility for accomplishing the agency mandate. If she relies on the members to keep the discussion flowing, they are likely to fail her. In some sense, having little faith in the group's ability to function is the worker's issue of trust. Also, the worker worries about involving all the members and being responsive to them so that they will all benefit from and return to the group. This is an important responsibility in beginnings, but too much focus on individual members can stop the worker from listening to the whole.

By dealing with the group as an evolving and interconnected entity rather than a series of discrete worker-to-member exchanges, the worker helps the group reach its goals. During the beginning phase of groups, members are constantly concerned about how others will see and think of them. Workers struggle with this evaluative process as well. The double-bind for workers is that they will be evaluated both by their clients and by their supervisors. Consequently, because she feels the need to keep the process alive, the worker ends up directing all the action rather than facilitating it.

To summarize, in the leisure time planning group, the worker identifies areas for work, engages individual members, and establishes the contract and norm for problem solving. Her concern and interest in the group are apparent throughout the session and seem to be keenly felt by all. However, she needs to move from the concrete to the thematic and help the group to focus on their work and develop mutuality.

Conclusion

In this chapter, we have presented material from several beginning sessions with distinctly different groups. Despite the differences in client populations and worker styles, we believe that the basic issue concerning beginnings is the same: to work through concerns about trust, thereby allowing the group to proceed with its work. Workers' understanding of their own feelings and their ability to use them to facilitate group process are fundamental. As we have demonstrated, there is not a right or wrong way to proceed but rather a number of alternative interventions that may be used. Workers' recognition of and respect for their own individuality and that of their clients determines the most effective interventions.

References

Erikson, E. H. *Childhood and Society*, 2nd ed. New York: W.W. Norton and Co., 1963.

Garland, J., Kolodny, R., and Jones, H. "A Model for Stages of Development in Social Work Groups." In *Explorations in Group Work*. S. Bernstein, Ed. Boston, MA: Milford House, 1975, pp. 17–71.

Shulman, L. *The Skills of Helping Individuals and Groups*. Itasca, IL: The Peacock Press, 1979.

5   IN THE MIDDLE

"Real isn't how you are made," said the Skin Horse. "It's a thing that happens to you. When a child loves you for a long, long time, not just to play with, but REALLY loves you, then you become REAL."

"Does it hurt?" asked the Rabbit.

"Sometimes," said the Skin Horse, for he was always truthful. "When you are Real you don't mind being hurt."

"Does it happen all at once, like being wound up," he asked, "or bit by bit?"

"It doesn't happen all at once," said the Skin Horse. "You become. It takes a long time. That's why it doesn't often happen to people who break easily, or have sharp edges, or have to be carefully kept. Generally, by the time you are Real, most of your hair has been loved off, and your eyes drop out and you get loose in the joints and very shabby. But these things don't matter at all, because once you are Real, you can't be ugly, except to people who don't understand . . . but once you are Real you can't become unreal again. It lasts for always."

Margery Williams
The Velveteen Rabbit (1922)

The Members' Issues

The second phase of group development is generally termed "middles" or the "work" phase. Although it cannot be identified as entirely separate and different from the earlier beginning phase and the later termination phase, it still has its own distinctive characteristics, which we address in this chapter.

Each stage in individual development can be thought of as possessing historical baggage: unresolved residual issues from previous experiences carried into the current stage. These unresolved issues may result in the inability to effectively meet the demands of the current developmental tasks. Old conflicts may reemerge when triggered by the current demands. If the initial foundation is structurally unsound, the later levels are compromised.

Similarly, in the growth and development of the group, unresolved issues of trust in the beginning phase limit the group's capacity to achieve the level of intimacy required to do the work of "middles." The presence of residual issues is not necessarily an indicator of the worker's lack of skill, but is rather a normal part of the developmental process in groups. The middle or work phase, the longest stage in the development of the group, is composed of three parts: (1) an early phase closely related to beginnings during which residual issues are evident; (2) a middle phase during which the group struggles to separate from the beginning issues and proceed with the work of the group; and (3) a final phase during which separation from beginnings is effected and group cohesiveness is achieved, which allows for working through all developmental tasks specific to middles. The stage is then set for termination.

The Early-Middle Phase

The members' issues in this stage include the beginning issues of trust, testing, approach and avoidance, and clarification of contract. Some sense of vulnerability, fear of exposure, and tentative exploration persist. In the beginning of the middle phase, group members move from a cautious, evaluative position to one that allows for more confrontational, competitive, and intimate behavior. In this period, group members slowly establish comfortable roles for themselves in the group, roles that are safe because they are a part of the members' historical baggage. At this point, members are gradually sharing more intimate information, paving the way for exploration of feeling areas.

A small vignette from a group session with adult relatives of alcoholics illustrates some of the issues so pertinent to this stage. In an attempt to push the group to a greater level of intimacy, the worker opens the session by requesting feedback regarding the process of the group.

Rose:	The group is important to me because it is a place to bring problems, a place to get what I need even if it is not what I expect, to listen to others as I share myself.
Rhonda:	I feel the same way as Rose.
Rose:	I prefer honesty to just chatting, and the group has sometimes made me frustrated because it isn't working.
Worker:	What do you mean?
Rose:	The group is sometimes like a coffee klatch that doesn't get down to work.
Worker:	What do you mean by work?
Rose:	It is when people talk about feelings and respond honestly to each other. I would like the worker to get the group working, but it is important to be able to state my frustrations, and this helps me grow.
Marlene:	The group has helped my growth. Without it I would be very isolated. Other relationships for me cannot be as honest.
Rose:	I would like more honesty in the group.

Worker: It sounds as if Rose would like others to risk stating their real feelings as Rose has when she has been frustrated in the group.

Rhonda: I have been honest, and people in the group seem more honest than they have been before.

Jenny: When I got angry in the group, I realized I could assert myself and be okay, a process which made me feel strong.

Marlene: I remember that time with Jenny. It was wonderful to hear Jenny express her anger. I would like to see more open expression in the group.

Worker: How do all of you feel about this?

Faith: I like things the way they are. I have great respect for all the members, who are very special people.

Worker: Is it possible to have angry or negative feelings about such special people?

Faith: I'm not sure.

The group struggles with how to be more honest yet stay safe. They discuss whether honesty and safety can coexist. Rose continues to push for both, and the worker supports Rose by summarizing the calls for honesty and the different points of view expressed. The worker remarks that it is sometimes scarier to imagine what is unexpressed than to confront difficult material openly expressed. Also, it appears that one group task, which has been an important underlying issue in the discussion, will be to decide how to become more honest.

After the session, the worker comments that the manifest content was the members' commentary on how the group worked or did not work for them. At the same time, latent content included change is scary so why rock the boat, and change is scary and necessary for growth. In general, this piece typifies the work of the early-middle phase. It includes a holdover of the residual issue of unresolved trust, a fear of exposure, an increased desire for—yet fear of—intimacy, and a time of group evaluation. An analysis of the process reveals the group's clear approach-avoidance struggle toward greater intimacy and the worker's attempt to gently push the group forward.

The Middle-Middle Phase

In this phase, the group moves to a greater level of spontaneity: clarifying, focusing, talking about intimate and emotional issues, sharing vulnerability as well as strength, risking exposure, and solving problems actively. They begin a less dependent relationship with the worker. This movement happens only after the complete resolution of the early trust issues and the resulting increase in the cohesive bond. In addition to greater cooperation among members in this phase of group development, an increased ability to risk exposure of self arises. This exposure may result in a more open expression of feelings, which sometimes leads to confrontation and open conflict.

Latent content begins to surface in a manifest way during this stage, and the group is now ready to identify this material and struggle with it. The norm that encourages and values self-disclosure and risk-taking is established. Roles, which had become more clearly identifiable, are beginning to change. Group members are no longer locked into one role and are more able to experiment, perhaps for the first time, with new roles in the group. In general, the struggle between group needs and individual needs is more apparent at this phase. Although individual group members have integrated many of the group's goals, they now differentiate their own goals or expectations for the group experience. They feel consonance with the other group members but also individual identity. Group members recognize similarities and differences among themselves and become aware of the unique qualities each of them brings to the group. Overall, a freer and more open flow of communication is established.

The End-Middle Phase

Much of the end-middle phase is a preparation for the separation and individuation stage of termination. At this point, the individual more clearly defines his or her independent goals and needs, but a fluidity exists between the meeting of group and individual needs. Issues identified at an earlier point in the group development are moving toward resolution with a heightened awareness and intensity in the work. Some of the group's goals are accomplished, thereby fostering a sense of empowerment, which catapults the group toward the completion of the remaining goals and into the termination stage.

The Worker's Role: Use of Self and Issues of Authority

In the middle phase, the worker assumes a less directive role than in the beginning or *termination* phase. Still, it is an active role, one that requires the worker to play a less pivotal part while developing group leadership and autonomy. In some sense, the worker must now relinquish control and help the group embrace it. This sometimes difficult process calls for the worker's ability to let go of power and authority in which the worker often feels invested. Some of this investment comes from the need of the worker to allay his or her own anxiety by controlling the group. For this reason, many workers find it particularly difficult to make the adjustment to the new role of worker in "middles." Ideally, the worker should become less a director and more a facilitator, reclarifying goals and purpose, supporting explorative work by the group, emphasizing the importance for the group to make its own decisions, and encouraging the development of positive group norms and cohesiveness.

Workers must use their selves differently from before, more openly challenging and confronting the group in its work. They must keep their groups "honest" by helping members to evaluate where the group is and where it appears to be going. They must encourage the groups to see where they resist change and growth. In the process, workers model how to engage in, grow from, and survive conflict.

Workers must strive to assist members to challenge each other and the worker. They must set limits to ensure that no one will be harmed or chased from the group as the intensity of the interaction heightens. At this point, the worker encourages, clarifies, analyzes, and directs what are often heated exchanges between members and between the group and the worker. The worker must remember that the expression of conflict is not an end in itself but a means for reaching the goal of addressing real feelings. For many workers, the middle phase is taxing and pulls at the worker's own fears about anger and impulse control. This stage demands the worker's constant monitoring and risking of self in order to encourage and regulate the level of conflict necessary for the group to mature but not self-destruct.

The middle phase requires specific worker skills such as clarifying communication; mediating; confronting; identifying commonalities to build deeper levels of cohesiveness, mutuality, and bonding; and identifying and respecting difference to build independence and individuality. The worker needs to support and value flexibility as a positive group norm in order to promote an arena in which members feel safe enough to change and to try on new roles. As the worker's role becomes increasingly one of regulator, facilitator, and assistant in maintaining the patterns and flows of communication, individual members emerge as leaders. The group is able to make its own decisions, to initiate plans for its own work, and to find its own direction. Thus, the group is empowered.

In this phase, the countertransference and transference issues are strong and frequently change and shift in multiple ways. Workers' use of self is crucial to identify what is being played out and not spoken among members in the group. By being aware of their own feelings, workers become barometers for their groups, allowing themselves to first feel, then pull away and analyze, and finally integrate and identify latent content for the group. The more knowledgeable workers are about themselves, the more effective they are in separating their own issues from group issues.

Mr. Barry is a school social worker in a high school for gifted youngsters. He has been working with teens for many years. Mr. Barry is an older person, balding and overweight, who often uses his size and obvious aging to make fun of himself, and in turn, to tease students about their inadequacies. Every year by midsemester, Mr. Barry develops a rapport with the adolescents in his leadership and school volunteer groups, which leads to their active participation. They adore him. He is often the happy butt of their jokes, which occasionally get out of hand, but which are met with an affable response along with firm guidance. Despite his sense of humor, Mr. Barry is quite forceful and demanding, confronts the youngsters, and does not permit them to avoid facing important issues.

When several boys in his group became the targets of an unreasonable teacher who had lost students' assignments and then failed them for not submitting their work, Mr. Barry approached the principal in defense of the students. Having validated the students' complaints about the teacher, Mr. Barry then worked with the students in helping them identify and take responsibility for their part in the difficulties with the teacher. He specifically noted how some had disrespectfully responded when the teacher had suggested that they had not completed their work. He also noted that those students were the ones who had failed and asked them what they thought about this. This balanced intervention enabled the students to draw a connection between their behavior and its consequences. The way in which Mr. Barry used his authority could only be accomplished in the middle phase when sufficient cohesion was established to tolerate the intensity in such confrontation.

An interesting, subtle way that Mr. Barry achieves trust and cohesion with the adolescents is his placement of an enormous jar of tootsie rolls on his desk for all to help themselves. The students do partake, but without even being addressed about it, only select a candy or two at any given time. By making the candy available without imposed restrictions, Mr. Barry communicates his respect for the students and his trust for them to use their good judgment in limiting themselves.

Mr. Lawrence is a counselor who also works with groups in the same high school. A man in his twenties, he is very conscious of the need to establish his credibility and control over the students. To achieve this, Mr. Lawrence asserts himself in an authoritarian manner; makes requests of the students, which students soon perceive as commands; and will not allow himself to engage in the banter and joking of his colleague, Mr. Barry. A number of the adolescents have dropped out of his groups and others speak about being dissatisfied with their participation. Although Mr. Lawrence is in the middle phase of group, he has not allowed himself to be less directive and active. His use of authority does not permit the adolescents to achieve the sense of independence so necessary in their developmental stage, nor does his controlling behavior indicate his trust of them.

Perhaps because Mr. Lawrence is so close in age to the teens, he fears that relaxation of authority will result in his not being taken seriously. It is common for some young workers to respond in this dictatorial way, and for some others to be unable to separate themselves from the adolescents sufficiently to establish themselves as an authority figure rather than a peer.

The Group as Mother

The following process record is fairly typical of a group in the middle-middle phase of group development. The excerpt is taken from a meeting of older disabled persons participating in an improvisation group within an extended care facility. The session illustrates the need these older persons have for mutual support, sharing, and intimacy in a setting that tends to be impersonal, institutional, and sterile. In some sense, the goal for all groups in this sort of setting is to function as a surrogate family, neighborhood, and community. In this context, the group can provide a warm hearth in what is otherwise an environment so large and bureaucratic that its very charge to help people is sometimes lost. In the group, people are seen again as individual persons with unique identities and histories, who still have a significant contribution to make to their world. Members resume once familiar roles as caretakers, providers, and nurturers. The group also grants permission for people to express sadness, anger, and pain and yet be accepted. Here, in this intimate, warm, and private space, members are again with others who care for them and for whom they care, to give each other enough strength to survive in a cold and sometimes harsh environment.

The mutuality demonstrated in the following excerpt is typical of middles where the group is truly the "loving mother." This is a poignant example of individual needs being met in the group context:

(Sally wheels Johnny, a blind, elderly man with a heart condition, into position to participate in an improvisation. She accidentally maneuvers the wheelchair so that it runs over Johnny's foot.)

Johnny:	My foot! My foot! . . . The pain, I can't stand it! I can't stand it! . . . The pain.
Sally:	Oh, I'm sorry, Johnny!
Johnny:	Oh, I hate everything! I hate everything! I'm going back to my room! I can't do this . . . I can't see . . . I don't want to do this anymore . . . I want to go back to my room!

(There is a momentary silence, and the group responds in empathetic unison.)

Group:	No! No! No!
Rob:	No, Johnny, stay, we need you . . .
Johnny:	(anger on the verge of hysteria) I wish I was dead! I wish I was dead! I'm no good . . . I hate . . . I hate everything! I should have died with those twelve guys in the fire. Why am I alive? I should have died . . . I should have died with the rest of the firemen. They were my friends, and I watched them die. I should have died.
Group:	(with great empathy) No, Johnny, no!
Fred:	No, Johnny, we need you here.
Rob:	(softly and gently) We need you, Johnny. We need you.
Johnny:	I wish I was dead . . . I'm blind. I'm no good . . . no good to anyone . . . I wish I was dead. (Johnny's body is trembling with emotion.)
Fred:	You're very important to the group. You're more important than you know.

Sally: No, Johnny, we love you . . . I'm sorry I hurt you . . . Don't leave us . . . what would we do without you?

Johnny: I hate everyone! I hate everything!

Alex: We don't hate you.

Mrs. Brown: (silencing Johnny) Shhh . . . shhh . . . Don't say that.

(Sally puts her arms around Johnny to comfort him.)

Joyce: (putting her hand on Johnny's arm) No, no. Now Johnny, what would we do without you? Remember the play? You were my son . . . I took care of you . . . We're going to do that play again. We'll both be in it.

Fred: You're good company, Johnny.

Flora: (walking over to Johnny and touching his arm to comfort him) We need you, Johnny . . . we all feel the way you do sometimes.

Johnny: (still fuming and trembling) I wish I was dead . . . I wish I was dead . . . I should have died on that gunboat in World War II. (Johnny simmers momentarily while Joyce, Flora, and Sally continue holding Johnny to comfort him. At this point, a flood of support comes from everyone in overlapping dialogue. Johnny no longer holds his foot in pain.)

Worker: Johnny, your foot seems okay now. (no answer) Johnny, you see, the group cares for you and wants you here.

Rob: (over and over again in a gentle, soft tone) We need you.

Worker: Come on, let's see the skit.

Fred: Yeah, let's see the skit. (As he speaks there is a sense of relief in the group and in Johnny, and the improvisation proceeds.)

Above all, this powerful excerpt suggests how significant groups can be in the institutional setting. Johnny's despair, the expression of which is triggered by his foot injury, is a concrete representation for the group of the misery of being ill rather than well, institutionalized rather than self-sufficient, and dependent rather than autonomous. Johnny's helplessness is underscored by his inability to maintain any control over his life, even in terms of his own movements as he is pushed about in his wheelchair. He recalls his vital days and remembers his past vulnerability and helplessness in the face of war and fire. War, fire, the institution: all are metaphors for the same theme. He and his fellow patients are not unlike him and his fellow comrades. Despite the depth of his pain, the expression of his anguish is permitted here. His feelings are accepted in an atmosphere of unconditional love. The others understand because they have been there too.

The worker seems to be almost absent from the scene and, as is appropriate in a group ready for this level of intimacy (in the middle phase), takes a back seat to the group members. On the one hand, her limited participation may reflect a conscious and skillful choice to sit with her own anxiety in order to allow the group to confront its feelings. This process empowers the group and empowers Johnny. In a very real sense, the work of healing and comforting Johnny by the other group members acts to heal and comfort them. On the other hand, the worker may be less active in this piece simply because the material is so powerful as to immobilize her. She says nothing because she, too, is in great pain and afraid of her own emotions.

It is essential for workers to be aware of their own feelings and to use their own internal struggles to benefit the group. The worker's feelings are, after all, a barometer for what others in the room may also be feeling. The worker might acknowledge her own pain: "This feels so painful to me; how much more so it must be for you." She might have verbalized and identified the feelings of both Johnny and the group: "It must be really awful for you, Johnny." She could have reached for further expression and moved the group toward establishing the commonality of the experience: "There's a lot of pain in this room." She might have more clearly verbalized the connection between his pain and theirs: "I wonder if Johnny is speaking for all of us here." The objective of reaching for a commonality of experience is not to dilute the individual's expression of pain but to emphasize the connectedness to others. Therefore, if the worker were to say, "How do other people feel about what Johnny is saying?" (perhaps an overly used phrase in reaching for feedback), then Johnny's special need for recognition might be undercut.

Although Johnny continually rejects the attempts of his fellow members to offer comfort, the support continues, sending him the message that even negative feelings are acceptable here. We agree with the worker's approach of allowing this process to unfold without her interference. When she does intervene, however, the intervention falls somewhat short of the most effective approach:

> *Johnny*:   I wish I was dead . . . I should have died on that gunboat in
> World War II.
> *Worker*:   (observing Johnny is no longer clutching his foot) Your foot
> seems okay now, Johnny. You see, the group cares for you
> and wants you here.

The comment about Johnny's foot feeling better appears to dismiss his pain. It probably would have been more helpful if the worker had said: "This has been a difficult time for Johnny and the group," recognizing his pain and that of the group, "but some things are just so lousy, and we can't change them." This comment acknowledges their realistic limits and gives a moment for the feelings to settle. The worker might also say, "You see that the group cares for you and wants you to be part of the play we're doing. Let's give it a try again." This statement propels the group toward its task, making a demand for the group's work while lending support for Johnny and the group throughout. Such comments would offer the group closure on the discussion without minimizing its importance.

Although the exploration of painful issues is essential to this group's process, it is not an end in itself. A goal for this group is to move beyond its pain by utilizing the positive task of participating in group plays. We believe a clear parallel runs between participating in a play and struggling with life issues as this group has been doing in its work with Johnny. The worker must establish a balance between adequate exploration of pain and movement forward. Also, in this particular type of group, a balance must be struck between exploration of feeling and accomplishment of the group's concrete tasks: participation in improvisations. The need for the achievement of concrete tasks is significant with any activity group and is discussed at length in Chapter 8.

Whatever the reason for the worker to intervene as she did, it is far better to have the support for Johnny come from the group than from the worker. First of all, the group benefits because their contribution to helping Johnny contradicts their feeling of powerlessness. Second, the member receives the supportive message as being real, for the others are in the same situation: "We all need you. We're all in the same boat." Third, the importance of each participant is highlighted by the others, "You're good company . . ." "Who would be in the play with me?"

A sense of the group as nurturing mother is apparent throughout this piece of process. In the institution, where painfully little opportunity exists for the physical expression of affection, this group is stroking, hugging, and patting Johnny to provide comfort. They offer solace to Johnny who also represents that wounded, crippled part of themselves. The healing is mutual. The touching brings back the quality of "humanness" lacking in the institution and is symbolic of unconditional love and acceptance of the members as they are.

This group has allowed the members to feel a part of a whole, to find a caring family and a renewal of life purpose. The session described could only have been possible after the group passed through beginnings, when issues of trust had been resolved. Now, in the middle phase, the cohesiveness, intimacy, mutuality, and bonding lead to confronting pain, healing, and moving forward. Above all, the existence of this group in an institution makes the suffering more bearable and the survival less lonely.

Working on a Shared Problem

The following excerpt is also taken from a session in the middle phase of a group. While this piece has a sense of mutuality similar to that of the institutional group, this group exhibits other characteristics common to middles: most apparently, problem solving and identification and confrontation of feelings. The process is from a group of latency-age, insulin-dependent, diabetic girls and their mothers. The purpose of the group is twofold: to educate both parents and children about diabetes and health so the children can achieve a greater safe level of autonomy, and to simultaneously deal with the psychological impact of chronic illness on the individuals and on family life. The group worker, herself an insulin-dependent diabetic for many years, is trained as a diabetic counselor-educator and as a social worker.

The portion of the session included here begins when the youngsters have gone to the bathroom, and the mothers are alone with the worker. Aware of an earlier and ongoing problem with the younger sister (Lisa) of one child (Maria), the worker begins the session by inquiring how things are going regarding Lisa. The children's mother, Rosa, has mentioned that Lisa is feeling a lack of attention. The discussion ensues with Rosa relating an incident in which Lisa was reprimanded in school for hitting another child. The behavior was repeated even after Lisa was scolded by her teacher. Rosa extended the punishment to restrictions at home for misbehaving in school.

As Rosa opens up in the group about her concerns, the youngsters return from the bathroom. They ask what is going on, are told about the worries concerning Lisa, and begin demanding their afternoon snacks. The discussion shifts to education about food intake and blood sugar level maintenance and away from Lisa. After considerable time, the girls mention snack time in school and how other children react to their special dietary needs. At this point, the worker is able to reconnect the discussion to Lisa's call for attention:

Worker:	Do you remember when Lisa was here? Remember some of the things she was saying about being hyperactive and wanting to eat special? What were some of the things she was trying to tell us?
Rosa:	When she did those things, it was because she felt lonely.
Worker:	Yes, lonely, because you had to give Maria a lot of attention.
Maria:	Is it because I'm diabetic?
Worker:	Yes, and when you were younger, you couldn't do a lot of things for yourself, but now you can, right? But what are you feeling, Maria? You're shaking your head.
Maria:	She's lonely because I'm diabetic, but I do need help sometimes because if I get shocky, sometimes they would be working, Daddy and Lisa, and then I would go into shock. Daddy would just leave her alone, and everybody would come around me, and everybody would be around me, and she would be left alone.
Lucy:	Yeah, that sounds lonely.
Tina:	Oh, yeah . . .
Rosa:	But Lisa helps also. She would help.
Worker:	But I think what Maria said is that there is a circle around her, and Lisa is left out and alone. Is that a strong picture for you?
Maria:	It's sad.
Worker:	Yes, it's sad.
Tina:	Maria is no different from Lisa. She just has a symptom that's nothing to worry about. She should just tell someone when she needs help.

Worker:	So when somebody gets shocky and starts to pass out, they should just tell someone?
Tina:	One person should be there, not a whole bunch of people. There are two kids and both need help, and one is diabetic and the other isn't. They shouldn't pay all the attention to one person.
Lucy:	It isn't fair.
Maria:	Remember last time we were in camp, and there was a basketball game, and Kay was shocking. Everyone was around her.
Tina:	I slapped her to wake her up, and she was dead asleep.
Worker:	Good for you. What did the nurse say?
Maria:	She wasn't helping at all.
Lucy:	They kept giving her honey and smelling stuff.
Maria:	But they couldn't get her awake. We were holding her, and she'd wake up and pass out again.
Tina:	No, she was faking.
Maria:	No, last year she was faking. This year it was real.
Tina:	No, she was faking; she was just faking.
Worker:	Okay, okay, but this year she wasn't. Let's come back for a minute to someone who isn't diabetic, who is younger and doesn't get as much attention, like Lisa. What you said about your Dad leaving her is very important. It's important for each of you to have special time with each parent.
Maria:	Somebody has to stay with Lisa.
Worker:	Yes.
Tina:	Well, I know, who has a quarter?
Lucy and Maria:	Not me.
Tina:	No, this is going to be very good because ... see tails would be Dad. Every day you flip a quarter and if it's heads, Mother works with Lisa, and if it's tails, you just change.
Worker:	Oh, I see; not a bad idea.
Tina:	If the quarter is never used, you just keep it.
Worker:	And the idea being, if Mom's working with Lisa, then if Maria has a reaction, Mom stays with Lisa?
Tina:	Right!
Lucy:	That's a really good idea.
Maria:	Once, I remember, I got really shocky, and my dad kept smacking me, and then my mother came in. She took me and ran so fast to the bathroom, made me sit down on something, and put cold water all over me and kept giving me juice and sugar. Lisa was working with Daddy, and he saw me lying down. He left Lisa and just took care of me, and Lisa was left alone.

Worker:	So you saw a lot of that, and when Lisa came to the group, she said that she did feel left out because she wasn't diabetic, and she keeps saying she wants to be diabetic. It sounds crazy to us who are diabetic that anyone who is not would want to be.
Tina:	Sometimes I don't want to be diabetic and sometimes I do. So I flip a penny, and if it only says heads, I'm not a diabetic, and tails, it is. And it's always tails.
Worker:	So if you weren't a diabetic, what would be different about your life?

The children begin to fantasize about what life would be like without the restrictions imposed on their diets and play and without the need for constant blood monitoring and medication. There is a feeling in the room, for the first time, of childish fantasy and freedom, pure glee in the thoughts of cotton candy and chocolate cake.

The preceding piece challenges any analysis as it is replete with important covert and overt messages for the group worker. The primary task of this worker is to balance the practical needs (the educational goals) with the emotional needs—a process that parallels the phase issue in middles of balancing problem solving with intimacy. Also, the worker struggles to meet the needs of both children and adults in this group, who should not necessarily share the group experience at all. The adults originally came to the group as escorts for their young children, and both adults and children probably have many beginning issues concerning trust. As the trust issues are resolved, parents no longer will remain in the meetings. They will soon be forming a group of their own. Once they depart, the youngsters are able to express some angry feelings more readily than before.

Because of the length and complexity of the excerpt, we have chosen to examine it using a nearly line-by-line analysis. The major issues for the diabetic children center on: (1) needing control yet struggling with helplessness; (2) learning coping skills, both emotional and practical; (3) finding an identity in a world in which they are different; and (4) fearing abandonment and isolation.

The themes of vulnerability, guilt, and fear of abandonment surface almost immediately when Maria asks whether her sister's loneliness is due to Maria's diabetes. The worker responds by identifying and reinforcing Maria's growth and ego strength while acknowledging the reality of the impact her disease has had on her sister: "Yes (your being diabetic required a lot of attention and that affected your sister and family), and when you were younger, you couldn't do a lot of things for yourself" (acknowledging the legitimacy of her need at that age and putting it in the past); "but now you can, right?" (reinforcing ego strength, growth, and independence). The preceding intervention might prematurely cut off expression of feeling by providing explanation and support too quickly. Often workers rush to teach or encourage rather than explore or stay with painful feelings. An alternative intervention would be, "Yes, that's true. Your diabetes required a lot more help when you were younger. I wonder how it makes you feel to hear that about your sister's loneliness." Here the worker would validate and legitimize the need but would also pull for the feelings.

In any event, the issue of feelings is not lost in the preceding process. The worker skillfully picks up on the nonverbal reaction of Maria to the worker's intervention: "But what are you feeling, Maria? You're shaking your head." This example of retrieving demonstrates how crucial it is to be aware of the client's responses, both verbal and nonverbal, to our interventions. The individual client and the group as a whole offer multiple opportunities to "hear" the truth and respond to it. Maria's response to the worker's query expresses her guilt at being so needy, her acknowledgment of her need despite her sister's reality, and her general confusion, ambivalence, and guilt associated with her special needs.

This expression results in empathy and support for Maria from her peers, who understand her situation all too well. Rosa, Maria's mother, has apparently been touched by the picture of isolation and loneliness Maria and the others have drawn of their experience (their isolation and loneliness is identified through Lisa). Rosa's reply—"But Lisa helps also. She would help"— almost appears as an attempt to lessen the power of the feeling. The worker holds to the feeling, refocusing on the loneliness and alienation via Maria. At the same time, she solicits understanding and compassion for the loneliness they all feel: "But I think what Maria said is that there is a circle around her, and Lisa is left out and alone. Is that a strong picture for you?" Maria confirms this need to stay with the feeling. "It's sad," she says. The worker replies, "Yes, it's sad," and sustains the feeling, validating it and giving permission for further expression.

At this point, the worker has many options. One of these is to more clearly draw the commonality of the isolation, loneliness, and alienation they— parents, siblings, and identified patients—all share. They are all different from their respective peers; they all feel a loss of "normal" lifestyle; they all feel controlled by something they cannot escape. Reaching out for more feedback from the group would take the group to a deeper level of emotional exchange, in keeping with the work of middles. The group would become more intimate while addressing the girls' developmental need to belong to others and counteracting the isolation of the illness. It is a good opportunity to reinforce and further develop the cohesiveness of the group, which is its ego strength.

When Tina comments that "Maria is no different from Lisa. She just has a symptom that's nothing to worry about. She should just tell someone when she needs help," the latent message is that the intensity of the feeling makes her anxious. She seems to be attempting to minimize and intellectualize the feeling so that it is less frightening.

The worker might respond by acknowledging Tina's apparent need to avoid the painful reality, thereby staying with the emotional content: "It sounds as if it's hard to talk about some of these feelings, being different or being sad."

This sort of intervention might encourage still more expression of feeling. When the worker recognizes that talking about the fear of expressing these feelings is difficult, it gives the group permission to address them. In other contexts than this group (with parents and friends, for example), these children often feel ashamed of what they perceive to be their weaknesses. One message they may receive is that the expression of certain feelings is shameful or even threatening to other people. Also, they may experience the need to protect parents from the feeling. The worker's intervention gives a message that it is safe, and even desirable, to talk about the feeling, and that the worker is strong enough that they need not protect her.

Another option for the worker is engagement of other group members in the process to reduce isolation and loneliness, and allow the group to become cohesive enough to do its work. The worker might say to the group, for example: "Do you really think Lisa's so different from us?" This draws other group members into the process, takes the focus off of Maria and onto shared problems, and returns the group to a discussion of feelings. By moving the group back to the painful areas, the worker communicates and reinforces the idea that the group is strong enough to tolerate and learn to deal with pain.

Examining the process excerpt, we see that the worker elected a course of action different from those we have suggested, perhaps respecting the movement of the group to safer ground. Tina, who voices the group's resistance to addressing pain, is also the group's most successful problem solver. The worker, by listening to Tina, responds in part to Tina's call and the group's call for caution when invading sensitive territories. The worker decides to move the group toward more active problem solving and education: "So, when somebody gets shocky and starts to pass out, they should just tell someone." This intervention could either express the worker's unconscious need to lessen her own anxiety or be a conscious effort to teach coping skills, thereby reinforcing a sense of control for the children.

The next part of the process develops into an elaborate problem-solving sequence. The girls, led by Tina, discuss sharing parental involvement with siblings, dealing with someone who has passed out, and using the diabetes to seek attention. These manifest issues disguise the children's latent concerns: helplessness and lack of control ("It isn't fair." "We were holding her and she'd wake up and pass out again"); vulnerability and dependency on others they are not sure they can trust ("She wasn't helping at all [the nurse] . . . But they couldn't get her awake"); fear of death ("I slapped her to wake her up and she was dead asleep . . . she was faking" [Tina's denial]).

This coded interaction reflects a natural, reflexive group defense against pain, a common survival mechanism for all living things. Within this safe moment, the worker attempts to give the group its space. She responds to its "caution," signaled by Tina, while working toward solidifying previous gains and strengths. After Tina's report of her quick and appropriate attempt to help a child having an insulin reaction, the worker replies with an enthusiastic, "Good for you," which encourages Tina's (and the group's) autonomy, self-awareness, and impressive knowledge. Moving toward independence is an age-appropriate developmental task, and it is especially important for these youngsters to also gain some independence with regard to their illness. The worker's question, "What did the nurse say?" may be an attempt to pull for feelings about adults on whom they are dependent (perhaps some transference to the leader).

The girls become tangentially involved in a discussion of pretend versus reality (perhaps symbolic of their own ambivalence in acknowledging their reality, or the group's denial in the here and now of the faking that is going on in the discussion). The worker then attempts to refocus on feelings and needs: "Okay, okay . . . Let's come back for a minute." It is clear from her response that the worker "feels" the group shift but struggles to get back to the feelings. She moves them back to a point in the discussion before they began the problem solving: "Okay, okay, but this year she wasn't," saying, in effect, "Let's get back to this year, to now." She continues, "Let's come back for a minute to someone who isn't diabetic, who is younger and doesn't get as much attention, like Lisa." This defines the point more specifically in an attempt to provide the focus to which she is returning them.

The worker proceeds, "What you said about your Dad leaving her is very important. It's important for each of you to have special time with each parent." The children respond feebly, but Tina's solution of flipping the quarter wins out, expressing their powerful need to have control over the uncontrollable. It is a wonderful solution: just flip a coin to decide which parent is to be with the diabetic child. But their pain is evident in Tina's longing for health: "if the quarter is never used, you just keep it." The youngsters know there will always be another reaction and plenty of use for the quarter unless they are either cured or dead (a powerful and painful reality). The worker allows the fantasy, which they all may need to maintain.

How else might the worker have responded? Sensing the shift from feelings to problem solving, it is appropriate for a worker to simply verbalize the feeling for the group: "We were talking about Lisa and those feelings. How did we get to this?" The worker thereby identifies the movement, redirecting the group's focus back to the feeling issues and asking the group to take responsibility for its own growth and independence. Taking responsibility and struggling with demands of reality are important tasks of all latency-age children. As workers, we need not know the reason for a shift, but if we feel it, identifying it opens exploration and keeps the group focused on its purpose and work. If the worker senses that the shift from feelings to problem solving is a resistance, she might make an interpretive intervention: "You know, it sounds as if it's difficult to talk about these feelings." The worker could take it further by clarifying: "It sounds as if it's scary, and it makes us angry. Does anybody ever feel these things?" With either of these alternative interventions, the focus stays with the feelings, giving the group permission to express their strong feelings while letting them know that the worker, unlike their sometimes frightened and confused parents, can tolerate the pain.

In the excerpt, group agreement on having "solved" the problem—"That's a really good idea"—signals to the worker that the children have gained control over the earlier fearful feelings from which they had retreated. At this point, it is safe to return. Maria does so by expressing her fear of dying when Dad couldn't help her, her need for her effective mother, and her fear of abandonment along with her ambivalence about her sister's needs also being met: "Once, I remember, I got really shocky [returning to reality], and my dad kept smacking me [fear of dying and no one being able to help], and then my mom came in. She took me and ran so fast to the bathroom, made me sit down on something and put cold water all over me and kept giving me juice and sugar [her dependency, neediness, and vulnerability]." Mom saved Maria, and Maria needs her. Maria fears the "toss of the coin" would result in dad caring for her [instead of Mom], and Maria's dying because of his inability to help her. Here is her helplessness set against a deeper existential terror she lives: the randomness of life and death. She concludes by expressing her confusion about getting her needs met—"Daddy left Lisa and just took care of me, and Lisa was left alone"—identifying with and feeling ambivalent about her sister's needs.

The worker first validates that confusion: "So you saw a lot of that." Then she attempts to move back to the feelings of being diabetic by connecting Lisa's wish to be diabetic in order to get attention with Maria's getting attention by being a diabetic. "When Lisa came to the group she said that she did feel left out because she wasn't diabetic, and she keeps saying she wants to be diabetic. It sounds crazy to us that anyone who is not would want to be." Tina expresses, for all, the mixed feelings and confusion: "Sometimes I don't want to be diabetic and sometimes I do" [for the secondary gains]. Desiring a choice where there is none, she returns to the magical coins, but they again fail her, ". . . so I flip a penny, and if it only says heads, I'm not a diabetic and tails, it is, and it's always tails." There is no magic, only the reality.

Here we feel their hopelessness, impotence, and grief in that painful truth. For whatever reasons (perhaps to inspire hope as she feels it fade, perhaps to protect herself and them from a pain she feels is too powerful), the worker chooses not to explore the expressed ambivalence about being diabetic but goes with the fantasy: "So if you weren't diabetic, what would be different about your life?" What results is, "a feeling in the room, for the first time, of childish fantasy and freedom, pure glee in the thoughts of cotton candy and chocolate cake."

Clearly the worker struggles to stay and deal with the powerful feelings of these children, which reflects her own countertransferential issues. Similar to the group members, she sometimes dilutes the feelings with premature problem solving or challenges reality with skillful concrete solutions. The pain and ambivalence about illness and dependency are often touched on lightly and not explored in depth. It feels as if the group is "saved" from falling into a pit of grief and despair, and we are relieved but question whether the feelings were abandoned.

Although the worker fails to more thoroughly explore some feeling areas she also demonstrates many positives in her approach. Recognizing that latency-age children grow through mastery and autonomy, the worker provides support for the children to cope with their illness and environment. She helps them maintain the normal child experiences of fantasy and make-believe that allow them to tolerate and cope with the harsh reality. She gives them specific concrete skills, such as how to bake a cake without sugar and what to do when they are feeling "shocky," which are part of her educational goals for this group. Information helps the girls to better lead close-to-normal lives and to exercise some control over their bodies.

Despite the movement into the educational sphere, the children are still able to return to their discussion of feelings and do so in the process excerpt to follow. This return to emotional content proves to us the children's need for this discussion and the importance for the worker to create an open and encouraging atmosphere in which such discussions are possible. The discussion returns to the concerns about monitoring blood sugar levels as Tina and her mother argue heatedly over Tina's use of a pricker machine. As it turns out, Tina's mother has not been insisting that Tina use the machine, and Tina has been using another method for monitoring her blood. The worker intervenes:

Worker:	(empathically) So, there are some other things, Tina?
Tina:	Well . . . But why do we have to be a diabetic anyhow and do all that?
Lucy:	Yeah, we can't have any fun.
Maria:	Yeah, we're like prisoners, too many rules.
Tina:	It's like God is punishing us.
Maria:	Yeah, like he doesn't like us.
Tina:	Just like I'm always getting punished for wanting things.
Worker:	Things?
Maria:	Yeah, like candy.
Lucy:	And cake.
Tina:	(speaking rapidly and in a frustrated tone) Yeah, but why can't we always have sugar? Why do we always have to test our blood and have insulin?
Maria:	Yes, and why do we have to exercise? Why can't we always just eat sugar?
Worker:	I wish we didn't know the answer to that—but we do.
Tina:	(sadly) Yeah, we'll get very high.
Maria:	And sick.
Lucy:	Yes, very sick, scary sick.
Tina:	What kind of sick?
Worker:	Have you ever been sick from being too high? It's the kind of sick you were when you first found out you were sick.
Mothers:	Skinny, weak, needing operations, going into comas . . .
Worker:	Yes, we don't want to be there again.

Tina:	(frustrated) But, but, I didn't, I won't, I mean I don't, I hate diabetes!! I think it's a stupid little . . .
Maria:	Thing—it's a thing!
Tina:	Yes, a stupid little thing, and it makes me so mad! I hate it! I hate it (louder). It makes me want to (looks around) hit a . . . (looks around) pillow.
Worker:	Hit it!
Tina and Maria:	(crying and hitting the pillows) Yeah . . . yeah!
Lucy:	(hitting the pillow) Yeah, I hate it!
Worker:	(encouraging) Yes, hit it! How about the moms?
Sonya:	I'm afraid to take a pillow because—I know this sounds crazy but—I'll hit Tina with it because she's the one who has the diabetes.
Worker:	Yes, sometimes you get mad at Tina and not the diabetes. So what do you want to do with that anger?
Girls:	Hit a pillow! (They continue to hit the pillows, and the mothers join in talking about their anger at their lives and its restrictions.)
Tina:	I think I feel like killing my diabetes.
Worker:	And what about you, Maria?
Maria:	I'm punching mine.
Lucy:	Me too!
Worker:	And what should I do with mine?
Girls:	Here, hit it! Hit it!
Worker:	But I thought I never get angry or feel not normal?
Tina:	You feel "frus-ter-ated!" (worker and mothers laugh).
Maria:	You don't like it. I think you get angry, too, I bet, when you get shocky like me . . .
Worker:	Yes, when I can't eat what I want.
Tina:	Yes, and I'm gonna beat mine up.

In the preceding piece, powerful feelings (primarily rage at their helplessness) surface. The worker helps the girls to redirect these feelings externally by expressing them verbally and physically (by hitting the pillows) rather than internalizing them and contributing to a negative self-image. There is already blurring between the children and their illnesses, a sense that all the hateful things about diabetes are associated with them as people, that they need to be ashamed of their weakness, that they deserve to be punished and deprived. Also note the camaraderie and mutuality of the group members who can finally express themselves here because everyone else can understand. As is typical in middles, the group takes over its own work with little need for worker intervention. In this segment, the worker respects the group's autonomy and is far more laid-back and nonintrusive in the process.

The excerpt begins with the worker's recognition of the latent message that something more than the pricker machine is at issue: "So, there are other things, Tina?" This immediately paves the way for Tina to express her feelings about the diabetes. Lucy and Maria, as well as Tina, soon share charged sentiments: "We can't have fun . . . We're like prisoners, too many rules. It's like God is punishing us." They protest the limits and restrictions imposed upon them by the diabetes. The worker's conscious minimal involvement enables further exploration and expression of the anger, which soon escalates to another level. The children question why they have to be different, "Why can't we always have sugar? Why do we always have to test our blood and have insulin?" Their questions follow their attempts to establish identities separate from their illnesses.

Again the worker introduces the educational piece, reminding them of the consequences of not following the rules: "I wish we didn't know the answer, but we do." Her attempt to balance acknowledgment of the fantasy and reality closes off some expression of feelings and focuses on the facts about the sickness. In response to Maria's question about why she cannot eat sugar, an alternate intervention would be for the worker to say, "It's really hard not to be able to do some things other kids do." This intervention responds to the latent content, sustains the feeling, and as a result, gives permission to move to a deeper level of expression.

Despite the short shift back to the educational piece, the feelings reemerge in an even more dramatic form: "I hate diabetes . . . I think it's a stupid little . . . thing . . . And it makes me so mad . . ." The worker now allows the feelings, supporting their expression as the children pummel the pillows: "Yes, hit it!" At the same time, she reaches out to unite the mothers and children: "How about the moms?" Sonya's anger at the diabetes has become confused with anger toward her daughter: "I'm afraid I'll hit Tina because she's the one who has the diabetes." The worker makes a helpful distinction by accepting the anger and thereby diffusing the mother's guilt while clarifying the differences between the child and the illness: "Yes, sometimes you get mad at Tina and not at the diabetes." The worker's follow-up comment, "So what do you do with that anger?" suggests that the anger should not be displaced onto Tina. Rather it should be expressed in some other way, perhaps by hitting a pillow or by sharing with other mothers in the group.

Having united the mothers and children in common expression of their anger and pain, the worker moves to bond and ally with them by de-idealizing her role: "And what should I do with mine [her anger]?" By acknowledging herself as a real object, the worker helps the group internalize a healthier self-concept. In a playful way, she questions the girls' distorted perceptions of her, enabling them to realize that negative or angry feelings are natural and not bad. Even she experiences them: "But I thought I never get angry or feel not normal." As the session ends, all join to fight the common enemy and, in so doing, achieve one purpose of the group.

We have reviewed, in some detail, interventions used and alternative interventions which could be used to explore some basic themes in the preceding excerpt. By no means has this analysis exhausted the possibilities for intervention or the variety of themes. A few of the secondary issues left unexplored include: themes concerning sibling rivalry, acted out between Maria and Lisa, and paralleled in the competition among group members; anger at parents, perhaps played out at the worker in the group; and secondary gains and manipulation for need gratification. We have also chosen to discuss only briefly roles in the group, a topic explored more fully later in this chapter.

The major lesson to be learned from this process is not found in the investigation of each individual intervention but is rather to be understood in terms of the whole: the group has an amazing capacity to continue expressing its needs and do its work. It gives the worker multiple opportunities to hear its cry and respond to it. If the worker misses key latent content, it will surely resurface, not necessarily in the same form, but always in a doggedly persistent fashion. She need only listen. Only after repeated attempts to raise important material go unanswered does the group begin to give up its work.

Obstacles

Numerous cues signal a group's failure to thrive. These include:

1. the worker's own feelings of boredom and helplessness;
2. group members' verbal and nonverbal expressions of boredom;
3. a sense of lethargy in the group's communication or activity;
4. primarily content-related discussion that is devoid of emotional material;
5. a pattern of absences and latenesses;
6. longer and more frequent periods of silence.

These factors generally connote some difficulty in group functioning. They may suggest that either the group's needs are not being met or the group is struggling with resistance. The worker's task is to evaluate which obstacle exists by asking for feedback from the members, studying when the symptoms show themselves, and consulting in supervision to elicit an objective view and establish a plan of action.

Resistance in groups may relate to the group's inability to confront painful and challenging issues. One of the worker's tasks in the middle phase is to help the group to be confrontational in a healthful way. Healthy confrontation is cathartic but not ego-assaultive; real feelings are expressed, which ultimately increases trust and intimacy in the group. Most importantly, confrontation promotes an honest awareness of self because group members receive valuable feedback about how others perceive them. This feedback affords each group member a more realistic perception of self and thereby enhances his or her capacity to change. The danger with aggressive confrontive behavior is that, if it is handled clumsily by the worker (that is, the worker fails to modulate the confrontation, and it becomes an attack), members can be hurt and thereafter less open to sharing because they no longer feel safe and able to trust.

Confrontation

The following illustrations demonstrate some of the strengths and weaknesses of workers dealing with confrontation. The first selection is taken from a substance abusers group in an outpatient drug treatment program. For this population, characterized by avoidance of reality and denial of problems, confrontation is particularly important. Although individual treatment is useful, it rarely has the impact of group confrontation to help the abusers access what they are doing to themselves. The commonality among group members prevents them from fooling one another about the reality of their behaviors. Their experiences have often led them to become distrustful and suspicious of any openness or camaraderie. A group that does not confront is devalued by members because they feel that their deceptions are believed. If treatment is based on a lie, group members do not feel helped.

We have chosen a sample session that includes some beginning confrontation. The group struggles with two related themes: responsibility for one's own actions and dependency on others. Given the degree of denial and distrust within this population, these are especially problematic themes:

Worker:	What happens to someone who has something important to talk about but is having a hard time getting it out?
Peter:	That's their responsibility, man. We're not mind readers. If you've got something to say, you're the one who has to deal with it and get it out.
Worker:	Peter, I bet you remember that's not so easy sometimes. Sometimes people sit for weeks with something they need to talk about.
Larry:	But that's awful. We should be able to help them or something. Did that happen to you, Peter?
Manny:	(angrily) That's when you were getting high, right? You had to leave for detox. Never said a word to us, just disappeared.
Peter:	And where has David been? He sat there for weeks sweating and not saying a thing.
Larry:	How long has he been out? Several weeks. I'm worried that we're losing people.
Peter:	(exasperated) Losing who? He's been out sick. He called in. And Barbara's out sick, too.
Larry:	There have been too many times when I got close to people, and they just bolted on me.
Manny:	David gets to me, too. I say things to him, and he gets all upset and defensive. He can't even admit he's an alcoholic.
Peter:	Yeah, man, that pisses me off.
Worker:	It's interesting that we're talking about David this week . . .
Peter:	What? You think it's like talking behind his back or something? That's not true.

Worker:	Well, I think it might be easier to say what you're feeling about David since he isn't here. But I wonder how it will feel the next time he is in group.
Peter:	No fuckin' way! I'll tell him to his face what I think is going on . . . You're right, though. We shouldn't stab him in the back.
Manny:	It's just that David has this thing, whenever I say something to him . . .
Peter:	Manny, not like this. It's not fair.
Worker:	Boy, Peter, you changed your tune pretty quick.
Larry:	You know what happened to me? Last week in the day room someone started telling me about them being high and stuff. And I said I really didn't want to hear it and that they should talk to their therapist or group about it.
Worker:	What do you think, group, about knowing that someone is high in the program?
Donna:	I guess you should talk to someone.
Peter:	I don't know. I have a hard time with that. I suppose it's for the person's good to tell staff, but it's that old street thing, though, you just don't talk no matter what.
Worker:	But you know, Peter, we have an agreement here among all of us. Street rules get left at the front door. This is drug treatment.
Larry:	I just don't want to hear about it.
Manny:	But maybe it was a way of asking for help.
Peter:	Or that he can't talk about it in group. People have lots of reasons.
Donna:	But I mean, how much can we really let out here? I don't know. It doesn't feel good sometimes.
Florence:	Right. Like I want to ask . . . Okay, Manny, say I know you're high, and I bring it up in group. How do you feel about it? Because the thing for me is, I don't want someone to get mad at me.
Manny:	No, no, you can do it, because it's for my own good. I trust Florence. I know you'd want me to talk about it.
Larry:	I'd feel two ways. First I'd be pissed, but then I'd be relieved.
Worker:	Relieved?
Larry:	Because at least someone gave a shit enough to think of someone else other than themself.
Peter:	Yeah, I go along with that. Maybe we should all agree right now that, in this group, anything goes.

In this piece, we see clearly how the worker sets the tone for direct and honest communication. The worker models constructive confrontational exchange by challenging the group's responsibility to its individual members:

"What happens to someone who has something important to talk about but is having a hard time getting it out?" He also holds the individual responsible for not denying his own conflicts and behavior: "Peter, I bet you remember that that's not so easy sometimes (being able to say what is on your mind). Sometimes people sit for weeks with something they need to talk about." Manny and Larry's responses show how the group confronts Peter in progressive degrees of directness. Manny becomes angry and approaches the issue of dependency and trust as well as that of responsibility: "That's when you were getting high, right? You had to leave for detox. Never said a word to us, just disappeared." Following the worker's model, Manny functions in a positive leader role. But Peter, symbolizing the group's denial and resistance and vying with Manny for the leadership role, avoids the confrontation by passing the buck to an absent member, David.

This discussion is typical of middles in all groups, where painful issues are played out in denial and resistance. Larry, serving as the spokesperson for the group's feelings and concerns, expresses the fear of loss associated with dependency: "How long has he been out? Several weeks. I'm worried that we're losing people." Larry's response demonstrates the attempt by some members to increase intimacy and bonding, again common to middles.

What follows is interesting. Peter—the negative leader, resistant to change and the voice for maintaining the status quo—becomes angry and denies the significance of the loss issue: "Losing who? He's been out sick. He called in. And Barbara's out sick, too." Larry persists. Like the others, he is frightened that dependency results in loss, intimacy results in pain, and trust results in deception: "There have been too many times when I got close to people, and they just bolted on me."

At this point, Manny attempts to confront the group and Peter in a more benign way than before. He displaces his anger at Peter's denial and lack of responsibility on the "safe to talk about" absent member: "David gets me, too. I say things to him, and he gets all upset and defensive. He can't even admit that he's an alcoholic." Manny's bit of unconscious dishonesty is quickly supported by Peter: "Yeah, that pisses me off." Thus Manny becomes a conspirator, and Peter effectively wins the leadership power struggle. The group's fear of dependency and responsibility wins out. Part of the task for any group in the middle phase includes jockeying for position in the struggle for leadership and autonomy from the worker.

The worker is aware of some of what is happening. He attempts to confront the move away from dealing honestly in the present, but his attempt proves ineffective: "It's interesting that we're talking about David this week . . ." This engages Peter in a defensive response, which quickly accelerates into an angry power struggle with the worker. Had the worker left David out and simply identified the move away from dealing with each other, the intervention would have been less provocative and more productive. Instead, he might have said, "We seemed to have switched gears here. We were talking about how hard it is to be honest and open in group, about being high and not talking about it."

The worker's role in middles is often to focus and clarify while encouraging the group's feedback. Even after Peter's angry challenge ("What? You think it's like behind his back or something? That's not true."), the worker might have clarified what he meant: "No, I didn't mean it's like talking behind someone's back. I just meant that it's really hard for all of us to be completely honest and open here." This intervention might have defused Peter's angry outburst.

Peter's expression is an avoidant maneuver (a defense) within which the worker gets caught. The worker produces a confused interpretation that moves the group further away from the here and now to hypothesizing about the future, when David will return: "But I wonder how it will feel the next time he [David] is in the group." Perhaps the worker's own issue of handling anger is triggered by Peter's response, a phenomenon not uncommon in working with this population and one which puts tremendous demands on workers. Peter raises the stakes in the negative confrontation for leadership. Perhaps sensing the worker's vulnerability, he speaks with a degree of intensity even greater than before: "No fuckin' way. I'll tell him to his face . . ." and goes on to claim leadership: "You're right, though. We shouldn't stab him in the back." Later Peter confronts Manny and takes charge: "Not like this. It's not fair."

Larry reintroduces the group's need to be direct by relating a story about advising a program member, who is high, about talking with a therapist or group. The worker struggles to use Larry's comments to return the group to more real communication in the here and now: "What do you think, group, about knowing someone is high in the program?" By his choice of the word "program" (outside) rather than "group" (inside), the worker weakens his intervention. Perhaps as a result of his own ambivalence concerning direct confrontation, he inadvertently gives the group a double message. Peter again challenges the worker by allying with members (the "street code") and putting the leader outside: "I don't know . . . you just don't talk, no matter what." The worker is again able to confront and restates the contract: "But you know, Peter, we have an agreement here between all of us [calling them together again and reuniting around their mutuality]. Street rules get left at the front door. This is drug treatment."

From here on, with the power issue somewhat less intense, the group is more directly able to verbalize its fear of confrontation, loss, and intimacy as demonstrated by Florence and Donna's comments: "I don't want someone to get mad at me . . . How much can we really let out here?" Manny surfaces as the positive leader once again: "You can do it (confront me), because it's for my own good. I trust Florence." Larry supports the comment: "I'd be relieved because at least someone gave a shit enough to think of someone else other than themselves."

The group reaches a consensus to confront despite their terror and forces Peter to join. In his characteristic fashion, he assumes (this time more positively) the leader's role: "Yeah, I go along with that. Maybe we should all agree right now that, in this group, anything goes." Although we are unsure precisely what he means, it appears that for now the group has reached some point of agreement about its purpose and method.

In this meeting, the group begins by confronting and then, fearing the intimacy, moving away from the confrontation to a safer level of discussing the confrontation. Finally, the group agrees that if it is to be worthwhile to its members, confrontation is necessary. As in most groups in the middle phase, this group has only reached a temporary plateau. Some movement has been made toward using confrontation productively, but the approach-avoidance behavior will continue until the group is finally able to reach the level of intimacy required to honestly explore painful issues.

As we have seen, confrontation can be frightening for workers as well as clients. Although we understand the necessity for and purpose in the direct expression of anger and other feelings, our ability to call them forth is often handicapped by our own residual fears of losing control. Will the expression of anger be a Pandora's box? Will we be able to channel what comes out, or will we be consumed by it? Will we be able to protect our clients from attack, or will we become as immobilized as they? All of us struggle at various times with issues concerning anger and its expression.

The following vignette is an example of a worker's struggle to deal with a particularly volatile and difficult group of adolescent girls. The group has a prior history of physical violence, and its members are engaged in a rather fragile alliance. The girls are foster children dealing with deep feelings related to abandonment by parents and others. Trust is a rare and delicate commodity. Feelings of fear and vulnerability are constantly present. The group is co-led by a senior worker and a student intern. The intern is scheduled to leave the group the following week, and issues of loss are surfacing:

Laverne:	Ms. T., you better do something about Elizabeth or else she is not walking to the bus station with us.
Michelle:	That's right. There must be something wrong in her head. She acts so stupid.
Worker:	Tell me what happened.
Laverne:	Well, we were walking through the Coliseum, and Elizabeth went up in front of a mirror and started jerking her body and neck all around. She just looked retarded, like this and that, I mean. What is everyone going to think, we are hanging out with crazy people?
Toni:	That's right, Ms. T., you know we all try hard to look good. You know when we walk down the street, people, I mean guys, say look at those fly girls. But with Elizabeth shaking this way and that . . . I mean I have a reputation to protect.
Intern:	I wonder why Elizabeth acts that way?
Michelle:	Because she's stupid—retarded. That's why.

Worker:	I think Elizabeth is trying to be your friend and is trying to do cool things.
Laverne:	No, Ms. T., that ain't working. You always try and protect Elizabeth. Why?
Worker:	Because I think she is always the one left out.
Vicki:	Well, that's her problem. She should do something about it. You don't always have to be sticking up for her.
Melanie:	That's not right, Ms. T. You know you can't be sticking up for one person. She is no better than all of us.
Intern:	Maybe it's easier to pick on Elizabeth than deal with real feelings about other things going on in your own lives.
Laverne:	Ms. T., what is she talking about? Does she think everybody gets along all the time? I mean, don't you and Ms. M. sometimes get angry with each other? What do you do?
Worker:	We talk about it.
Michelle:	Figured white people would say something like that.
Laverne:	Yeah, well, if you don't do something Ms. T., we will.
Elizabeth:	(stands up, throws her chair back, and punches Laverne) Yeah, and what are you going to do about it?

Several important themes emerge in this piece. Here are young girls struggling with an internalized negative sense of self represented by the scapegoated member, Elizabeth. Elizabeth is a part of all of them, a part they are ashamed of and blame for their rejection by those who should love them, a part that is frightening. The conflict is whether to accept or reject this part of themselves. The theme plays itself out in the desire to be rid of Elizabeth and receive the support and protection of the workers, one of whom is about to desert them. No doubt, the repeated changes in workers and the fact that one more is about to leave heighten the intensity of the interaction in this meeting.

The workers, in turn, struggle to stop what they believe to be a potentially explosive situation from developing. They attempt to lessen the scapegoating by increasing the girls' understanding of their feelings about themselves. Instead, the group never gets beyond the manifest content to the underlying feelings. The session explodes in a physical expression of frustration, pain, and anger, which parallels their feelings about their lives in general.

The girls indirectly express their struggle to accept the negative part of themselves by requesting the leaders help them deal with the deviant member: "Ms. T., you better do something with Elizabeth or she's not walking to the bus station with us." They then express their fear of the part of themselves that is crazy, irrational, unlovable: "There must be something wrong in her head. She acts so stupid." Sensing that they have more to say, the worker opens the discussion for exploration: "Tell me what happened."

What follows is an outpouring of their fear of rejection, their low self-esteem, and their shame: "She just jerked her body and neck all around. She just looked retarded. What's everyone going to think, we are hanging out with crazy people?" (How are they viewed by others, as crazy?) "Ms. T., we want to look good . . . but with Elizabeth shaking this way . . . I mean, I have a reputation to protect." Again the fear of not being accepted surfaces. In adolescence, when conformity and acceptance by peers is so important, these girls have the additional hardship of being foster children, a built-in burden because they are different from other children. At this point in the process, themes concerning their self-images and worries about acceptance and rejection could have been identified by the worker simply by labeling what they said: "It sounds as if you are concerned about how people see you."

Instead of using this approach or another approach to address the girls' issues, the intern further identifies Elizabeth as the problem: "I wonder why Elizabeth acts that way." Perhaps this was an attempt to help the girls understand Elizabeth's need for attention but, as we see, it allows the frustration and blaming to intensify. Michelle expresses her rage, and the worker, perhaps recognizing the building tension and fearing it, attempts to explain Elizabeth's behavior. The girls perceive the explanation as the worker's protection of Elizabeth and become more angry, which further entrenches Elizabeth in her role as scapegoat: "You always try to protect her (but not us) . . . You don't always have to stick up for her . . . That's her problem . . . She's no better than all of us . . ." This reaction continues until the group pushes out the workers, blaming the workers because they are white (or blaming themselves for being black, Latina, and rejected).

In reality they are saying, "You don't hear us. You can't help us with what feels so awful." The intern makes one unsuccessful attempt earlier to reach out to the girls by commenting that, "Maybe it is easier to pick on Elizabeth than to deal with real feelings about other things going on in your own lives." The comment is too general and somewhat confrontive and, consequently, is misunderstood by the girls. None of the interventions succeed. The entire session ends with Elizabeth's physical expression of anger and frustration.

The competitive issues between group members (sibling rivalry) and the need for workers' (parents') love and acceptance go unaddressed. The departing worker's abandonment and its meaning for the group is not touched upon. Even the self-hatred and the resultant scapegoating, which the girls are apparently feeling, is not focused on directly. In all, the major conflicts and themes get lost in pursuing the defense of Elizabeth.

When the workers are accused of protecting Elizabeth, they might have tried to explore the girls' feelings toward the workers for rejecting them. Such an approach would allow the girls to express directly their anger at their rejecting parents rather than displace it on each other or blame themselves. Also, it would have been useful to bring Elizabeth, the scapegoat, into the discussion, including her instead of reinforcing her difference by leaving her out. Early on, when the girls first express their frustration with Elizabeth's behavior, the worker might have asked Elizabeth how she felt and what she thought was going on. Some of the feelings connected to the behavior in the group may also relate to issues of loss generated by the anticipated departure of the student intern. Loss and rejection are dominant ongoing themes for children in foster placement. Clearly, some direct discussion of the worker's leaving would have been helpful. In short, it is necessary to address feelings or they are likely to be acted out.

The following treatment group for anorexic inpatients uses confrontation successfully and is further along in its development than those previously discussed. The reader should note that the segment does not even include a worker (although she was present) but shows a group functioning autonomously as a healthy mother working with one of its members, Wendy. She has just submitted a premature request for discharge from the hospital.

Carey:	Now that you're planning to leave us, I'd like to know what's going on with you. You haven't said anything since you've been here.
Wendy:	I don't think I need to stay here. I'd like to get on with my life. I'd like to get back to work and continue working on myself outside the hospital.
Zena:	How can you be better in such a short time? I've been in and out of hospitals, and I was always released too soon. And besides, your opinion isn't the only one that counts.
Carey:	The program gives you a chance to focus on yourself. Many of my friends could be characterized as borderlines, and they would love to have this opportunity.
Wendy:	The groups are a joke.
Karen:	If you haven't participated in them. You get what you give.
Gilda:	It's not just what the groups do. Your participation is necessary. It gives the team a chance to observe you in different settings.
Bea:	You say you've gained weight, but I still see you sitting there in those skinny little pants.

Following the session, Wendy withdraws her sign-out letter.

Conclusion

This chapter offered an overview, a taste of the complexity and variety of middles, including:

1. the early-middle phase of a group of adult children of alcoholics engaged in a very tentative exploration of themes concerning openness and sharing;
2. the middle-middle phase of a group of older, physically disabled, institutionalized people struggling with the depersonalization of institutional life;

3. the middle-middle phase of a group of diabetic youngsters reaching for autonomy despite their physical illness;

4. the early-middle phase of a group of drug abusers testing the acceptability of confrontation;

5. the end-middle phase of a group of foster adolescent girls confronting negative self-images associated with loss and rejection;

6. the middle-middle phase of a group of anorexic inpatients using their new skills to confront a member in crisis.

In discussing the phase issues in middles, we recognize that process does not necessarily follow a particular program. One cannot always define exactly what phase or part of a phase is demonstrated in a particular piece of work. The creative reader can make a case for including particular illustrations in phase categories other than those we have suggested. We use the phase demarcations simply as guideposts for some key concepts to recognize in understanding middles.

The special task related to the use of self in middles is for the worker to become flexible and sensitive to the need for change over time. At times the worker needs to be directive and, at others, to pull back; the worker may need to confront or to encourage the group to confront. We focus on the needs of those populations included in the analyzed excerpts because we cannot possibly address the needs of all populations in this text. Clearly, the more limited the social skills of a given population, the more actively involved the worker will have to be. For some groups, there will be points when it is necessary to bypass process in favor of education or task completion. Everything depends upon the goals of the group, the group's purpose, and the needs of its member.

6 ENDINGS

If Winter comes, can Spring be far behind?

Percy Bysshe Shelley
"Ode to the West Wind" (1820)

The Members' Issues

The final stage of group development is appropriately called endings or the termination phase. The ending may be for an individual member, the current worker, or the group as a whole. Whichever ending occurs, however, the group as a whole and its individual members all experience some sense of loss and need for adaptation to a changed situation without the group or with a differently constituted group. The more profound the group experience, the more significant and meaningful the loss, and the greater the need for adjustment. In the ending phase, the importance of striking the right balance between preserving what has been gained by the group experience and successfully breaking away from the past cannot be underestimated.

While the final termination occurs in the last meeting in a group, issues regarding termination occur throughout the group's sessions from the beginning phase. In fact, beginning questions about trust are heightened by the early awareness of the temporary nature of group relationships. As we discussed earlier with regard to the end-middle phase, the group usually, for several sessions prior to the actual ending, addresses and struggles with termination issues.

In the study of individual development, we have learned about the importance of the separation and individuation phase. This phase begins in a baby's early movement away from mother and is repeated later in other forms as individual identity is established, evolved, and redefined in latency, adolescence, and throughout the rest of life. The termination stage in groups is similar to a separation and individuation process in individual development. Just as the individual must successfully master the separation-individuation process in order to develop self and good future relationships, so, too, must the group experience success in mastering endings for the sense of self and the positive connection to new relationships afterward. In effect, the goal for the ending stage of all groups is to smooth the way for healthy and fulfilling participation in other groups and in other contexts.

The approach-avoidance that characterizes other stages of group development (moving toward and away from intimacy, longing for connection yet fearing exposure) manifests itself again in termination. Group members appear simultaneously indifferent to the group experience and intensely involved. The expression by group members that the group was not so important or significant to them often betrays the truth. Losing the group is so painful that one defends against the loss by feigning its unimportance, a classic denial. The ending period is often characterized by excessive absence and lateness for members, a sort of trial for the final separation. If the group or worker is going to "desert," some members may abandon the group first to shield against hurt.

In some groups, endings become a period of frenzied activity and relating. More openness and work occurs as the group comes to a close than has ever occurred in past meetings. It is as if members hope to get every last bit from the experience before it ends. Perhaps an unconscious hope also surfaces that sharing with others, and particularly expressing deeply felt troubles, will force the worker or departing member to recognize the neediness of the remaining group members, thereby compelling the individual to stay with the group. The continued expression of neediness may also be an unconscious avoidance of confronting the separation.

Communication in the ending phase generally flows easily and readily with much evaluative discussion, review of the group's accomplishments, and reminiscences about the shared experiences. Along with this discussion comes talk about the changes members have been experiencing in their lives outside of the group and the influence the group may have had on their behavior in other situations. Because of regret for the loss of the group or worker, and because of some anxiety about members' future directions, some conversation may be strained. It may be particularly difficult to talk about the perceived abandonment by the worker. Some angry and sad feelings may be played out in regressive behavior within the group, a defiant return to old, dysfunctional ways of relating which the group appeared to have overcome successfully. The regression may also relate to fearing the loss of the group. By demonstrating continued neediness, the members unconsciously avoid the separation.

One group for teen mothers in a vocational training program demonstrated its anger about its worker's departure by offering her a farewell celebration featuring beer and pizza. Discussions about responsibility and the use and abuse of alcoholic beverages had been the focus of many earlier meetings, and a number of the group members were minors. The choice of beer for the ending party was a not-so-covert expression of their rage, a regressive acting-out that needed to be confronted and explored.

The cohesiveness so distinctive in successful middles often wanes during the ending stage as group members prepare for the weakening of bonds. As ties weaken, group members may find renewed satisfaction in relationships outside the group. When termination proceeds in a positive fashion, they will move in a constructive way to other groups and relationships.

The Worker's Role: Use of Self and Issues of Authority

The worker's role shifts from the beginning phase in which she or he must enable the group to trust (the engagement), to the middle phase in which she or he helps the group attain the autonomy and cohesiveness needed to do its work, to the ending phase in which the group is empowered to deal with the ambivalence regarding loss and to move to other experiences. The worker's major task in endings is to help the group maintain its gains. This process is made possible, in part, by the group's acknowledgment of the meaning of the loss and recognition of its achievements and continued areas for work. Group members and the worker are certain to have ambivalent feelings about the ending. The successful group, after all, usually has become a fairly predictable and secure place in which strong connections have been made between the worker and members and among the members.

In endings, as in all other phases, workers must be aware of their own feelings and must monitor those feelings while assisting with the appropriate interventions. Workers should encourage group members to express all feelings, including anger and sorrow at a worker's leavetaking or the disbanding of the group. Sometimes, it is useful for workers to admit their own sadness when members are reluctant to do so. This admission can begin the review of some of the high points and difficulties the group has shared. Again using their own sense of what is happening in the session, workers can help their groups to verbalize feelings that are hard to express. One of the aims of workers is to help the group end with the honesty it has developed over time, to add some completion to the process that is true to the spirit of what has been accomplished.

It is important to begin exploring the meaning of the termination long before the final endings. Rushing this stage and leaving the discussion of loss to the very end are means for workers to allay their own anxieties about discussing issues that are often painful for workers as well as for their groups. Workers' feelings are likely to include their own dissatisfactions about members who were not helped or goals left unachieved. They may finish by encouraging a flurry of discussion to cover all remaining topics before the end. Such discussion is impossible to pursue fully and is generally disappointing. For workers, the termination process may arouse unresolved conflicts concerning their own earlier losses; it may raise issues related to control, grief, and anger. Powerful countertransferential reactions are often experienced more intensely in the termination period than in the early stages of group development.

Although workers need to help their groups reflect on evaluation, ambivalent feelings concerning the past, and the termination, they also must help their groups focus on the future and where the members will go from here. The future should relate to some of the skills learned in the group; continuity must be maintained from the current group to the next group or worker, if appropriate, or to experiences outside of the group. It is the worker's responsibility, as much as possible, to alert the group to future agency plans, whether the group will be reinstituted and, if so, when and who will be the new worker. The worker may also help the group discuss goals and areas it wishes to explore in a future group with a new worker.

Andrea has been working with a group in a psychiatric day program for many years. She recently received the news that she will be promoted to an administrative position in the facility and will need to terminate with her group. When asked about the promotion by group members, Andrea reassures the members that they will still see her around in the program and that they really do not need to be concerned. Group members exhibit a number of regressive behaviors, they are often absent, and several of the group members decompensate. After one more session, Andrea leaves without addressing any of the issues.

Andrea's difficulty in exploring the feelings of abandonment associated with her leaving reflects the issues most workers have with their own unresolved conflicts concerning loss and abandonment. Commonly, workers offer false reassurance, in effect denying the real painful feelings. This process inadvertently denies the member an opportunity, perhaps for the first time in a therapeutic and healthy environment, to explore and hopefully resolve longstanding conflicts around loss, grieving, and separation. These conflicts often underlie many dysfunctional components of personality. If the worker is able to tune in to her own feelings, then she can use her authority to actively direct the focus of the group toward the discussion of feelings about her leaving and, more generally, about loss.

Although we all recognize that not everything can be dealt with in the group, it is particularly problematic if the worker colludes with the group in failing to address termination issues or giving these issues short shrift at the group's conclusion. Few issues are likely to be left fully resolved at a group's ending, but the process toward resolution has been started and should be acknowledged. Worker and group must struggle together to allow the termination period to be a positive, growth-producing experience.

Termination of a Member: A Group Issue

The following piece is excerpted from a group session with alcoholics in the final stage of treatment. The group meets weekly on an outpatient basis. The participation of members ranges in length from four months to three years. Members, all of whom have high-level jobs, are unusually articulate and intellectual. They attend voluntarily. The session is the final one for Ron, who has attended regularly for nearly three years. We see how the issues of termination for one member reflect the issues of all members. In such open-ended groups, beginnings and endings are a constant part of the flow. Older members such as Ron represent hope in having successfully completed the program but also represent the loss of the group's stable components. Ron's leaving triggers fear for some members about "making it" and having to survive independently:

Leon:	Well, this is it, Ron; you've done it. I'm really glad for you, but we're going to miss you in the group.
Ron:	Yeah, I have mixed feelings, too, but I'm ready. It's been a long time here, a lot of work, but I feel prepared.
Helen:	What supports are you going to use once you leave here?
Ron:	I plan on hooking up with that psychiatrist I told you all about for individual, then I'll continue to use my spiritual thing, you know, Amity services; and I'll go to one AA meeting a week as usual.
Leon:	Only one AA meeting? Is that all you think you'll need?
Ron:	That's what I've been doing for a long time. I don't feel the need for any more since I have the other things.
Sue:	It sounds like you now feel that you can back away from the supports that got you sober. That's a little grandiose, don't you think? I don't know of too many people who can make it with just one meeting a week.
Ron:	Look, if I ever begin to feel the need for more, I'll go more often. It's just that I've got so many things going now that I really have to budget my time.
Leon:	Wow, you really have got your priorities mixed up. I'd like to hear what Ned [the worker] has to say about this.
Worker:	It seems to me that Ron has made himself clear, and I wonder why some of you won't accept his plan.
Leon:	You mean to say you accept what he's going to do? You aren't concerned that this man is walking out of here planning to go to only one AA meeting a week? You should be really into him, I think, trying to talk some sense into his mind.
Ben:	Well I don't see what all the fuss is about. I'll admit I might be biased because I don't go to AA at all, but I think Ron has enough sense to know what he needs and to get it when he needs it. I don't see anything wrong with his plan.
Leon:	You know, I'm really worried about this. I know for myself that I couldn't make it without at least one meeting a day, and I'm surprised that Ned is letting this slide.
Worker:	Why are you so sure that Ron's needs are identical to yours? What's going on, Leon? You seem really worked up about this . . .
Leon:	I guess I'm just putting myself in Ron's place, and I know I'd feel kind of shaky if I weren't making more meetings.
Worker:	Well, are you in fact in his place? How far are you from "graduation"?
Leon:	As a matter of fact, I was just thinking about that. How come you've never raised that with me?

Ken:	I think you're raising the question for yourself right now. It looks as if you're going through your own termination, Leon . . .
Leon:	Well, I'll be darned. Let's see, I've been in this group, how long? A year and nine months. Maybe it's about time.
Ken:	It's been a while since I've been wondering when you two would be "graduating." It's obvious you're way ahead of the rest of us.
Leon:	That's really strange to hear you say that, but it feels good. When I came here to this group, there were some guys here that I could see were ready for graduation, way ahead of where I was at that time . . .
Worker:	Okay, let's step back a little to look at what's been going on here tonight.

What was the group really telling Ron? What was Leon saying about where he's at?

In the initial exchange between Leon and Ron, Leon expresses his, and probably the group's, mixed feelings about Ron's "graduation." Hope and joy are felt in recognition of Ron's accomplishment of taking control over his own life. But the group members also experience a deep sense of loss because Ron is leaving them: "Well, this is it, Ron; you've done it. I'm really glad for you, but we're going to miss you in the group." On an even more profound level, group members mourn the loss of the old part of themselves, dysfunctional as it may have been. The delight in the newly found self, and the fear and sadness in the loss of the old familiar self-pervade the discussion in a way that is typical of the termination phase in groups.

Ron acknowledges the commonality of the mixed feelings, not really elaborating or identifying them, but verbalizing his own ambivalence: "Yeah, I have mixed feelings, too, but I'm ready [the new self]. It's been a long time here, a lot of work [sadness and acknowledgment of his struggles], but I feel prepared [embraces the new strength]." The worker chooses to remain nonintrusive at this point, allowing the group to carry the process on its own. The worker could pick up on the "mixed feelings" comment and explore it openly with a simple request for clarification—"What are the mixed feelings you're both having?"—followed by "What about others?" Such an approach would solicit each member's response and open a path for verbalization of feelings. The group would identify more specifically their issue of dependence and independence as well as their ambivalence in desiring health yet fearing letting go of old familiar pathological forms of relating. This kind of early intervention is enough to accelerate the process without being so threatening as to stop it.

The worker's decision to sit back opens the issue in a different manner: the group members are allowed to respond. They question how Ron (how they) will make it without the group (the supportive nurturing force): "What supports are you going to use once you leave here?" Ron identifies an apparently solid plan to continue his work, but the group challenges it: "Only one AA meeting. Is that all you need? It sounds like you now feel you can back away from the supports that got you sober. That's a little grandiose, don't you think?" Sue's anger at his leaving is apparent. "I don't know many people who can make it with just one meeting a week." She expresses her fear and the group's fear of regressing when they leave. Ron holds on to his reality, but the group members reject it; the dependency pull is strong.

Leon, who is particularly upset, tries to receive confirmation from the worker that Ron's plan is a poor one. Instead, the worker not only supports the strength of Ron's separation but also confronts the group on their inability to let him go: "It seems to me that Ron has made himself clear, and I wonder why some of you won't accept his plan." Leon avoids the confrontation and attempts to solicit the worker's support as the superego, "You mean to say you accept what he's going to do? You aren't concerned that this man is walking out of here planning to go to only one AA meeting a week? You should be really into him, I think, trying to talk some sense into his mind."

Ben supports both the worker and Ron, which pushes Leon to admit the real issue—his and the group's fear of not making it, of separation and failure: "You know I'm really worried about this." Leon refers to Ron's plan to leave (the concrete issue) and Ron and the group's ability to separate and remain in control of their own lives (the latent issue): "I know for myself that I couldn't make it without at least one meeting a day, and I'm surprised that Ned is letting this slide." Leon's comment suggests his anger and confusion at what he experiences as the worker's abandonment.

The worker responds by reinforcing the concept of individual difference and need—an important ingredient for all groups in the termination phase—in preparation for the separation: "Why are you so sure that Ron's needs are identical to yours?" The worker continues with this idea and notes Leon's affect, compelling Leon to examine his own feelings and further supporting the concept of separateness: "What's going on, Leon? You seem really worked up about this." This statement forces Leon to be even more specific: "I guess I'm just putting myself in Ron's place." Leon verbalizes his identification with Ron: "I know I'd feel kind of shaky if I weren't making more meetings." The worker identifies the issue clearly, finally focusing on Leon's fear: "Well, are you in fact in his place? How far are you from graduation?"

This direct confrontation helps Leon to finally verbalize his competitive feelings and his concerns about his own termination: "As a matter of fact, I was just thinking about that. How come you've never raised that with me?" Leon actually asks the worker for reassurance. He is not so much concerned about stopping Ron but about being okay himself. Modeling the worker's style, Ken confronts and clarifies for Leon: "I think you're raising the question for yourself right now." Ken reinforces Leon's own ability and deemphasises his need to depend on the worker: "It looks as if you're going through your own termination, Leon." The termination focus switches from Ron to Leon here with Leon now able to directly verbalize his sense of movement and his readiness for change: "Maybe it's about time . . . That's strange to hear you say that [referring to Ken's statement that Leon is ahead of the others], but it feels good. When I came here to this group, there were some guys here that I could see were ready for graduation, way ahead of where I was at that time . . ." It appears that Leon is ready to begin the process of evaluation and identification of change when the worker stops the process to help the group analyze.

It may be argued that the group needs to experience the process rather than analyze it, that more exploration of the pain is appropriate, that the expression of the unconscious feelings frees the individual to move forward. Perhaps the worker, a bright and highly verbal man, was more comfortable (as is often the case) in the intellectual realm. Termination issues of loss and change are painful for both clients and workers. Often, as appears to be happening here, workers opt to move away from those painful feelings by engaging in an intellectual analysis of the process.

One result of the worker's request for analysis is that the discussion of Ron's departure is lost. Although the move to Leon's concerns and the concerns of the group is legitimate and although the feelings are in need of expression, the entire discussion is actually defensive in nature, a way to avoid discussing the departure of Ron. The current feelings of loss associated with one member's termination are avoided in favor of the discussion of a future, less real, and less immediate feeling.

When the worker, by pursuing Leon, is able to break through the group's defense against feeling the pain of loss and the fear associated with separation, it would have been helpful to go one step further. The worker might have connected Leon's feelings with those of Ron, validating their feelings of sadness and fearfulness, and then generalizing their feelings to the group. Such an approach would help the entire group to say good-bye to its member. One way of encouraging the group to express its concerns while including Leon and Ron would be to say, "So, Leon, I guess your fears of Ron's not making it are your own fears about not making it. What about other people? Is it a fear others have? Ron, do you?" This sort of intervention would move the group to a more specific discussion about the loss of the member, about leaving and being left. The worker might follow this by reiterating the group's comments, "I guess making it means having to leave others behind and having others leave us. I wonder how you feel about leaving us, Ron." After Ron has had a chance to respond, the worker might ask the group to voice their feelings about losing Ron and their thoughts about how the group will be different. By using this approach, the worker assures that Ron's departure is addressed and that the group, in its mourning, is able to work through and verbalize some of their own fears of leaving and separating.

The key is to stick with feelings, solicit feelings, and explore feelings. Issues of loss and dependency are always the glue preventing healthy separations. Addictive behavior is often a way of holding on to the past. The worker's task is to free up energy that is generally tied up in pathology. This energy then becomes the force behind successful separation.

Lost in Feelings

Unlike the preceding piece, the following excerpt allows discussion of feelings to the point where it is sometimes overwhelming. Evaluating gains, identifying growth, and acknowledging loss are crucial during the termination phase. These interventions act in the same way as reminiscence enables the letting go process to begin and to build other supportive networks for when the group ends. It is also vital to encourage the expression of a range of feelings including anger, despair, loss, joy, anticipation, fear, anxiety, emptiness, and hope. While some workers only allow limited expression of feeling before closing off the interaction, others find themselves drowning in a sea of feelings and grasping for life rafts.

The following excerpt is an example of a worker whose current function and history with a group of blind or deaf aged persons in a senior center program has allowed for a free expression of feeling. The worker's problem is what to do with the depth and amount of feeling she is able to solicit. The pain of loss and endings stalks all of us, worker and client alike, but with the disabled elderly, it is a constant force waiting to be triggered. Each loss is symbolic of the ultimate one they are approaching.

Worker:	I just want to remind people that after today, we have three meetings left. Our last group is on May 11, and we've decided that on that day we're going to have a party. So, we need to spend some time planning. But before we get to that, last week we closed by thinking about what we've accomplished and shared in this year we've had together, and we planned to discuss it here today. What have you been thinking about what has happened throughout the year?
Ellie:	I enjoyed you very much. You made it possible for us to make two tapes.
Thelma:	You discussed different things. I always had a pleasant Monday. (A discussion of the videotaping as a highlight of the program continues for a few minutes.)
Ellie:	Elaine, we are talking about making the tapes. Do you want to add something?
Elaine:	No, I don't want to say it . . . (A hush falls over the group.)
Worker:	Why is everyone so quiet?
Sol:	Well, Ellie said most all of it. Whatever subject you brought up was interesting. It was very good.
Giuseppe:	I was thinking about destiny. When I like someone and they leave, I feel bad. I loved you and when this . . . Forget about

it. This is going to be in my mind a long, long time until something else comes to make me forget. It makes me feel like crying. You're going to go away, and I have you in my memory a long, long time.

Worker: I am touched and feel a deep sadness. I will also remember you, Giuseppe, for a long time.

Giuseppe: I wish the one comes after you be just like you. I remember one worker was nice, but she really didn't seem to have time for us. (The group begins a discussion about the other social workers who have worked with the group who have not helped them at all. Everyone seems very agitated.)

Worker: I understand that everyone here is going to miss me, and I'm going to miss everyone also. But Giuseppe was saying that sometimes when someone leaves you care about, it's hard to think about it ever being a good situation again, till someone else comes along. Maybe some of you are having some negative feelings because you're thinking that next year, you won't have someone you'll like. (The group members begin to talk about their fears and worries about who will replace the worker.)

Orlando: Maybe whoever replaces you won't be good.

Ellie: Yeah, or maybe no one will replace you.

Elaine: When you go, I'm not interested in coming here anymore. There won't be anything here for me anymore. When I first came here, I was very disturbed. You came, and you opened up my life. You have tried everything under the sun for me to get advanced (enumerates a long list of services). God should bless you for whatever you do. I don't know what to say. You have done wonders and miracles. I'm going to fight for my rights. I thank God I know you. This is the truth. I don't lie to people.

(changing to an angry tone) I don't argue with nobody unless they push me. If they do, I push them back because I'm as good as the next party. Don't think that because I can't hear that you people have to think for me. I have to do my own thinking. I don't relish this place no more. Everyone rubs me the wrong way (said with great anger in her voice). I'll stay until . . . I'll see. I don't have to say it now, but I know I will not stay. People rub me the wrong way.

Worker: Do you remember, Elaine, that you felt that way at the beginning of the year?

Elaine: I only remember what she did!

Ava: What did I do to you?

Elaine: Nothing. Forget about it.

Ava:	What did I do?
Elaine:	Nothing. I'm here to enjoy my day.
Ava:	What did I do?
Ellie:	You don't talk to her.
Ava:	What do you mean? When I come in the car, do I say good morning and so long?
Sol:	Yes.
Ellie:	That's as far as you go. With the others you chat.
Ava:	(getting out of control) With who? How much talking do I do? I'm not a talkative person.
Ellie:	Yeah, with Giuseppe you can talk all morning . . .

The session continues from this point with heated and seemingly disconnected exchanges, with an outpouring of emotion and a difficulty in settling on any direction or focus. The termination phase is characterized here by much regressive behavior. The worker struggles to put it all back on course.

The worker begins the meeting by identifying how much time the group has left to work together, "I just wanted to remind people that after today we have three meetings left. Our last group is on May 11, and we've decided on that day to have a party. So, we need to spend some time planning." By restating the temporal limits of their work together, the worker clearly defines the ending and the work yet to be accomplished. In so doing, she provides a sense of safety and control with structure, purpose, and continuity. She then pulls the members back into the present by using a bridge to last week's session: "But before we get to that, last week we closed by thinking about what we've accomplished and shared in this year we've had together, and we planned to discuss it here today." In addition to providing continuity, her intervention skillfully focuses the group on the work of termination: evaluation, sharing of feelings, and reminiscence. The invitation is clear and the group responsive.

Ellie shares a personal feeling for the leader and notes her favorite program, the videotaping. Thelma's expression of feeling is more guarded but still positive: "I always had a pleasant Monday." The group members discuss their favorite project—the making of the tapes—and reminisce about the fun they have had. They recapture for themselves moments of accomplishment and pleasure. Member helps member, a sign of a developed group. Ellie reaches out to a deaf member, Elaine, pulling her into the group by telling her what they are discussing and inviting her to share her feelings. Elaine is not ready: "I don't want to say it." The worker decides not to push Elaine but attempts to explore the group's silence following Elaine's comment. Instead of addressing their silence, the group counters with a defense of Elaine "Well, Ellie said almost all of it. Whatever subject you brought up was interesting. It was very good."

Giuseppe, however, needs to express his feelings more affectively and enters into a moving speech about his love for the worker. The feelings are powerful and real, a statement about the accepting atmosphere the worker has created in this group. She is genuinely touched and sad and chooses to share these feelings: "I will also remember you, Giuseppe, for a long time." With much sensitivity, the worker reaches inside and uses her feelings to extend the message that expression of feelings is acceptable and to confirm and validate the exchange that has taken place in their lives. Giuseppe has given and received, and the worker has given and received. This tender and loving exchange can remain for both to draw upon in the future.

An important part of termination and the entire process of work with clients is to acknowledge to ourselves and the client that the giving is mutual. The acknowledgment of Giuseppe suggests that the others also have given to the worker. Those who are more analytically prone can make the case for remaining the "objective object," but we believe that part of what is destructive in human relationships and development is the denial of self-worth and the worth of others. By acknowledging that she has gained something from the group, the worker demystifies her role and enhances healthier, more realistic, object relationships. Additionally, she increases her clients' self-esteem by recognizing that they too have something to give. This enhances their sense of self-worth and autonomy. To deny that our clients add to our lives is to deny the mutuality of relationships.

After this exchange, Giuseppe leads the group to discuss "what will happen to us." He compares previous workers with the present one and expresses fears of not getting enough and of being abandoned: "I wish the one that comes after be just like you. I remember one worker was nice, but she really didn't seem to have time for us." The worker's response is interesting here. She states in her record that she senses the group's nervousness about what the new worker will be like, and her intervention shows that she connects the nervousness to the group's anger. Specifically, the worker fails to connect the group's anger at her for abandoning them.

The worker responds, "I understand that everyone here is going to miss me [validates, indicates responsive listening], and I'm going to miss everyone also [reiterates her feeling for them in an effort to slow the process down to where it was clearer]. But Giuseppe was saying that sometimes when someone leaves that you care about, it's hard to think about it ever being a good situation again, till someone else comes along [reiterates the loss issue and begins to address their feeling unsafe]. Maybe some of you are having some negative feelings because you're thinking that next year, you won't have someone that you'll like." This last sentence suggests the presence of negative feelings but eliminates the worker's role in the situation. It is she who is leaving and creating the new situation that frightens them. Her message is confusing and ends up sounding as if they are angry because maybe they will not like the new worker. In fact, they are angry because they feel abandoned. They feel guilty saying it because of the positive feelings expressed earlier by both members and worker (the analytic argument against the worker's sharing of her feelings). They are fearful of being able to transfer the gains they have made because they attribute those gains to the worker.

As is often the case in the termination phase, the group regresses to a dependent position, viewing the worker as being all powerful and the members as helpless. Therefore, when the worker leaves, members feel they lose their strength. It is necessary for the worker to help members own their accomplishments. The worker in this excerpt attempts to reach for what she calls the "negative feelings" but instead delivers a signal that she cannot hear negative feelings. She does this by giving a vague and confusing interpretation. Because the word "negative" has a pejorative quality, it may further contribute to shutting off expression. Even though the group cannot express anger at her, they do express the fear that the agency will not give them what they need. Here again are the abandonment and poor self-esteem themes: "Maybe whoever replaces you won't be good," or worse, "maybe no one will replace you." They are really saying, in part, that perhaps the agency will see them as old, blind, and consequently undeserving of service.

The worker has another opportunity here to slow down the accelerating fears. She needs to confirm that her departure is unrelated to continued service and that there will be another worker. Then she must explore the members' fears and feelings of abandonment. She might say, "I hear people being frightened and angry. Let me first reiterate that there will be another worker assigned to the group and that the group—all of you—will continue to meet. But I am leaving, and it sounds as if people feel that when I go, I take away something we've achieved here, that somehow it's mine and not yours." Such a comment helps address the need of the group to let go of the leader and consolidate their independent gains. This is an important task in ending. The worker could focus more directly on the anger at abandonment if she added something like, "Boy, I'm taking it all and leaving you alone. How does that make you feel?" or "Sometimes people feel angry when a worker leaves them. Maybe people feel that here, but it's hard to say you're angry with me."

One task in endings is to examine distorted perceptions involving themes of abandonment and loss. If this examination is not successfully completed, members are prevented from establishing new relationships. The worker's role is to solicit and explore feelings associated with abandonment and loss in order to ensure that members can move on after the worker leaves. If members are allowed to idealize workers and consequently devalue themselves, they become more dependent and invested in the worker's omnipotence. Elaine's comment illustrates the point: "When you go, I'm not interested in coming here anymore. There won't be anything here for me. When I first came here, I was very disturbed. You came, and you opened up my life." The reader can feel the pain of Elaine's loss and her sense of growth but sees how she credits the worker alone for her progress. Elaine idealizes the worker and devalues herself: "You have tried everything under the sun for me to get advanced. God should bless you for whatever you do. I don't know what to say. You have done ... miracles." In effect, she has given away her gains to the worker, attributing her growth to the worker and not to herself.

As a result, Elaine is left where she was when she began the group: angry, defended, distrusting, and alone. In the following comments, the reader can feel the rage and distrust, the isolation and the helplessness associated with dependency and abandonment: "I don't argue with nobody unless they push me (in an angry tone). If they do, I push back because I'm as good as the next party. Don't think because I can't hear that you people have to think for me. I have to do my own thinking." Elaine has returned to where she began. The worker feels the regression, and she attempts to confront it: "Do you remember, Elaine, that you felt that way at the beginning of the year?" The attempt to point out the connection between how Elaine feels now and how she felt before suggests that the regression is related to the loss. Although it is a perceptive intervention, it gets lost as the group proceeds to discuss anger at those who have been hurtful and who have denied hurting them. This is an opportune time for the worker to connect their anger with the worker's leaving (and, consequently, hurting) them. Unfortunately, the worker gets seduced by the content rather than the affect, and the group's anger accelerates in an increasingly irrational manner, which ends in a displaced attack on another member who is, interestingly enough, accused of abandoning Elaine. The worker struggles to get a hold but cannot. The group literally gets away from her and engages in a series of arguments.

Becoming lost in the group's resistance is unfortunately all too common in work with groups. We know well the rapid-fire pace the group can set. Reflection is not always possible. What can we do to help? We can stop the action, help the group to focus and slow down. When the worker starts to feel lost and as if things are going too fast, she can use the feeling: "Wait a minute. Let's slow down. I'm getting lost." She can then backtrack and review, "We were talking about negative feelings about my leaving and now suddenly everyone is fighting." The worker may choose to follow up by suggesting a connection, "Do you suppose it's easier to be angry with each other than it is to be angry with me?" She can ask the group how they understand the shift, "What do you think this is about? Why is there so much tension here today?" Although many different styles are effective, the worker should always help the group to continue doing its work even at the ending. The work of the group is to promote honest communication through exploration.

Staying with Feelings

No matter how clear the purpose of the group, even if specially geared to help clients terminate, the resistance to separation presents itself powerfully. Such is the case in the following piece taken from an open-ended discharge planning group in an inpatient unit at a state psychiatric facility. Although the group is meeting to discuss their concerns about ongoing termination from the hospital, the worker senses the group's resistance and struggles to help them confront their fears. She points out that each time some members broach the subject of termination, others divert it by engaging the group in a seemingly unrelated and lively topic such as the Leonard–Hagler fight. The worker succeeds in refocusing and keeping the group working in the present.

Worker:	Hmm . . . Does anyone else notice that every time we get on the subject of discharge, the subject seems to immediately change to something else? (silence, a few smiles) I wonder why that's happening so much today.
Bob:	Well, you know the big championship fight was on last night, and a lot of people watched it and were betting on the outcome and everything. That's all.
Worker:	Right. That's true . . . But do you think that's the only reason we're getting off the subject?
Terri:	Yeah. I already talked about my discharge plans and everything is set with that. Like I said before, I'm looking forward to leaving and starting a new life.

(Bob heaves a conspicuous sigh and shifts uncomfortably in his chair.)

Worker:	Bob, you seem kind of uncomfortable. Is there something on your mind?
Bob:	No, no. Not at all. I'm fine. Just a little tired today maybe.
Worker:	Uh huh.
Bob:	And there are a lot of things going on around here.
Worker:	Oh? What kinds of things?
Bob:	Well, you know. People coming and going all the time.
Worker:	Uh huh. And that must be difficult when you find that you've become attached to people and then they leave. (silence)
Terri:	(looks kind of embarrassed) Yeah. I've gotten to be pretty close with some of the people here (looks at Bob), and I'll be sad to leave them. (Bob playfully pokes Terri lightly on the arm. Terri playfully returns the gesture.)
Bob:	OW! (joking, but revealing his true pain) You hurt me. Look what you did; I'll never be the same again!
Terri:	(embarrassed) Oh, Bob don't be ridiculous. I hardly touched you. (silence)
Worker:	Maybe Bob isn't talking about his arm. Maybe he's really talking about how he feels about you leaving.
Terri:	Oh? Are you?
Bob:	Well. Yeah, maybe. But I'm happy for you, too. (silence)
Worker:	It's tough though, isn't it, when you feel both happy and sad about something?

The worker's intervention, "Hmm . . . Does anyone else notice that every time we get on the subject of discharge the subject seems to immediately change to something else," clearly identifies the process of interaction. It focuses the group's attention on the movement or flow of their communication. In effect, the worker says, "We were here and then we moved. How come?" "I wonder why that's happening so much today" implies that this pattern is unusual for the group and demands attention. This interventive technique forces the group to step outside of itself, to function in the capacity of observing ego. The statement is a pull, a demand for health.

Another possible approach is to address the latent aspects in the content of the conversation, to relate to the concrete message by identifying a symbolic connection. One might say, for example, "It sounds as if there is a real battle going on with people in this ring." Such a comment takes the concrete content of the boxing match and connects it with the worker's sense of the group's battle with resistance. This technique is discussed more elaborately in the chapter "Manifest and Latent Content." Its use requires considerable skill and the ability to hear with a third, inner ear. Commenting on the group's movement or connecting the latent and manifest contents both call upon the group to examine its behavior and question the interaction. Such approaches maintain the function of the group up until its end and prevent premature termination. The resistance to dealing with the pain of separation sometimes manifests itself in a failure of the group to do its work. This failure is equivalent to group members not attending or coming late to ending sessions. These acting-out behaviors are common to the termination phase.

In the previous excerpt, the silence and smiles that follow the worker's query about what the group thinks is happening indicate that something else is going on. Bob challenges the worker's interpretation by defending the concrete communication. The worker acknowledges the reality of the content ("Right. That's true") but, in a skillful and nonthreatening manner, pursues the point. She allows for more than one possible meaning and calls the group to work: "But do you think that's the only reason we're getting off the subject?" Terri's response, "Yeah. I already talked about my discharge plans . . ." tells the worker that she is on the right track and refocuses the group on the issue of termination.

As the subject is reintroduced, the worker identifies some nonverbal responses (perhaps in an attempt to help the group verbalize more of the negative or ambivalent feelings behind the "battle"). Referring to Bob sighing and shifting uncomfortably in his chair, the worker says, "Bob, you seem sort of uncomfortable. Is there something on your mind?" This attempt to connect with the feelings appears to work, even though it is a fairly open-ended intervention, which can sometimes be too vague and allow for a vague response. Rather than "Is there something on your mind?" following the identification of Bob's nonverbal communication, she might have asked a more specific question: "Is there something about what Terri said that made you uncomfortable?" Or she might have asked an even more focused question: "Is there something about leaving that makes you feel uncomfortable?" Either of these questions would move more pointedly to the feeling level.

In any case, Bob is ready, and the worker's nonthreatening explorative style, "Uh huh . . . Oh? What kind of things?" opens the path for the verbalization of the key issue: "Well, you know. People coming and going all the time." The worker seizes the moment and verbalizes the feeling for Bob and the group, specifically identifying their struggle, "Uh huh [validating]. And that must be difficult when you find that you've become attached to people and then they leave." The silence validates the feeling of emptiness associated with the loss issue the worker has identified. The worker skillfully sits with the silence, allowing the group their pain and trusting in their ability to come out of it. Terri moves the group directly into the present: "Yeah, I've gotten to be pretty close with some people here and I'll be sad to leave them."

The exchanges which follow, both verbal and nonverbal, are particularly potent. Bob and Terri poke each other, physically touching perhaps in an unconscious need to connect again for the moment and, in so doing, ward off the isolation, reassuring themselves that others are there. Bob's comment, "You hurt me. Look at what you did; I'll never be the same again," is symbolic of the most painful of truths: to allow ourselves to be touched by others exposes us to the pain of loss. Lost is our old self, for we are never again as we were, and the future holds the inevitable loss of those by whom we were touched. This is a seminal issue for the termination phase.

The worker interprets the latent feelings beautifully: "Maybe Bob isn't talking about his arm. Maybe he's really talking about how he feels about you leaving." This interpretation focuses the group in the present, making it consciously aware of its pain and not allowing it to hide behind unconscious symbols. This focusing lessens the real loss because it gives group members conscious awareness and control. By being consciously aware and by expressing real feelings, the feelings are not lost to group members even when the relationships end.

In this excerpt, the group is able to acknowledge its feelings and its ambivalence. "But I'm happy for you, too." The worker identifies and verbalizes the pain and mixed sentiments of the group. She helps the group to stay with the feelings and gives group members a strong message that feelings are valid and that, as painful as some are, the members can survive them. The worker demonstrates trust in the group's strength by allowing those feelings to be explored. In effect she is saying to the group, "You are okay. You can feel and survive. You can separate and be okay."

The worker's excellent approach with Bob and Terri falls somewhat short because it fails to recognize their struggles as a group issue. The other group members are absent from the interchange. Perhaps not as dramatically as Bob and Terri, they are also addressing the group task of discharge planning. The worker might have pulled for the group's feelings by saying, "How are other people experiencing the 'comings and goings'?" This comment would not dilute the focus on Bob and Terri but might draw others into the discussion. Similarly, a statement such as, "I wonder if it is as difficult for some others of you to think about the leaving as it is for Bob and Terri," might be effective in involving other group members. The importance of using a technique to include others in the group is that it increases cohesiveness and allows support through the process of separating.

The ultimate goal of keeping current feelings conscious is to provide a healing and healthy replay of early losses and separations that were traumatic and served to developmentally fix the individual in the past. Dealing with this is the primary task of the termination phase. How the members act out their feelings around termination reflects, for the worker, the members' previous separations. It provides a golden opportunity for the worker to consciously connect the past and the present by asking how this termination is like other losses in the member's life, how it is different, and what it recalls. This time a chance exists for the leavetaking to be different from past separations and a chance to move the individual from the past into the present so that she may exercise control over her own life.

Termination and Regression

As mentioned previously, certain behaviors are characteristic of the termination phase. Among those we listed were the group's sudden regression to previous forms of relating and an increase in absences and latenesses. The following piece involves a long-term psychotherapy group from an outpatient clinic in an inner city hospital. The patients, from various ethnic backgrounds, are diagnosed as borderline personalities. The group is in the termination phase, and the worker has become aware that the group is focusing on concrete and superficial issues and having a significant increase in absences. She assumes that this behavior is a way to avoid dealing with feelings associated with loss. As evidenced in the excerpt, the worker has a parallel struggle with these same issues.

Although earlier in the month the worker broached the subject of her leaving and the consequent termination of the group, the group resists any in-depth discussion of the topic. Instead, members focus their attention on superficial issues, and their attendance has become inconsistent. The following segment is taken from the third meeting following the worker's announcement that she will be leaving:

Nathan:	Where's Edith?
Norm:	I think she has an appointment. Her daughter is sick.
Worker:	Who else is missing?
Nathan:	Julieta is missing. I wonder what's happening with Nilda. She's been out, too.
Norm:	Yolanda is here. She's in the community room. Can I go get her? I don't think she remembers the time for group. Don't lock me out. I'll be right back! (Norm leaves to get Yolanda without waiting for a response from the group.)

Yolanda:	(enters with Norm) I just can't seem to remember the time for the group on Fridays.
Nathan:	(joking with Yolanda) Now Yolanda, we cannot get senile. Remember you want to be able to go back to work. (There's laughter among the group members.)
Worker:	It seems as though people are having a hard time getting here.
Merco:	Jorge, did you return to work?
Jorge:	Oh, yes, I've been working.
Merco:	But weren't you out sick?
Jorge:	Yes, but I returned on Tuesday.
Merco:	So you worked three weeks and was out three weeks sick and just returned on Tuesday?
Jorge:	Yes. I'm trying to make up for the time because my volunteer work ends in December.
Worker:	Are you having a hard time being here because you will be leaving the group soon?
Jorge:	Well, I took a test to go to school. I may start college in December or January.
Worker:	We have heard what's going on with Jorge. I wonder what's going on with the other members in the group?

The process opens with Nathan and Norm inquiring about the missing members. The worker amplifies the signal with further exploration: "Who is missing?" Nathan appears most conscious of the losses in the group and identifies two other absent members, Julieta and Nilda. The worker has an opportunity to pursue Nathan's concern about people being out and to begin the exploration of the group's feelings about loss and abandonment present and past. However, the process moves quickly, particularly with Norm who needs to deny the losses, "Yolanda is here. She's in the community room. Can I go get her? I don't think she remembers the time for group." On some level, Norm attempts to protect Yolanda and the group from its real feelings. Norm's need to keep things as they are, thereby preventing the forthcoming change, is heard in his exiting plea, "Don't lock me out. I'll be right back." It is also evident in his impulsive withdrawal from the room—a desperate attempt to literally pull the group together again. With Yolanda's return, the group—led by Nathan—consents to deny the significance of Yolanda's forgetfulness by making it a joke. Clearly the message is not to confront the mixed feelings around leaving.

At this point, the worker's comment, "It seems as though people are having a hard time getting here," is an attempt to identify the feelings connected to the acting-out behavior, lateness, and absenteeism. It is a good effort, but the group seems to bypass the comment and engages in a discussion about other matters. However, closer examination of the exchange between Jorge and Merco reveals the content as a veiled discussion about endings and absences:

"Did you 'return' to work?" "Yes, I've been 'working'." "But weren't you 'out' sick?" "Oh yes, but I 'returned' on Tuesday." "So you worked three weeks [you were 'in'] and was 'out' three weeks sick and you just 'returned' Tuesday?" "I'm trying to make up for the time because my volunteer work 'ends' in December." Every sentence in this exchange is replete with terms related to endings. The reader can almost feel the swinging back and forth and the approach-avoidance, but of course, the issue remains hidden in the safer content of jobs rather than of group.

Feeling the tug-of-war between staying and leaving, the worker might say, "You know, Jorge, it feels as if you really had to struggle to be at work and get what you could before the job ends. It doesn't sound as if it was easy for you [validating the struggle with resistance], but you know it feels very much like the struggle in our group [relating his comment to the present and the group experience]. It's hard for people to be consistently here as we approach the end [connecting the feelings to the behavior and connecting the manifest with the latent, making sense of their communication and demystifying it]. I wonder if it is hard to be here knowing we're going to end soon [opening up and exploring as well as verbalizing feelings]." This approach is slightly different from the worker's direct interpretation of the coded messages because it appears less exposing. It offers a bridge between the latent content and the manifest content, in which members feel less of a sense of the worker's seeming to say "aha, I caught you!" The subject needs to be handled with a finesse often missing in interpretive remarks. The worker using this alternate approach is able to point out some of what is happening without suggesting that the clients have done something wrong.

In the excerpt, however, the worker makes a direct attempt to stick with the feelings: "Are you having a hard time being here because you will be leaving the group soon?" But as Jorge begins to acknowledge that possibility—"Well, I took a test to go to school. I may start college in December or January"— the worker abandons him. She says, "We have heard what's going on with Jorge. I wonder what's going on with the other members in the group?" The worker's response, although it appears to be an attempt to draw in the rest of the group, feels more like a run from the feelings about to emerge. Perhaps because of her own feelings about leaving, the worker loses the group to superficial and coded interaction, which appears safer for them all.

A lengthy and detailed discussion about where to buy shoes, how to manage with health problems, and how to file a Medicaid application follows. While this discussion also relates to the termination theme, worker and group become lost in what appears to be tangential chatter. Even at this point, the worker may pursue many approaches to retrieve the lost discussion of feelings. The trick is to remain fresh, creative, and open to playing with some of the ideas. When Yolanda speaks about her swollen feet, could she really be indicating how hard it is for her to walk away from the group? Could the discussion of filing for Medicaid relate in some way to support in illness or to the fear of not being able to take care of oneself when one is ill and there is no more group? What might have happened had the worker said, "It sounds as if it might be painful for you, Yolanda, to walk away from the group?" Relating to the issues about Medicaid, the worker might have said, "It sounds as if people are concerned that they won't be taken care of if they become ill." One could speculate endlessly about the sorts of responses such questions might generate. It is really only important to recognize the possible creative avenues the worker might use to reach deeper levels.

One of the worker's termination tasks is to help the group members connect their group experiences with future plans. The worker could have used Jorge's comments about returning to school to bring in the rest of the group members and help construct a bridge to the future. She might have said, for example, "Jorge, that sounds terrific [supporting his ability to move on]. Who else has some plans after the group [reminding group members of the ending and connecting to the future]?"

The worker never reached the deeper level of communication desired in this group session; communications remained coded, and absences continued to be a problem in the following session. Despite this, she kept with it and was gradually able to be more comfortable with the leaving herself. She moved to a point where she was able to provide some interpretation of the feelings of loss based on her own experience in having a favorite boss leave her job. The worker related this story to the group's anger and sadness at her for leaving them and causing the disbanding of the group. This process opened the door for the group to mourn its many losses, both past and present, which they were reliving. In effect, when the worker was able to face her own feelings, she could allow the group theirs. She gave the message that all feelings were safe. The worker no longer needed the content to hide in, and the group was finally able to give it up as well.

Conclusion

In some ways, the termination phase is also a beginning, a preparation for whatever is to come. As a result of the group experience, members are different from what they were before: they may have acquired particular skills and supports in coping with important social relationships. In some groups, members are profoundly aware of internal changes that provide insight into functioning and assist them throughout life. They fear that through leaving, the valuable understandings they acquired will be sacrificed, understandings that exist for them in some magical spirit found only in the group. One task for the worker is to help members realize that whatever they gained in the group experience can accompany them beyond the group.

Some theorists suggest that terminations are part of a cycle moving back toward beginnings. Even in work with dying patients, one could suggest that, as members leave the group, they assume the beginning of a different sort of coping with their impending deaths. Workers hope that, after the successful group experience, group members feel less isolated, more supported, more accepting, more in control over emotional and concrete matters, and generally less terrified. In all groups, while the particulars may vary, the letting-go is difficult for both worker and client. For both, termination triggers memories of unresolved endings and the accompanying losses. Just as a tree sheds its old leaves in the autumn to allow for new growth in the spring, so, too, people must relinquish the old to allow for new growth—again the task of termination. As with the seasons, the process is not sudden but gradual. As with the seasons, sometimes the process moves in spurts and is more erratic.

In the first excerpt discussed here, the group for alcoholics, the termination of an individual member from the group stirred feelings about loss and fears of the future for others. The worker's task was to help members see the relationship between their feelings about one member's leaving and their own conflicts around termination.

In the second process, a blind, older persons' group struggled with their increased sense of vulnerability and powerlessness exacerbated by the worker's leaving. These feelings triggered regressive behavior and a flood of overwhelming emotion, the nature of which the worker needed to identify and focus. Important in this piece, as with all termination sessions, were the countertransferential issues for the worker, who was feeling overwhelmed by guilt in her perceptions of abandoning the group.

The third process excerpt again dealt with the termination of one member, this time in a discharge planning group from a psychiatric inpatient facility. As with the alcoholics, the client was graduating from the program in some sense, but where the first group focused on what their own future would be like once graduated, the discharge group struggled with being left behind after having risked intimacy with each other. Again, the worker had to reinforce gains to allow the members to move on and separate.

The last piece presented, that of an outpatient psychiatric group, spoke to the issue of an entire group terminating as a result of the worker's departure. Both the worker and group had difficulties in coming to grips with the termination. A salient point in the analysis was that the worker could not effectively assist the group until she had worked through her own sadness and anger.

In beginnings, the hardest issues concern establishing trust and moving toward disclosure. In middles, the hardest issues concern reaching toward intimacy and deeper levels of understanding. In endings, the hardest issues concern solidifying gains yet moving on and surviving the loss.

7 GROUP PLANNING

As you have sown, so shall you reap . . .

Cicero
De Oratore (55 BCE)

Historically, the rationale for developing a group service in many organizations was motivated more by economics than by client needs. To provide services to many clients at the same time was simply less expensive than to staff individual contacts. Many agencies are reimbursed by grants and other special funding based on the number of clients seen by each clinician. This reimbursement arrangement has little to do with the importance or value of the group experience for clients. Group treatment work with veterans returning shell-shocked from the world wars (the beginning of the social psychology movement) originated for reasons of practicality rather than as a part of good clinical treatment (Konopka, 1963). Bringing the soldiers together for treatment demonstrated that the group method was a powerful tool in restoring health—for some soldiers perhaps even more helpful than individual treatment. Groups have been started for the wrong reasons and have been successful. How much more valuable groups might be when adequately planned and when the many facets that can be investigated beforehand are considered.

Often it is assumed that a group can serve a panoply of needs for any population at any time, but little thought is given to teasing out the specifics concerning the structure of the group, its purpose, members' needs, and other factors related to content, population, and agency. To ensure the survival of the group and to maximize its accomplishments, it is necessary to work out the details. One useful model, developed by Kurland (1978, 1982), assists workers to structure their pregroup thinking. It considers seven areas as essential to planning: needs assessment, identification of purpose, considerations regarding composition, establishment of structure, identification of key content, methodology in pregroup engagement, and examination of agency context. In this chapter, we use the Kurland model to demonstrate a thorough preplanning approach that maximizes the opportunity for a successful group.

Needs Assessment

The full gamut of client, agency, and worker needs should be examined as a first step in any analysis. If clients do not perceive the group as meeting their needs, they will not attend. If attendance is involuntary and clients still do not perceive the group as meeting their needs, the work of the group will not proceed. If workers are forced to run groups that they do not find fulfilling, their participation may slacken. If, instead, the group is convened solely to meet the worker's needs and not those of the clients or the agency, the group is likely to fail. The needs of the agency must also be met to encourage an atmosphere of acceptance for the group.

The process of assessing the needs of clients, workers, and agencies is a complicated one. Evaluating population needs involves general knowledge about the population served. This includes factors related to culture, ethnicity, developmental stage, socioeconomic class, age, and special situation issues. Assessment of worker needs must include a tuning-in to one's own feelings. How do I feel about working with this population? What emotional responses are stirred in me when I relate to them? How will this enhance my job, lead to my promotions, be regarded by my colleagues? The worker must consider ethical and philosophical issues, such as what contribution, if any, she or he will make to the population, agency, and perhaps, society by developing this group. The worker must also assess the agency needs in establishing the group, considering whether the group is in keeping with the agency mandate. Is this group part of what the agency sees as its responsibility in serving its community? What will be the impact of this group on agency image? Will the agency be willing and able to utilize its resources to support the goals of the group? The worker must determine whether plans for the group could be perceived as threatening to the existing distribution of power.

The worker obtains general information regarding client, worker, and agency needs by listening and questioning, both formally and informally. The worker needs to ask the following questions:

1. What important needs of the clients does the agency serve, and how does the agency's perception jibe with the clients' perceptions of their own needs?

2. How do other workers understand these needs?

3. What significant cultural and social factors are present that influence clients' needs? For example, in a new immigrants' group with many Asian participants, recognition of the clients' cultural need for privacy and respect for authority is essential to facilitate productive communication among group members. The worker's presentation of self may need to be modified accordingly—not probing too soon, not expecting early self-disclosure, and maintaining a somewhat more formal professional posture.

4. What are the developmental needs of members? One developmental need of latency-age children is mastery. As such, the worker with this population would want to include activities that allow for cognitive as well as emotional growth.

5. What is the worker's need in developing this group? This need is an important issue because it obliges the worker to note possible countertransferential issues from the very beginning of the group's development. The passion of the worker will no doubt affect the passions of the group.

6. How can the proposed group meet the needs of clients?

Purpose

The purpose of the group must be clearly defined in the worker's own mind before the initial meetings, with the additional recognition that the purpose will evolve with the clients' input and their expression of needs. The group will continue to question its purpose. Goals will be redefined, and evaluation will be constant throughout the course of the group, but the initial explorations of purpose must be clearly stated. The worker should consider the following questions:

1. How is the purpose of the group related to the needs of the clients?
2. What structure best addresses the purpose of the group: counseling, activity, social action? The purpose of a tenants' group, for example, would dictate the choice of a social action orientation as opposed to a psychotherapy orientation, even though the group might have therapeutic elements.
3. How do potential group members perceive the group purpose?
4. How will the worker evaluate whether the purpose has been achieved? In some groups, the evaluation procedure may be a formal one. A questionnaire might be useful to evaluate a training group but inappropriate for a psychotherapy group.

Composition

In many settings, it is impossible to select exactly the perfect combination of group members based on appropriate commonality, heterogeneity, and size. It is helpful, however, to be able to formulate an ideal construct despite the realities of agency life. Although we cannot always achieve the ideal composition, we will be aware of the implication of not achieving that ideal and act accordingly.

1. How many members will be invited, and with how many does the worker anticipate beginning? What would be an ideal number of participants for the group to conduct its work? Considering the average no-show rate of one third in most groups and that, in certain groups, some dropping out and absenteeism occurs, registering ten would guarantee a number approaching six to eight persons. This would ensure enough participants for a good exchange but not so many as to interfere with the development of intimacy.

2. Who will be in the group? How will the worker balance the need for commonality and heterogeneity with regard to ascriptive or inherent characteristics such as age, gender, and racial, ethnic, and socio-economic status? A general rule for developing a group is to avoid selecting a single member of a group with characteristics greatly different from those of the other members.

    What is the rationale for the worker's choices of certain members and for electing homogeneity of membership over heterogeneity or vice versa? For example, severely disturbed adolescents find coed groups too stimulating because these clients struggle so hard with their sexual identity issues. It is necessary for them to have less intensive contact with the opposite sex in order to feel safe enough to explore these issues. Homogeneity of gender for this population is preferable. With healthy adolescent groups, however, coed groups might be desirable. A widows' bereavement group should be restricted to persons who have been recently widowed. Diluting the focus of the group by including those long widowed, divorced, or separated would diminish its effectiveness to deal with grief issues. A singles' group with a more general focus could include people of various single statuses.

    How will the worker consider behavioral characteristics—those characteristics that relate to social functioning—as a factor in the choice of certain clients for the group? For example, an entire group of depressed clients would be dysfunctional; it would lack the energy and affect to provide sufficient interchange to do the work of the group.

    How will the worker's own gender, race, ethnic background, and socioeconomic status be considered as a factor in group formation? Commonality with the group in terms of these ascriptive character-istics may serve as either a way to develop good and comfortable rapport with group members or a hindrance to maintaining worker objectivity. The Italian-American worker who overidentifies with her Italian clients' expression of their anger at their intrusive mothers will be unable to help these clients understand their own roles in intimate relationships.

    Differences in ascriptive characteristics between worker and clients create other issues. The white worker, who ordinarily may have difficulty confronting the resistant behavior of her adolescent clients, may struggle particularly with confronting resistant behavior on the part of adolescent black clients with whom she is attempting to ally. Part of the reason for this reaction may relate to her concern with being seen by the client as the white oppressor. The worker's own internal prejudices may be influencing her perceptions. She may experience ungrounded fears of clients' responses, which may prevent her from intervening appropriately. Other issues concerned with race and ethnicity are elaborated on in Chapter 11.

3. How many workers will be in the group, and what will be their characteristics, and why? In a couples' group, it might be helpful to have male and female co-therapists who, in effect, model good communication between persons of both sexes. With an acting-out population in residential treatment, two workers might be desirable to help maintain control. One worker would certainly be appropriate and effective in many groups where the considerations regarding gender modeling, behavior controls, and worker continuity are less pressing. Issues of co-therapy are discussed at length in Chapter 12.

4. If this group is open-ended, what characteristics will be considered in the selection and introduction of new members? Selection and introduction of new members should relate to an assessment of where the group is in terms of its developmental level and what the introduction of a new member will mean to that process. Would a newly identified substance abuser fit into a group that has been in treatment for many months? Some might argue that the new member offers the group the opportunity to confront anew the parts of themselves still not healed. Others might contend that the new member could have a regressive influence on the group.

Structure

Some arrangements for the group structure, such as time and place of meeting, staffing, and fee arrangements, will be determined by the agency without worker input. But, as much as possible, the worker should control factors with conscious regard for preplanning. The worker must always recognize the need for advocacy around issues vital to the success of the group.

1. When and how frequently will the group meet? How long will each meeting be, and how many sessions will be held, and why? For instance, a senior citizens' group would not draw members to evening sessions because of the difficulties in going out at night, while a multifamily group held during the day would have difficulty in attracting members because of work and school schedules.

2. What are the physical arrangements for the group and their rationale? The size of the room (too small or too large) and the setup of the furniture (with or without the protection of a table between members) are significant variables in treating a psychiatric population with issues concerning intimacy and boundaries. While a small room provides feelings of security, boundaries, and control, it can feel intrusive and consuming for some persons. While allowing for more freedom and expansiveness, the overly large room can precipitate fears of the dissolution of self and loss of control. In a large room, it is also easier for some members to become distracted.

3. What arrangements will the worker need to make regarding intra- and interagency communications and sharing of information?

4. Will the group be open-ended or closed to new members, and why? One factor to be considered when deciding whether to maintain groups as open-ended or closed should be the clients' capacity for tolerating change and loss. For example, in a battered women's group, which focuses on severe traumatic and painful stigmatizing issues, a closed, short-term approach might allow for more disclosure and intimacy than would likely occur in an open-ended, short-term group.

Content

What will actually transpire during group sessions, whether an internal structure for sessions will exist, and who will decide that structure must all be considered as part of the planning process.

1. What will be the content of group meetings: discussion, didactic material, other program media? Why? How will the content be used to stimulate group interaction? For example, some parenting groups use a format in which a short lecture by an expert in the field of child development leads off each meeting. This lecture may be used to help the group become engaged and begin focusing on pertinent issues.

2. Who will plan the content for meetings? How will this planning be achieved? What is the rationale for the approach selected? In a therapeutic community for psychiatric patients, for instance, participation in planning the content of community meetings helps to give a sense of mastery and control to people experiencing an acute sense of loss of control and power. A formal structure for planning the content of meetings helps group members to feel more secure and capable.

3. What, if any, supplies and equipment will be necessary?

Pregroup Contacts

Little attention has been given in the literature to issues regarding pregroup contacts between worker and client and the means by which potential members hear about and are introduced to the idea of group participation. A thoughtful consideration of these matters is essential in the planning process.

1. How should the worker recruit or reach out to potential group members, and why? Should the worker offer a general invitation, advertise on agency fliers, post signs inside the agency or in public places, or should the worker recruit selectively by speaking with other agency personnel? In a breast cancer inpatient group, for example, one might want to screen patients in terms of diagnoses to avoid mixing participants who have undergone mastectomies with those who have

inoperable cancers or who will receive alternate treatment. Since the prognosis, procedures, and treatment of patients from these two groups (mastectomy and non-mastectomy patients) are quite different, their needs are consequently different and probably would be best addressed in separate groups. The worker would be ill-advised to advertise a breast cancer group with a general open invitation, attract potential participants, and then be forced to send some away—unless one is prepared to provide more than one group based on diagnosis. To avoid the rejection of any person, given the related cancer issues, is essential.

2. Who will evaluate clients for a group, and what will determine their suitability? In certain groups (a group of parents of retarded children, for example), the worker can assume a degree of health and appropriate self-selection with a commonality among members regarding shared problems and needs. In such a group, the formal intake process may be less necessary to create a working group. Without a formal intake, the group members may be able to move more quickly to an equal footing with each other and the worker.

    The intake can create something of a dyadic relationship between client and worker prior to the group experience, which could then sabotage the sense of groupness. Also, the worker who has met the client on a one-to-one basis prior to the group meeting is likely to have some reactions that may color the worker's picture of the client's functioning and hamper the worker's ability to be as open to the group process.

    If a formal intake procedure is omitted, a member who is unsuitable for the group may attend and then have to be removed later; such a process will likely be difficult for all concerned. Additionally, a pregroup contact is valuable because it provides an opportunity to orient the prospective client to the group.

    Even with the formal intake process, however, workers often make mistakes in selecting group members. In certain groups, intake is usually advisable. In a group for psychiatric patients, for example, clearly some intake procedure is required to assure a workable mixture of health and pathology to allow for growth and change. For some of the same reasons, workers may or may not find it desirable to read client records before meeting with clients in groups. Case records may bias workers or may prepare workers. When reading case records, the worker should look for prior indications of the client's ability to function socially. This includes a history of aggressive behavior or impulse control problems, ability to verbalize, cognitive development, and ability to focus and concentrate. Generally, a mental status or psychosocial workup will provide this information.

3. How should the worker secure and utilize referrals? In many agencies, starting a group raises important turf issues, particularly when

individual therapy is conducted by professionals other than the worker. Questions regarding who is the primary therapist, what material will be discussed, and where and how information will be shared will certainly arise. It is always worthwhile to develop some informal networks that facilitate good working relationships. These minimize the possibility of clients being caught in territorial disputes among staff.

Agency Context

No group begins in a vacuum. Overtly or covertly, an agency may encourage or discourage the formation of a particular group, may be philosophically opposed to the whole notion of group treatment, or although supportive of the idea of group, may be afraid of moving in the direction of new groups. The atmosphere in which groups thrive and are nurtured and workers can be fulfilled and, in turn, successful, must be a hospitable one. The poorly heated or cooled agency, the agency with inadequate space, or the unmaintained agency, wars against the achievement of therapeutic goals. Workers who receive inadequate supervision, inadequate time for reflection, or inadequate supports, are not sufficiently nurtured to perform at optimum levels. Energy is sapped by these stressors, and groups suffer. The agency and the larger political and social environment influence the potential success or failure of particular groups.

1. What is the agency's philosophy, attitude, and experience regarding work with groups? How will these have an impact on its commitment in terms of staffing, funding, space, time, and other resources to the development and maintenance of groups? Sometimes measures of commitment level are so subtle as to be missed. For example, an employee assistance program (EAP) that fails to assure a group meeting place in a space separate from the worksite is insensitive to the issue of confidentiality and is communicating a lack of commitment to the service.

2. What is the relationship of the agency to the community? How will this relationship have an impact on the recruitment and participation of clients? For instance, knowledge about an agency's responsibility for removing children from abusive and neglectful families might discourage participation in a parenting group offered by that agency. Issues concerning confidentiality and trust would surely be problematic during the planning stages.

3. How does the agency view the needs of clients, and is that view different from or similar to the worker's view? Again, an example from an EAP is appropriate. The EAP may receive referrals for the group from the employer whose goal is to punish employees who have job performance difficulties. The worker may see her or his role as helping the troubled employees resolve a variety of conflicts, some of which may be hindering their job performance abilities.

4. How can the worker help develop an agency climate receptive to groups? This question is central to the planning of most groups in settings not necessarily conversant with the idea of group treatment. For many agencies, the whole notion of group work is foreign, frightening, and threatening. In such settings, the worker must prepare, even more thoroughly than in receptive agencies, the answers to all the preceding questions so that she or he can respond in a reasoned, thoughtful, and reassuring manner to objections and concerns.

Utilization of the Kurland model—needs assessment, identification of purpose, considerations regarding composition, establishment of structure, identification of key content, methodology in pregroup engagement, and examination of agency context—by no means assures the development of a successful group, but the model starts the worker off on a firm footing that acts as a predictor of group success. At each point in the early planning, the worker struggles to maximize the proper blending of factors. She or he considers the needs of potential members and the best ways to implement a group to serve those needs.

The following excerpt from the log of a student worker on a cardiac surgery floor of a large teaching hospital illustrates some of the pitfalls that can occur even with seemingly careful planning.

Student's Log

I had been working on the cardiac surgery unit for about six months, becoming familiar with the procedures, staff, and the emotional needs of the patients, when I began to observe that patients were making informal contacts with each other to discuss their concerns about the upcoming surgeries. Those who were scheduled for operations, which mostly consisted of bypass surgery and heart valve replacements, were eager to talk with those who had survived the procedures. Most of the surgery candidates were understandably apprehensive and needed to know how others had coped and made it through. Those recovering from surgery were also pleased to tell their stories, to offer comfort and information to others, and in so doing, to feel more positive about their own progress. Nurses on the surgery floor were so aware of the need for families and patients to share their experiences that they introduced prospective patients (at the hospital for preadmission screenings) to patients nearly ready for discharge. It seemed that patients who were well prepared emotionally as well as physically for the surgery had better outcomes and recoveries. I believed that this was a natural and hospitable place for a group to be developed to formalize what was already happening somewhat haphazardly.

In individual discussions with patients, their families, and the nurses, I learned about their specific concerns. Patients and families needed desperately to discuss their fears, to have some concrete information about pain, the life-support machinery, about physical capabilities after surgery, about the hospital routines and approximate length of stay in the hospital, about continuing treatment and restrictions, and in general, needed to talk about their powerful feelings regarding the experience of life-threatening surgery.

Dr. Stevens, head of the unit, assigned a special cardiac surgery nurse to provide general information to all patients in individual interviews. The nurse answered patients' questions and provided some written material about cardiac surgery as well. From my viewpoint, the major flaws in the individual interviews were that the emotional component was peripheral to the intent of the meetings and was seldom explored, and the information given was difficult to absorb all at once, either emotionally or cognitively. Some patients told me that on awakening in the cardiac intensive care area—where they remained for several days with hookups to numbers of machines—they were certain of their impending deaths. Family members also imagined the worst. The individual interviews had included information about the intensive care, but patients were apparently unable to hear what was being said. It was simply overwhelming.

In discussing patient needs, my supervisor and I developed a plan for instituting a cardiac surgery group. Patients would attend the group as part of their initial preadmission screenings. The outpatient screenings were scheduled for Tuesdays and Fridays of the week prior to admission. Surgery was performed on Mondays and Thursdays. On admission, each patient would attend a second group meeting. Approximately a week following surgery, if possible, patients would attend another meeting and then two or three more meetings in the course of their remaining hospital stays. Meetings would be held in the floor lounge, and I would take responsibility for gathering those unable to walk unattended to the meeting. At any given time, six to eight patients would be on the unit at various points in their treatment and several more would be involved in the preadmission process.

We decided that I would co-lead the group with a nurse who could provide more accurate information regarding the medical aspects and routines about which the patients might be concerned. The nurse, Ms. Woods, and I determined to have a fairly tight structure, covering some basic information with the group before launching into a more open discussion. Our intent was to help group members deal with their concerns and fears and to be educated and thereby more in control of their situations. We planned to conduct a group with a similar format and schedule for family members.

My supervisor and I were enthusiastic about the idea. What we did not realize at the time, however, was that we had neglected a key element in the planning process and one which I, as a relative newcomer to the bureaucracy, had never even considered. Hospitals, even teaching hospitals, are host settings for social workers. I was a guest and, worse yet, a student guest. Dr. Stevens, head of the unit, barely knew who I was and had no intention of my tampering with groups of his patients. He was presented with a completed plan, never consulted for what probably would have been his invaluable input, and never enlisted in the planning phase to determine whether our schedule for patients was appropriate considering the seriousness of their conditions. Furthermore, Dr. Stevens' nurse, whom he trusted and felt was doing an excellent job in preparing patients for surgery, was completely overstepped in our process. Besides everything else, Dr. Stevens was skeptical about formalizing the sharing of information among patients, when much of what might be said could be inaccurate or not the same for everyone. He opposed the group, and as the head of the unit, his decision was final.

I still believe that the creation of such a group on the cardiac care service would have been an asset to patient care. Dr. Stevens was not unreasonable in his opposition. It was we who had failed to realize the complexities of the system. Had we approached Dr. Stevens from the beginning and asked for his assistance and his opinions about how to address the needs we had observed, I am certain that he would have been less resistant. Presenting him with a finished plan denied his importance to this process and increased his suspicions about us. Dr. Stevens, not even knowing us, imagined we were playing with his often very ill patients. We had not even looked at the history of handling the preparation of patients and the vital role of the special nurse and incorporated the method or perhaps the person in our design. Most importantly, we had not understood the agency context or the key players.

The Kurland model notes the worker's responsibility in pregroup planning for recognizing resistance to groups in some settings. The preceding excerpt indicates that a planner's failure to understand the significance of the agency system can result in a failure to get a group started. The vignette also suggests how vital appropriate supervision is to the beginner in negotiating the system. The supervisor should have been more aware of how to help the student worker recognize key individuals, their authority, and their power.

Planning a Group for Persons with AIDS

We have chosen a planning piece that illustrates the use of the Kurland model to develop a group focusing on people with AIDS. In this age, when AIDS has become an omnipresent problem (showing itself in every sort of setting), many groups for people with AIDS and their significant others are certainly needed. Unfortunately, despite a growing demand, inadequate services are available to face this epidemic. Our hope is that the presentation of this model in work with people with AIDS will provide the impetus for developing and promoting groups to realistically address the needs of this population. This planning piece involves the development of a support group for people with AIDS within an agency servicing gay men and committed to providing the full spectrum of care. This spectrum ranges from concrete services to education, counseling, and advocacy for people with AIDS, their significant others, and the general public.

Needs

The clients' perceptions of their own needs can be assessed in the pregroup interview. The words of potential group members during the early screening process are revealing:

> "I want to talk with other gay men. They understand me—what it's like to be gay and have AIDS, to feel like a leper, to feel heterosexual hate."
>
> "I don't want to feel that I'm bad, that I deserve this like my father says."
>
> "I feel so frightened, so vulnerable. I need to talk and be with people who have this too but who are fighting."
>
> "I need someone to hear how scared I am and not run from me."
>
> "I don't want to be alone in this. I don't know what to do. I don't know where to go, what to expect."
>
> "The only place I've ever felt loved is with other gay men."

The agency views the clients' needs in a similar way. A support group would offset the isolation and alienation the person with AIDS feels in the larger homophobic society. The severe societal stigmatization that the gay man experiences can be, and often is, internalized, particularly during the despair that accompanies a diagnosis of AIDS. This internalized negative image can act to isolate and push the person with AIDS further away from needed support systems, ultimately decreasing his will and ability to survive (Kübler-Ross, 1987). By creating a "commonality of culture" (Rochlin, 1982), a group of accepting others can reinforce and develop a positive identification necessary to counteract this negative self-image.

The larger society, lacking knowledge regarding the disease and consequently fearing contagion, can also isolate the person with AIDS. Often families abandon, friends become sparse, and social opportunities become fewer. As the disease progresses, the ability of the person with AIDS to function independently decreases, and his needs increase. The eventual decline in self-sufficiency along with the continued acceleration of the disease create new needs. He eventually requires the provision of concrete supports associated with daily survival, including help with household chores, transportation, food preparation, finances, and legal matters (Gambe and Getzel, 1989). The person with AIDS experiences a dramatic increase in his emotional needs and physical needs and, at the same time, a sharp decrease in independent functioning and the availability of support systems.

In developing the group, the worker must anticipate these client needs and recognize ways in which the group might address these needs. The support group can be thought of as acting as an alternate "healthy family" (Gambe and Getzel, 1989). The group is fully accepting, loving, and capable of helping the person with AIDS to problem solve in a manner that strengthens his sense of self-worth. In the group, he belongs, he is not alone. In the group, others feel as he feels and struggle as he struggles. He is validated, cared for, and assisted in all areas of importance. A fellow group member helps with the details of writing a living will or gaining information about homemakers. Others provide an ear for the expression of painful feelings.

According to recent Center for Disease Control Statistics, the major cause of death for young men between the ages of thirty and forty-four is AIDS. What we commonly recognize as the developmental needs and tasks for this age group—work, creative fulfillment, the development of mutually rewarding and gratifying relationships (Erikson, 1963)—are radically altered by the diagnosis of AIDS. At the potentially most productive stage of his life, the person with AIDS is cut short. He is prematurely pushed to confront the meaning of his life with a sudden urgency. He must explore any and all options that could enhance the quality of his remaining time, and he must face the fear of his nonexistence daily. All of these factors should be considered as part of a needs assessment in establishing the support group.

Purpose

The purpose of the group is to help members cope with a life-threatening illness and to maximize their current life experience. Various individual and group goals include the following:

- to provide a mutual support system to counter the devastating effects of isolation;
- to help members identify and express feelings arising from their frequent physical and emotional crises and to confront and resolve long-standing negative feelings associated with the role of being a gay man in a straight society;
- to provide concrete services and practical supports during periods of increased emotional and physical need;
- to offset feelings of helplessness and worthlessness by being part of a mutually supportive system;
- to provide an emotionally available atmosphere in which to face one's own mortality.

Content

The content of the group reflects the members' needs and the group's purpose. Therefore, the group should be set up as a combination of supportive counseling and education. The educational aspects would center around the exchange of the latest medical and legal information. Content could include a discussion of new drugs and treatment, financial management, insurance problems, entitlements, and more. The counseling component would help members explore, express, and resolve emotional issues. Overall, the focus of the group should be on the here and now and should enhance the quality of each member's present situation with content to address current needs.

Composition

Planning considerations include the group's size and the nature of its membership. This group ideally should include between eight and ten members in order to maximize the process of discussion and the exchange of information and ideas. This number provides enough variety for active dialogue but is not too large or too small to prohibit intimacy. Too large a group may allow members to hide and be lost; too small a group may be experienced as too threatening and demanding of self-exposure. It is also important to have a large enough membership to allow for absences when members are unable to attend due to illness.

Generally, in groups of this sort, it is preferable to have two co-leaders. Co-leadership guarantees continuity and security by preventing cancellations of meetings due to unexpected absences or planned vacations for the worker. The stability of the group is essential; the group must always be there, a powerful and necessary symbol for members experiencing the rest of their lives as unpredictable and out of control (Gambe and Getzel, 1989). An additional benefit of co-leadership in a group for people with AIDS is that co-leadership gives the worker a partner with whom to share the burden of his own pain and countertransferential feelings. Possible difficulties with co-leadership include the additional time needed for processing the group and problems for the relationship between the workers as they deal with sensitive material (see Chapter 9). Another consideration regarding one or two workers is whether it is desirable for one or both workers to be persons with AIDS. The issue of sameness and difference between worker and members regarding a common problem is discussed at length in Chapter 9. We recommend two workers to ensure the continuity necessary for this group, at least one of whom is symptom-free.

The pregroup interviews provide an opportunity to address members' feelings regarding worker and member characteristics. If any reservations or preferences surface about the presence of a heterosexual male or female as a group worker, these can be explored. Additionally, concerns about member characteristics may be verbalized. The worker will have to evaluate the wishes of group members in deciding who will be part of the group. Will members prefer that other members be gay men rather than IV-drug abusers or their sexual partners who are straight? Some groups successfully mix these populations, and workers see the AIDS diagnosis as an overriding commonality. However, we believe that the success of a mixed group depends on the prescreening process and the worker's ability to select those potential members who have a high degree of commonality in other areas. These areas might include the client's ability and willingness to verbalize and confront feelings, the aftershock status and time since the initial trauma of diagnosis, the mental status, the capacity for exploration and problem solving, the ability to relate to others, physical condition, and level of denial.

It is our experience in most groups that ethnic differences enrich the group if the socioeconomic distinctions among members are not dramatically different and if the ability to express feelings and use the group is strong. Another composition issue concerns the inclusion or exclusion of care partners and significant others in the support group for people with AIDS. While we recognize the importance of addressing the issues of care partners and significant others in some forum (either separate groups or a group with the people with AIDS), we believe that the people with AIDS still require a group themselves.

Structure

A modified closed group is the most appropriate structure for the people with AIDS support group. The modified closed group allows for new members to join the group in order to replace members who leave. Such a structure demands an ongoing commitment to the group on the part of members once the decision to join is made. This structure also allows the perpetuation of the group's life although the membership may change. It is necessary to contract clearly with new members to prevent instability and unnecessary loss in a group that will face far too many losses in its life. The group should meet once a week—again, to maintain continuity and stability. More frequent meetings may prove too taxing for members with limited energy and with difficulty in traveling.

Since many people with AIDS continue working, the group should be scheduled in the early evening after work hours. Later evening hours are inadvisable since members may find this too physically draining. Meals or snacks may be served to help supplement healthy diets, particularly if the sessions are held during dinner hours. Of course, the ability to provide food is largely determined by the agency resources, and food need not be a priority.

The structure of the group may include periodic guest speakers: experts in insurance benefits, legal, or medical issues, in accordance with the needs and wishes of the group members. At all sessions, time should be made available before and after meetings to allow members to seek individual private assistance as necessary. The focus is both on group and individual needs. Arrangements for keeping the group available to those members who become homebound may include the use of a speakerphone or even sessions in the homes of members who cannot get out. For those with difficulty in traveling, transportation may have to be provided.

Agency Context

The initial proposal for the group will have to include some exploration of agency funding, particularly to assess support for transportation. If no funds are available, volunteer systems may need to be developed to assure that disabled members can attend meetings. The workers in a support group for people with AIDS must always recognize the importance of consistency in group and worker attendance. Every effort should be made during the planning process to assure optimum participation.

Although the proposed group is being offered through an agency that provides a full range of services to people with AIDS and their significant others, one cannot assume that the worker will have the full support and cooperation of the agency in establishing and maintaining the proposed group. Stated commitment is often quite different from actual commitment. One simple indicator of a lack of support is the failure of the agency to staff adequately. Because of the severe stress on workers who deal with people with chronic or terminal illness, the agency should focus on adequate back-up services, support, and supervision for workers, and sufficient time for workers to reflect on their work and on their own needs. Additionally, funding, supplies, philosophy, and agency politics will always have an impact on the worker's ability to be fully creative and should be considered in the planning process.

In an agency with a strong informal network, the exploration of all of these issues must take place informally. Lunch with other senior workers, coffee pot chats during the day, exchanges at staff meetings—all provide opportunities to assess where the formal and informal power lies. Learning about the proper channels in the formal system also avoids alienation of potential allies and helps assure success in planning for the group. In the AIDS support group or any other group, the worker's proposal must demonstrate a keen awareness of the benefits from the group to the client and the agency. Peer and agency resistance may be limited by noting the usefulness of the group in reducing caseloads, increasing billable contact hours, and decreasing client waiting list time. These factors help to sell the group. Additionally, the open exchange of information between the group worker and the individual worker regarding the goals, purpose, and possible content of the group can help to reduce resistance from staff in making referrals to the group. The worker's awareness and readiness to address all of these factors helps to create a positive and receptive climate in which to develop the group.

Conclusion

Effective planning of the support group maximizes the opportunities for its success. The worker must understand needs; consider composition, structure, content, purpose, and pregroup contact; and then present the complete package clearly in an atmosphere already made receptive by previous efforts. The process of pregroup planning is a complicated struggle to balance multiple factors and reduce resistance.

References

Erikson, E. H. *Childhood and Society*, 2nd ed. New York: W. W. Norton, 1963.

Gambe, R. and Getzel, G. "Group Work with Gay Men with AIDS." *Social Casework*, 1989, 70(3), 172–179.

Konopka, G. *Social Group Work: A Helping Process.* Englewood Cliffs, NJ: Prentice-Hall, 1963, pp. 1–22.

Kübler-Ross, E. *AIDS, The Ultimate Challenge*. New York: Macmillan Books, 1987.

Kurland, R. "Planning: The Neglected Component of Group Development." *Social Work with* Groups, 1978, 1(2), 173–178.

Kurland, R. *Group Formation: A Guide to the Development of Successful Groups*. Albany, NY: Continuing Education Program, School of Social Welfare, State University of New York at Albany and United Neighborhood Centers of America, 1982.

Rochlin, M. "Sexual Orientation of the Therapist and Therapeutic Effectiveness with Gay Clients." In *A Guide to Psychotherapy with Gay and Lesbian Clients*. J. Gonsiorek, Ed. New York: Harrington Park Press, 1982, pp. 21–26.

8 THE USE OF PROGRAMMING IN GROUPS

Heard melodies are sweet, but those unheard
Are sweeter; therefore ye soft pipes, play on;
Not to the sensual ear, but, more endear'd,
Pipe to the spirit ditties of no tone . . .

John Keats
"Ode on a Grecian Urn" (1820)

We are swaying together, worker and clients, arms gathered around each other and hands holding in a barely conscious reaching out, past the music and beyond the surroundings, thirty or forty or even fifty years into memory. The place is a senior citizens' center. A Runyanesque figure—his hat, whether summer or winter, worn as he must have in some nightclub of the thirties—plays his piano. His hands flutter, bird-like, across the keys. Some lyrics return, some are forgotten, but the mood is fixed in the moment.

Every week the scene is recaptured. The program begins with the variety showcase. It is an attempt at a professional performance in which the seventy-plus-year-old Italian-American emcee banters with the mostly Jewish audience in Yiddish. She holds her tiny yellow plastic bat threateningly against interruption and gracefully introduces the series of aging performers, one song to a customer. Three hundred or so are in the audience, and approximately twenty volunteers get their chance to perform. A soprano with a tender voice transports the audience to a romantic era of "Embraceable You." No one seems to notice that she is wide in the hips and has terrible teeth. Before she begins, the emcee offers a public pep talk, "She's a little scared. Let's give her a big hand. She's great—introducing Mary!" Ironically, "Embraceable You" seems to require that Mary be hugged through the first few bars. This routine beforehand assists several through their performances, which are nearly all followed by thunderous applause.

One highlight is a Sigmund Romberg tune sung by an elegant ninety-one-year-old woman who seems transformed by her singing into a young flower of a girl. Both her age, a sort of proof that there is hope for everyone here, and her achievements are applauded by all, no doubt the high point of her week. The tough accompanist, a mimic of Sophie Tucker, the Red-Hot Mama, guides each performer through every number. Playing perfectly by ear is an especially fortunate talent for this pianist since she is slowly going blind and can no longer see to read the music.

The program goes on for an hour or two. Few leave before the final notes when all the participants, many of whom were immigrants, join in for a last round of "God Bless America." The room empties. Twenty or so remain, gathering in groups around the piano. The feeling changes. The sing-along begins. The Red-Hot Mama yields her piano to the smooth magic of Cole Porter, subtle and delicate even when the music moves to a more upbeat rhythm. Some bring sheet music and offer solos to the group. A song is played, and someone says, "That would be great for Joe to do. Joe, why don't you try it?" A certain democracy is evident. While a sense of individual accomplishment pervades here, one feels more the harmony (both literally and figuratively) of the group. What theorists call cohesiveness and mutuality is all communicated in the singing and touching.

The preceding vignette comes from a real-life group that has developed over time into a surrogate family for its members—a group meeting that feels like a weekly family gathering. Through the common activity and the shared history, an atmosphere is created to transport these older people to an earlier and, at least in their rose-colored memories, to a happier time. Members feed on the mutual giving and feel intimate in both the present and through their shared past. Through the support of the group, they receive sustenance and are no longer alone to meet the present demands of their lives. Group activity is the therapeutic vehicle.

The words "group therapy" conjure up all sorts of mystical and exotic images of persons engaged in deep analytical and troubling discussions to work through pain to health. Many social group work settings, however, have a different therapeutic focus. Through play; through recreation; through competition; through the acquisition of concrete skills; through literature, music, art, and dance; and through shared learning and growing, clients—members, patients—move to healing, a renewed quality of life, personal development and satisfaction, and fulfilling social relationships. Therapeutic activity, infrequently identified as such, has been central in the work of organizations as varied as the Boy and Girl Scouts of America, the Veterans' Administration, and the Associated Neighborhood Houses. Activity groups have been used in children's programs, hospitals, mental health in- and outpatient facilities, nursing homes, community centers, prisons, shelters, and in nearly all other social service agencies. Why is activity needed? How can it be therapeutic? How can programming skills be applied to clinical issues? When and which activities should be used? This chapter addresses all of these concerns.

As waves of European immigrants arrived in the United States in the early part of the twentieth century, some early social group workers recognized the need for acculturation as a part of survival in the workplace and, in turn, in the larger society. These group workers introduced English classes, sewing classes, home economics classes, and others to help the newcomers adjust and, in as much as they wished to be, Americanized (*Encyclopedia of Social Work*,

Jane Addams). As the immigrants acquired jobs, afterschool programs were started to provide both child care for working parents and opportunities to learn sports, crafts, music, and more for children. Both generations of newcomers thrived as they participated with others through the crisis of being strangers in a strange land.

This pivotal episode in the history of social group work holds many lessons for us today about the usefulness of program pieces to help people realize their potentials and feel good about themselves. Child development experts suggest that some learning about "who I am" relates to learning about "what I do." In doing, the sense of self emerges. Theologians, too, emphasize the importance of doing as a part of being. They suggest that early ritual training, even without understanding the meaning of that learning, is necessary for the religious experience to become intrinsic to the individual's being from the beginning.

Self-worth, self-esteem, and a sense of mastery and control all can develop as one achieves life tasks. The baby handles his own spoon, takes his own steps, and moves from mother to his own independent achievements, activities which identify him as a separate being. Again, in doing, the self flowers. Watching the growing child, one sees how early activity strengthens the child's understanding of who he is and what he can be. A child's first adventures with finger paints, reading, and nature start her or him on the road to both individual recognition of self and feedback from a social environment that acts approvingly or disapprovingly of this individual's behavior. In this process, a social self develops.

In earlier chapters, we described how the group environment nurtures the individual, how group members learn from and support each other. The members in groups described earlier found it possible to get what they needed from the group experience by talking with each other. Many clients we see, however, find this kind of communication impossible. They are unaccustomed to expressing deeply felt emotions directly, particularly in the presence of strangers. They struggle to clarify their thoughts and feel inadequate and self-conscious about being less sophisticated than other group members or the worker.

Some populations find alternate ways of communicating feelings to be more natural and comfortable. Children, for example, express themselves more naturally in play and fantasy. A foster children's group assignment to make a picture autobiography becomes a tool to address the terrible grief these youngsters feel about the loss of family. Other groups may use music as a means of expression. Residents of a shelter for the homeless, people who are often unable to sustain social relationships, regain a sense of dignity and belonging by participating in a band. For many, physical activity becomes a means of communicating that helps connect feelings and is a powerful source of vitality. A baseball league for male methadone patients who have long felt out of control and powerless replaces those feelings with vigor, masculinity, and usefulness.

Activities may be utilized for various purposes:

1. To reach out to clients who are uncomfortable or unable to express themselves verbally. Multifamily group members learn a great deal about themselves through a programmatic technique called family sculpting. In this method, group members who are unable to verbalize feelings about each other place their family members in poses to illustrate their relationships.

2. To teach specific coping skills. A cooking-and-shopping-for-one group might be an important part of a program for widowers. While providing an opportunity to share feelings in a period of bereavement, this group also teaches specific skills needed for survival in a changed environment.

3. To help clients to feel competent, worthwhile, and—through mastery —spiritually, emotionally, and intellectually rejuvenated. A newspaper writing group in a nursing home allows patients to express themselves, be creative, and feel capable of making a contribution to the larger nursing home community.

4. To sufficiently distance threatening subject matter in order to address it and problem solve around it. A popular group for psychiatric inpatients uses soap opera programs as engagement material. The patients are able to talk about the television characters with an openness impossible if they were asked to speak about themselves. The discussion, which begins with the fantasy, progresses to real-life situations and the patients' issues. The group provides its members with a socialization experience, develops problem-solving skills, and can hopefully lead to insights for patients concerning their own functioning.

5. To learn to share and work cooperatively toward common goals. Many groups with specific concrete goals fail to reach them because group members find it difficult to share tasks and work together in a constructive manner. These difficulties may be seen in employee groups within organizations, in social action groups, and in volunteer groups. Training exercises, group puzzle assignments, and other activities may be useful to mobilize a tenants' rights group, for example, to accomplish a unified effort to a common end.

6. To engage clients selectively around an area in which particularly problematic or painful material creates resistance. Adolescents struggling with sexual identity issues may find such matters hard to discuss. A coed basketball game may be a way to bring boys and girls together in an activity that involves some physical closeness within clear rules for conduct. For adolescents less able to tolerate the physical intimacy of a game such as coed basketball, another sport such as baseball may be appropriate. The recreational element can lessen the discomfort and provide an arena for discussion later.

7. To help clients express socially unacceptable or conflictual feelings in a socially accepted manner. A puppetry group allows abused children to act out frightened, violent, and angry feelings. Unexpressed, some of these feelings are likely to manifest themselves in problematic antisocial behavior or in severe depression.

8. To help develop higher levels of frustration tolerance. Emotionally disturbed youngsters need to acquire essential skills, such as waiting for one's turn, concentrating on a task, and being competitive yet in control. A simple game of Pickup Sticks can help children to master these skills. In the game, each child takes a turn at dropping a stack of colored sticks on a table and then attempting to pick up each stick one at a time from the pile without disturbing the other sticks. The player to collect the most sticks without moving the remaining sticks is the winner. For more sophisticated groups, sticks with certain colors may be given point values. For young children or those with great difficulty in tolerating frustration, the game can be modified to allow two or three mistakes before passing the sticks on to the next player.

9. To provide individuals with an opportunity to experience new roles and unexplored parts of themselves. Psychodrama activities have been used successfully in many groups to stimulate discussion and help individuals to new levels of understanding about themselves. Role playing enhances multifamily and parenting groups in which walking in someone else's shoes provides a valuable new perspective that hopefully improves communication.

10. To act as a prelude to permitting successful movement toward verbal communication. Organized physical exercise programs can be useful in reducing tensions, releasing energy, and relaxing group members who may be agitated and unable to focus. Dancing or listening to music may also be therapeutic and assist in calming clients (including psychiatric patients and hyperactive children) in order to pave the way for more introspective work. Similarly, activities may be used as a reinforcement or reward after a productive discussion. A game and snack period might follow a gradually lengthened discussion period. The game may also be used as a way to practice the skills expressed verbally. For example, the group may talk about conflict and then work it out in a competitive game.

11. To aid in diagnosis, interpretation, and treatment. By seeing clients engaged in group activities, the worker can assess patterns of functioning, some of which may reveal behavior in other social settings.

Manipulating Aspects of Activities to Meet Clients' Needs

Part of the assessment process, and one that demands a great deal of creative and analytic thought, is the manipulation of specific factors in any activity. Factors include high and low power roles, group environment, level of tension, amount of frustration tolerance, degree of intimacy, availability of new experiences, and allowance for acting-out behavior. Every activity must be regarded in terms of the specific needs of the group's specific population, and every factor should be considered accordingly.

Power Roles

Games involving high and low power positions for group members can help change dysfunctional roles. By placing a low-status child in the role of leader through such games as "Simon Says," "Red Light, Green Light," or "Giant Steps" (see glossary in the Appendix), the leader can elevate the group member, thereby increasing the child's confidence and importance in the group. Similarly, by selecting an activity that the worker knows will expose a particular member's talent or skill, a withdrawn member may be allowed to become engaged and admired. Again, manipulating the activity to permit power shifts enhances individual development. The worker must always consider the group phase and the need to take a more active, and consequently more powerful, role in beginnings. Gradually, the worker provides less direction in the activity as the group moves toward a middle phase.

Group Environment

The worker has the opportunity to vary the environment in a manner that works with the activity and the client needs. A structured art activity might be conducted using several tables with chairs arranged in groups of four around each table. Group members might be assigned to various tables. This structure and formality encourages some group members to feel safe and secure, particularly in the beginning stage of group development when trust is an overriding issue. When more freedom and greater informal interaction are desired later in the group's development, the worker might eliminate the tables and chairs and place paper and paints on the floor. Lowering lights or using soft music in the group might also create an atmosphere consonant with what needs to be achieved in that group. In all groups, the activity must take place in an emotionally and physically safe environment that considers the individual needs of the population being served. Numerous possibilities for varying the environment exist and should be considered.

Tension Levels

Activities can also be varied to reduce or increase tension in order to meet therapeutic goals. Helping group members use physical activities to discharge energy permits quiet discussion afterward. Placing group members in competitive situations can elicit a more open confrontation around issues that must be addressed but are otherwise avoided.

Frustration Tolerance Levels

By playing with the degree of task-difficulty within a given activity, the worker can help members to learn improved socialization skills such as waiting one's turn, not always succeeding at a task, and controlling one's temper. The more ego-impaired or immature the clients, the simpler the beginning tasks should be. One hopes, as the group develops, that these activities can become more challenging in accordance with emotional growth.

Also, a longer and more sustained time period for any activity is possible. For some groups, particularly young children, activities should be very short and should be changed frequently. As capacity for concentration and focus, and tolerance for frustration increase, the activity can last longer. Early on, however, it is better to leave the activity too soon rather than hold on to it beyond interest.

Degree of Intimacy

Games that require physical closeness among members may help to create bonding. A storytelling hour in which preschoolers sit in a close-knit circle, or a dance program for older people in which touching and holding is possible, dispels isolation and provides an atmosphere that leads to openness.

Availability of New Experiences

Groups have varying capacities for trying out new experiences, particularly those involving risk, challenge, or change. The worker should determine a group's readiness for such experiences before launching into demanding activities. Both the nature of the population and the group's developmental stage has to be considered. Experimenting with emotionally laden role plays as part of a training group in its early sessions would likely cause increased resistance and interfere with the learning goals of the group.

Allowance for Acting-Out Behavior

The worker needs to determine how much control group members can exercise over their own behavior and how group activity can best be used to avoid chaos and to promote mutuality and cohesiveness that lead to growth. Establishing rules to allow for otherwise unacceptable behavior may be necessary under certain circumstances. Group members may be helped with contracting to permit swearing, walking around the room during meetings, or withdrawing from the activity when the emotional intensity necessitates it. Sponge balls, bop bags, pillows, and bean bags may prove useful tools in channeling aggressive behavior.

The way in which these factors can be manipulated to meet client needs at various stages in the development of a group is illustrated in a simple group activity chart involving a baseball game (see Table 8.1 at the end of the chapter). Although the activity used in both examples is baseball and although the population served by each program is adolescent, the different characteristics of each group demand a particular adaptation of the factors.

Overall, a pattern develops in which emotionally disturbed adolescents require more structure, attention to individual needs, emphasis on cooperation rather than competition, and a slower-paced game than do adolescents who are not emotionally impaired. The worker is more active throughout each phase when working with disturbed youngsters and is particularly aware of the need for support during termination. Coping with loss and separation is difficult for all adolescents, but the impaired adolescents have fewer coping mechanisms. Consequently, they are likely to have a more problematic termination from the group.

Storytelling, an activity with many variations, can be used in work with both young and old. To illustrate the ways in which factors of a storytelling program can be manipulated to serve different populations, Table 8.2 compares a preschoolers' group with a senior citizens' group (see end of chapter). One should note, while looking at the two groups, that key differences have primarily to do with developmental needs. Storytelling helps young children communicate their needs more clearly through the expression of feelings and, through fantasy, permits a sense of power and connectedness with others. For older people, storytelling is also a means of empowerment but, this time, often through reminiscence, a reaffirmation of past accomplishments and present ability.

The Group Mural

An examination of several different uses of program techniques further illustrates the value of programs in work with groups. The following excerpt is taken from a meeting of young adult psychiatric patients in a day hospital program who participate in an art therapy mural group. The purpose of the group is to help patients to express feelings through the art. For this population, feelings are associated with potential threat, and feelings of intimacy or rage, particularly, are often experienced as dangerous. Although frequently present, these feelings often are not verbalized. Patients may repress their feelings but act them out later in some behavioral gesture. Drawing gives patients a safe way to express their feelings. Once drawn, the feelings are experienced as being separate or detached from the patient. The goal of the worker is to help the group express feelings and resolve issues that remain powerfully present but have not been previously expressed.

The following excerpt was preceded by the decision of group members about the topic for the group mural. The topic is a significant one since the group members and not the workers selected it. Consequently, it is truly the group's issue. The topic, the escalating war in the Mideast, suggests conflict within the group. The worker has indicated that many subtle antagonistic feelings remain among the members. Prior to drawing, the antagonism was not addressed but merely acted out in disruptive and chaotic exchanges. The choice of topic at this time suggests the group's readiness to now deal more openly with the conflictual issues.

(Kevin is the first to go up to draw and silently draws a bomber plane dropping bombs on a building on which he has written "Madison House." This is the name of a residence in which many of the patients live. There is general snickering.)

David:	(draws a cannon shooting down the plane and its pilot) I'm shooting down your plane, Kevin. I'm shooting you down. (laughs nervously)
Mike (the worker):	Well, what do you think about that, Kevin—about David shooting down your plane?
Kevin:	I don't care. I mean, it's not real. (After several others have drawn pictures, David returns to his picture and embellishes on what he has drawn earlier. He draws fire hitting the plane and setting the pilot on fire.)
Ellen (the co-worker):	Wow! Something is really happening up there. You really mean to shoot that pilot down?
David:	Yeah, I guess so. (sounds nervous)
Mike:	What's going on, David? Are you trying to tell Kevin something?
David:	Yeah, I guess so. I mean he makes me mad, you know? No, I mean really. I don't like the way he's been treating me, and he's been goofin' on me. He's nasty, and I'm nice. I mean, I didn't do nothin' to him or nothin', an' I'm tired of it, ya know? An' I'm not gonna take it any more. (All of this is said facing Mike, the worker, and not looking at Kevin who is sitting right next to David.)
Mike:	Well, why don't you tell Kevin that?
David:	(turns to Kevin) I'm tired of the way you act to me, and I'm just not goin' to take it no more. (He repeats this sentiment several times. Kevin sits silently through David's complaints.)
Eli:	Yeah, Kevin, you is mean!
Eddie:	(draws a newspaper with the headline, "War over, no more war")
Mike:	Eddie, you want to put a stop to the war?
Eddie:	I hate war. We don't need no war. Tell them to stop . . . stop . . . stop the fightin'. No war no more, war no more . . . (stuttering and rhyming)
Mike:	How can we stop this war?
Ellen:	Which one? The war in Iraq, or the war in this room?

Mike:	I think it's too frightening for the group to admit that something heavy is happening here. Kevin, David is telling you something about yourself. Do you want to respond?
Kevin:	Naw, I hear him.

(Ellen allows for some silence and then draws a picture of a weeping figure.)

Eli:	What you drawin', Ellen? Someone cryin'? (various comments from the other group members sympathetic to the "poor lady" who is pictured)
Eli:	Why you draw that, Ellen; someone sad, crying about the pilot?
Ellen:	This is a picture of someone mourning the pilot's death.
Mike:	Is it so surprising to think that someone might actually feel sad for Kevin because of the damage he is doing to himself when he puts other people down? (group is silent for a moment)
David:	Oh, all right. I'll take away the cannon and the fire. (crosses out the fire and cannon) There, okay, Kevin?
Eddie:	Are they really going to fight each other? (Eli draws a white flag of truce.) There, sign the surrender.
Mike:	Feel better now, Eddie? You're not the only one who wants peace.
Kevin:	(crosses out his picture of the bombs dropping on the building, chuckles) There, I hope it's not too late.

The group concludes with some exploration and resolution of the conflicts. The workers had several directions to pursue regarding the issues of anger and conflict expressed in the drawings. The explosive expression of rage—the bombing of the building where the patients reside—can be thought of as an expression of anger at their home. Home symbolizes the patient's primary family, and home also refers to the current place of residence. As a sort of spokesperson for the group as well as himself, Kevin expresses his aggression. His drawing of a plane dropping bombs on Madison House could also represent anger at mental illness symbolized by the residential home. In addition, if one takes an interactionist view, the drawing might express conflict in the group among members, perhaps involving themes of roles, power, and competition.

The seemingly simple acts of choosing a topic and drawing the first picture are filled with meanings. The workers here wisely decide to sit back and wait for the group's reactions to those first drawings. The initial response to Kevin's picture is seen in David's drawing of a cannon shooting down the plane. In part this is an expression of David's hostility toward Kevin and, in part, perhaps an indication of David's discomfort with any expression of anger. The workers take note but attempt this time to explore underlying feelings.

One worker, Mike, directs his inquiry to Kevin in an attempt to solicit some verbalization of feelings: "What do you think about that, Kevin, about David shooting down your plane?" Kevin denies any problem, "I don't care. I mean, it's not real."

Rather than challenge Kevin and make the process too threatening, the worker accepts the need for the distancing and allows the group to go on, determining its own direction. Premature interpretation of feelings often cuts off further expression. It is generally preferable, as the worker does here, to permit the process to evolve. The workers' investment is in soliciting as much expression as possible and not in validating their own interpretations. The activity of making a mural has been selected precisely because it is so difficult for these patients to express themselves verbally. To press them to do so can sabotage the purpose of the activity.

David's embellishment of his drawing clarifies his intent and leads Ellen, the co-worker, to cautiously pursue David. She reacts by recognizing the action: "Wow! Something's really happening up there." The second part of her statement interprets the act: "You really mean to shoot that pilot down?" This manner of interpretation is effective, for it identifies David's anger in a nonthreatening way. The comment holds no accusation and is nonspecific in nature; it allows David to express his anger in a safe way and in a way that is not acted out. Ellen has linked David's anger to "the pilot" and not yet to Kevin.

Now the worker skillfully separates the act from the feeling by asking David if there is something he wants to tell Kevin. David is now able to acknowledge his anger and frustration with Kevin. Here the activity functions as a vehicle to allow the client to connect with feelings long harbored inside. What he was able to draw he was never able to say before. Still, David's comments are not directed at Kevin. Mike gently encourages David to talk to Kevin. Finally, David is able to be direct: "I'm tired of the way you act to me, and I'm just not goin' to take it no more." Following the interchange between David and Kevin, Eli joins in to express his feelings, "Yeah, Kevin, you is mean." The group conflict has surfaced and, through the drawing, has moved safely into the open.

Despite the progress the group has made in expressing real feelings, direct and open confrontation remain threatening for this population. Eddie's picture suggests the group's fear that once the anger is expressed, the group will be unable to control it. The newspaper headline drawn by Eddie calls for a stop to the confrontation. Anxious about the escalation and expressing the group's fear, Eddie says, "I hate war. We don't need no war. Tell them to stop . . . the fightin' . . ." It is important to note that Eddie is the largest and potentially the most physically powerful member of the group. His physical appearance is in direct contrast to his seemingly meek and fearful style of relating. How frightened he feels and how fragile he really is are illustrated by his regressive stuttering and rhyming.

After Eddie's request, the workers decide to give permission to stop the war. Perhaps this move is in recognition that Eddie's primitive level of defense is faltering and that he may soon be out of control. Also, the workers may wish to put a cap on potentially explosive feelings and give control to the group. The workers may also have stopped the confrontation because of their own discomfort with the emotional intensity. Often the worker's own internal barometer is a reliable measure of what is happening in the room.

Instead of simply putting an end to the discussion, Mike asks the group to come up with an idea for dealing with the problem: "How can we stop this war?" The word "we" appeals to the members' problem-solving strengths and abilities to be in charge of their own destinies. Ellen makes a final attempt to stick with the confrontation in the present by asking the group which war they are addressing: the war in Iraq or the war in the room. Mike also reaches out to Kevin, allowing him to respond to David, and Kevin seems to have a resigned acceptance of David's message. Whether this acceptance and understanding are truly integrated by Kevin is uncertain, but some movement is apparent, even if it is only limited communication between the two group members.

A silence follows during which Ellen feels a weeping figure that she proceeds to draw. Her motivation is unclear. Her drawing appears a visceral response to the sadness she feels in Kevin and the group's struggles. Perhaps she hopes to use the picture to further engage the group members to express sad feelings that she believes are present. Whatever the intent of the worker, the group members are moved and somewhat confused by the worker's exposure. Eli asks whether someone is sad, "crying about the pilot." Clearly there is an empathic association with the figure. Mike, in a highly skillful move, interprets the sadness as empathy for the self-destructive part of Kevin. Perhaps like all of them, Kevin wants to be with others, yet he feels undeserving of their caring. Consequently, Kevin pushes people away with his bad feelings and hurts himself by being left alone or, to paraphrase Mike, damages himself when he hurts others. The group resolves the conflict by erasing the anger. Once they confront it, they are able to stay intact. They even offer hope for change as Kevin, having erased his dropping bombs, states, "I hope it's not too late."

Saying Good-bye

The issues dealt with in the preceding piece were clearly middle phase issues. Let us now examine a programming piece concerned with termination phase issues in a socialization club for emotionally disturbed older adolescents and young adults who are meeting with a student co-therapist to prepare a gift for a worker who is leaving the agency. The worker had been working with this group for many years and developed close ties with each of its members. The members are creating a photographic collage that includes each member's picture and features snapshots of the group's activities. This project stirs the painful discussion of the impending loss. For some members, the gift becomes a way to distance themselves from the harshness of the reality. The gift allows members to feel a continuing connectedness with the worker who takes a part of the club (the collage) with her in her departure. The concrete representation further offers the members a transitional object into which they can pour their feelings of loss. As the members create the collage, a discussion of the pictures permits a more direct avenue for addressing the emotional issues.

Programming has been an integral part of this group throughout its evolution because the limited capacity of its members to tolerate intense feelings required less threatening means of expression. In its initial stages, when relationships were tenuous at best, the group was encouraged to gain some closeness through activities such as social dancing, trips, and picnics. The majority of these were planned by the worker with limited involvement of members. In this sense, the feeding was, in the early stages of the group's development, the responsibility of the worker.

As the group developed greater intimacy during its middle stage, preparing, planning, cooking for, and sharing holiday events—feeding each other— became possible. Now in the final stage related to this worker, the group once again comes together. This time it shares the pain at the ending and offers a special part of itself to the worker, a concrete expression of feeling—the collage. The group, having grown, is able to give rather than merely receive.

Group:	Did you bring the pictures? (taken the week before) Let me see them. I want to see them.
Worker:	(as the group members gather around the pictures) I said that everyone will have a chance to see them. These pictures are pretty important to you, aren't they?
Nick:	I don't care about the pictures. I just care about Carole leaving. Nobody feels the way I do. All they care about is the pictures.
Worker:	Well, Nick, let's ask other people. What are some of the rest of you feeling about Carole leaving?
Terri:	(said repeatedly throughout the process) I need to make a phone call. I want to put the pictures back in the frame.
Worker:	Sounds like things feel all mixed up for you, too, Terri.
Terri:	I've really got to get to the phone.
Nick:	I don't give a shit about the pictures or the friggen' phone. All I care about is Carole leaving.
Pearl:	Can we frame the pictures now?
Worker:	It sounds like everyone is having a hard time with all these confusing feelings, wanting to look at the pictures but feeling sad at the same time; wanting to talk about it but having a hard time talking. (starts to rearrange the pictures and invites others to start the framing process)
Terri:	(assisting with the pictures) I'm sad. I'm nervous and sad. I'm nervous about Carole leaving. No, I'm sad about Carole's leaving. It makes me nervous that I'm sad.
Worker:	Being sad is frightening for you.

Terri:	I need to make a phone call.
Worker:	I hear what you're saying. It's hard to stay here, but do you think we could all work together for a few more minutes?
Aldo:	No one cares about me. No one realizes how lonely I feel when I see those pictures.
Worker:	You feel very alone, Aldo. I wonder if other people here feel lonely.
Phil:	We've got to laugh it off. We got to stop staying with this.
Worker:	You would like laughing to help make the hurt go away?
Phil:	Well, inside I got the feelings, too. It don't feel good that she is leaving, but I guess I laugh to make it better. Come on, Aldo. Don't be that way.
Worker:	Is it hard for you to see Aldo in pain?
Phil:	I don't think he should be that way about it. Come on, Aldo, take it easy.
Aldo:	That might be easy for you to say, but I don't want her to leave. I love Carole. I don't want her to go. (he picks up the picture of himself with Carole)
Worker:	We can really see that in this picture of you together. That's a lovely remembrance for Carole to take with her. Would you like to help me paste it in the collage? (Aldo and worker paste the picture, and the worker picks up a picture of himself with Carole.) I remember the first time I came to the group, and Carole introduced me to everybody. I was feeling very enthusiastic about working with all of you. (worker pastes the picture)
Nick:	The pictures are beautiful. Look, they're in Technicolor. Look at them. They're beautiful, so bright. Look, there we are at the bowling alley. Wasn't that great?
Pearl:	Yeah, we really had a lot of fun that day. (Nick and Pearl paste the bowling alley picture.)
Terri:	I'm never going bowling again. I won't be able to bear it.
Worker:	What's that all about for you, Terri?
Terri:	When I see the pictures, I think about how it used to be with Carole, how it will never be the same.
Worker:	It will be different, but this group can still go bowling.
Aldo:	I don't care about those pictures. I care about Carole leaving.
Worker:	It's still very painful for you, Aldo. Nick, how do you feel about Carole leaving?
Nick:	It bothers me that she's leaving. It isn't good. She's been here a long time. But now we have John O'Hare.
Worker:	So Nick, you're feeling a lot like Aldo, but you're also looking forward to meeting the new worker?
Terri:	I need to use the phone.

Pearl:	Me, too. What's happening with the framing of the pictures? We have to get them right.
Worker:	Yes, we need to choose the right pictures for the collage. Maybe we should find one of Terri on the phone! (group laughs)
Terri:	I don't like it that she's leaving. Aldo, I don't like it either. You ain't the only one with those feelings. I don't want her to leave.
Phil:	Now, now, you don't have to get upset.
Terri:	Can we frame the pictures now? (looks for a picture of herself and pastes it)
Phil:	I don't want to get involved.
Worker:	With what?
Phil:	No one should get so upset about Carole's leaving. She got another job, and she got to go. What you gonna do about it?
Pearl:	We can't do anything but give her something so she won't forget us. (pastes her picture)
Worker:	I'm sure that Carole will never forget you.
Aldo:	When Carole leaves, I'm going to be in real trouble again. I might even end up in the hospital.
Worker:	I wonder if anybody else ever feels that way, that the feelings are so strong that they can make us sick and put us in the hospital.
Phil:	That ain't gonna happen, Aldo; that ain't gonna happen. Look at this picture at the party. We're having such a good time.
Worker:	Even though Carole is going, this group is still here, having a good time and caring about each other, helping people to stay well.
Terri:	Do you think I could make my phone call now?
Pearl:	Some things will never change. (the group laughs)

The preceding excerpt involves the integration of a program piece with a powerful expression of sadness and loss at termination. Although the feelings might have been expressed without the collage, the activity facilitated a more positive and direct transition to termination.

As discussed at length in Chapter 6, the primary tasks of termination are:

1. expression of ambivalent feelings around loss and change;
2. evaluation of accomplishments and areas of remaining work;
3. consolidation of gains in preparation for the future;
4. separation and moving on.

All of these are seen clearly in the preceding process.

One characteristic of the termination phase is the regression to earlier abandoned forms of behavior, an unconscious attempt to hold on to the worker or group by indicating that the work is not yet accomplished, that the client is not yet well. This characteristic is apparent in the preceding material when Aldo says, "When Carole leaves, I'm going to be in real trouble again. I might even end up in the hospital." A second characteristic, denial, a means of devaluing the significance of the group in order to lessen the pain of the loss, appears throughout this segment as well. Phil's comment, "She shouldn't get so upset about Carole's leaving. She got another job, and she gotta go," is typical. Terri's continued need to leave the room to use the telephone recalls still another characteristic common to termination—avoiding dealing with various feelings, most notably anger and sadness. Although here it is simply a matter of leaving the room, in many groups avoidance manifests itself in absences and latenesses, a way of saying, "I'll leave you before you'll leave me," or "I can't come anymore; it hurts too much."

Reminiscence—a process of reviewing past group experiences, which internalize accomplishments to be ego-supportive in meeting the challenges of the future—is also apparent throughout the excerpt. The message is, "*Look what we were able to do. Look what I will be able to do now.*" Reminiscence also instills a sense of meaning and feelings of past mastery, which can translate into an acceptance of the present letting go. In general, the process illustrates how each of the termination tasks is addressed by using the activity and how the issues of termination are brought to the surface in the process of creating the collage.

The specifics of the activity—making the collage—generate a means to deal with the loss. The fact that the collage includes pictures of each group member engaged in activities with the others and with the worker aids in the reminiscence and evaluative processes: "Yeah, we really had a lot of fun that day." Furthermore, after Terri vows she can never go bowling again because she is unable to bear it, the worker's intervention acknowledges the feelings of loss and change but does not allow those feelings to immobilize the group: "It will be different, but we can still go bowling."

The use of the concrete object becomes the vehicle through which the worker models a means of letting go. By recalling his own early meetings with Carole and the group, by taking his own picture and placing it in the frame, the worker suggests a way members can express themselves. As he selects the picture, absorbs its meaning, and then pastes it in the frame—in this sense releasing it (separating)—he permits the other group members to do likewise. Each group member is then permitted an individual connection to Carole, a picture, and a memory. As each member pastes his or her own picture, the separation from the group is effected symbolically. The frame becomes a structure to once again, both figuratively and literally, draw the group members together permanently. The collage becomes a metaphor for the permanent way in which the group is part of each of them. Giving the gift to Carole assures that they will not be forgotten by their beloved worker.

A special feature in this session is the worker's use of humor (the joke about Terri constantly needing the phone). The humor diffuses some of the anxiety and lowers the intensity of difficult feelings to permit the moving on. It also renews the sense of being bonded together by their shared experience. In general, the shared joke reminds the group of the accepting and loving atmosphere, a sense of warmth that they and the worker will carry always.

Acting out Feelings

Our next process is taken from a beginning group for boys age five to seven whose parents recently have been divorced. The boys have been referred to a family agency because of behavioral problems, apparently stimulated by the events at home. A fruitless discussion and a lack of receptivity to a story about divorce have preceded the decision to give the children a chance to do a puppet show. The subject of the show, as designated by the worker, is divorce.

Jonathan:	Yay, we can put on a puppet show for you two! (grabs the two puppets and sits down) This is the father and this is the mother. (takes the father puppet and yells) You stupid idiot! I'll knock your head through the wall if you don't shut that big mouth of yours! (pretends that the mother puppet is speaking) Oh, yeah, I'll show you who's stupid, you big dummy. Don't talk to me like that or you'll be sorry. (replies with the father puppet) You're the one who is going to be sorry when I knock your block off, you stupid bitch! (Puppets begin to hit each other, yelling, "You take that," and "you take that.")
Worker:	What do you think about this puppet show, boys?
Peter:	That's just like my house before Mommy and Daddy got divorced. One time after, my mom's boyfriend put a knife to her throat, and said, "I'm going to kill you."
Worker:	So what did you do?
Peter:	I was so scared he'd hurt my mommy that I kicked him down there. (points to his penis)
Jonathan:	It was the same thing at my house.
Worker:	What's been happening with you, Jeremy?
Jeremy:	My mother and father hit each other, too. I was scared. (Jonathan grabs the puppets once more and takes over.)
Peter:	Give me a chance. I want the puppet.
Jeremy:	Yeah, Jonathan, this isn't just your show.
Rickie:	I'm tired of this. Isn't there something else to do? Hey, give me that puppet . . .
Jonathan:	(The others try to wrest the puppets from him.) Stop it! Cut it out! This is my puppet show, and you'll get your turn next. (grabs some additional props from the other boys)

	Gimme that! I don't want it that way. Get away from here. (Jeremy and Peter try to steal the puppets from Jonathan and to work their ways into the plot.)
Rickie:	(becoming distracted and disconnected from the scene) I need to go to the bathroom. When will the group be over?
Jonathan:	(continues with the show) So the father died because the mother shot him . . .
Jeremy:	(furiously grabs the father puppet and makes him talk) Ha, ha, he's not dead! See? Take that! Take that. (Has the father puppet hit the mother puppet?)
Peter:	(Screams and cries, runs toward Jeremy and the father puppet and hits Jeremy in the face. Peter and Jeremy are both hysterical, and the workers find it necessary to separate the two boys. Peter faces the cement wall, sobs, and cries out.) Mom, help me. Mom, come and get me. Help me! Mom, where are you?
Worker:	(hugs him) Mom is right outside.
Jeremy, Jonathan, and Rickie:	(have been huddling together on the opposite side of the room and now cautiously approach Peter) We just wanted to make sure Peter was okay. Is it all right, Peter?
Jeremy:	(hands the father puppet to Peter) Here's the father, Peter.

The preceding piece of process illustrates the intensity of emotion that can be elicited by the use of program in work with young children. The excerpt comes from a first session in which the issues around trust, vulnerability, and exposure are typically present. The worker's clear agenda is to get the boys to directly address their feelings about divorce, but the children are unwilling to discuss the topic of divorce at first. They refuse to participate in informal talk or to listen to a story concerning divorce. Although the boys have expressed themselves clearly, indicating that they are not yet ready to discuss this issue, the worker plunges ahead, forcing them to address it in the puppet show.

The worker seems invested in helping the group focus on what she knows to be an important issue for them. However, she is so committed to her agenda that she bypasses an essential part of the process in the beginning phase: establishing trust and creating a safe environment before proceeding to the work of the group. Although she believes that her intervention is a means to empower the children by helping them express themselves, she actually reinforces their feelings of powerlessness. Such feelings are also associated with their roles as youngsters in divorcing families. Despite the limitation of requiring that the topic of divorce be addressed, the power of the puppets leads to a much-needed ventilation of feelings.

In general, even if a worker is overly anxious or has poorly timed an attempt to engage clients in a particular area of discussion, there are means by which the process still can be fostered. In this case, the worker might employ specific techniques to help youngsters feel safe, even with the selection and promotion of her own agenda. While choosing the topic, the worker could still permit the boys to pick the puppets they wish to use and design their own scene together. In part, the purpose of giving the children more control in this, or any other situation, is to make the experience feel safer by increasing the individuals' power. Adequate planning of the activities used can certainly assist in that process.

Since this group is in the beginning phase, rules need to be established, and the boys need to have a role in developing these rules. This participation will increase the children's sense of control over a new and frightening experience. In the case of the physical fight between Peter and Jeremy, the worker intervenes as the authority figure. Had children together with the worker established the rule that no hitting was allowed, the rule and the agreement could have been mentioned when the boys were separated by the worker. The agreed-upon contract would serve as the arbiter. Despite the violation, the statement of the rule and its origins could help the children feel somewhat in charge of the group. Making rules does not ensure safety. Rules are likely to be broken, but formulating them does provide a basic structure within which appropriate behavior is defined and expectations clarified.

Another rule the worker would probably have to suggest, and which might have been helpful in contracting with this group, is that every child is to have a chance to participate in the group in his own way. This rule only could have been played out programmatically if a sufficient number of puppets had been provided so that every child could choose one if he wished. In this group, the fact that only two puppets were provided heightened the competitiveness and emphasized the problems with sharing and deprivation (general issues for this age group). Additionally, the competition paralleled conflicts in the children's family situations—the competitive themes in divorced families. We do not know whether more puppets might have made Jonathan any less monopolistic, but enough puppets for everyone at least would not contribute to the competitive and, thereby, less safe environment.

Furthermore, the worker might have decided to either distribute the puppets to the boys or allow the youngsters to pick for themselves. Self-selection reinforces feelings of empowerment and may also be useful from a diagnostic point of view. Who picks the bunny puppet and who chooses the lion puppet gives the worker some insight into how children see themselves in the group and in their families. At some later point in the development of the group, the worker may use puppets to help the boys assume roles in the play for which they might not otherwise opt (e.g., helping the bunny to be more of a lion or vice versa). The program can thereby assist the youngsters to explore unexpressed parts of themselves and see other perspectives.

Different ways of selecting a topic for the puppet show rather than assigning the topic of divorce could yield a greater sense of trust, safety, and control for participants. One method for choosing a puppet-play subject is for the worker to elicit some choices from the group and then have the members take a vote as to which topic interests them most. In early beginnings, before youngsters are clear about expectations, the worker may decide to offer her own choices for a vote. Empowerment is gained in the act of voting even when group members have not contributed to the choices. Voting can be problematic in small groups where individual members may have made suggestions in which they are particularly invested. In larger groups, with greater anonymity, voting may be experienced as less threatening. Secret ballots also decrease threat and competitiveness.

Another method for selecting a puppet-play subject is for the worker to put all the choices (the worker's and the children's) in a hat for random selection. This technique can be enhanced by creating a game out of the process. To make the selection fun, and in some way cooperative, the choosing might be preceded by some sort of fanfare. Random selection eliminates competition.

In the excerpt, most of the action seems to develop without consideration of the factors outlined above. Jonathan grabs both puppets, the other boys jockey for position, and the worker moves away from the program piece into a short discussion of what she selects as the theme. Program is used here as a catalyst to talking about divorce rather than as a means to address the issues. Different approaches use the program more directly. The worker might have introduced herself as a character in the puppet show, responding to the action depicted by the children. The purpose in joining the play could be to clarify, explore, or focus feelings; to assist in the problem solving; or to be a voice for reality or reason. For instance, in one play in which feelings were being denied, a creative worker entered as a mythical spokesperson for truth and justice, and the group was helped to verbalize its feelings. Another technique might be for the worker to take some puppets and develop an answer play in which she could model effective problem solving or alternate solutions regarding the issues suggested by the children's performance.

Since these youngsters are so full of the painful feelings generated by their chaotic family lives, the expression of intense emotions is inevitable, even in these beginning stages. Despite their differences, the boys quickly move from being strangers to having a strong empathic connection with each other. This is demonstrated clearly by the concern they finally show to Peter and by Jeremy's acknowledgment of the puppet character's significance for Peter. When Jeremy hands the puppet to Peter, he shows apparent understanding of its meaning and certainly illustrates his compassion. The puppets, with all the squabbling and commotion they create, still offer a particularly apt vehicle to help the boys to express themselves and describe their struggles.

Play is, of course, a natural means for reaching children. We have already noted some of our criticisms and suggestions about ways to proceed more effectively using the puppet theatre to engage the boys and allow them to feel safe. We want to be clear, however, that despite the difficulties described in this process excerpt, puppetry is an excellent means for eliciting feelings, working through hard emotional realities, developing new perspectives, and finding solutions for problems.

Use of the Small Group in Large Group Settings

The use of activities in groups often necessitates the dividing of a larger group into several smaller groups. This need to break the group down may occur when a worker is in an agency in which large populations are being served at the same time. Some examples are camp settings, educational institutions in which classes are large, or various hospital settings—chronic inpatient units or day hospital environments.

Seemingly a simple task, the selection of members for each small group is a complex matter. Workers need to address the process as carefully as they would any aspect of composition. Issues of trust, exposure, rejection, acceptance, and the many "risk" factors involved in forming the small groups need special consideration, especially in the beginning phase of the small-group development. In a training seminar, for example, the group might include twenty-one participants. To demonstrate a particular aspect of group dynamics, the trainer might require that this large group be broken down into three smaller groups. Members of each of these three groups could work cooperatively in developing an exercise to share with the larger group later in the training session.

One easy and often-used method to divide a larger group might be used here: asking the members of the large group to count off by threes and having all the number ones constitute one group, the number twos the second group, and the number threes the third group. This dividing technique minimizes risk and exposure for the members since the leader has directed it. The technique is random, safe, and efficient; it prevents subgroups of friends, who are seated together in the larger circle, from all being placed in the same small group. The random nature of the small-group selection also leads naturally to a distribution of group members including various ages and ethnicities.

This approach, however, does little to set the tone for working in the small groups. It fails to provide any atmosphere of anticipation, fun, or enthusiasm which might serve as a prelude to the small-group activities. In order to provide a more stimulating atmosphere which sets the tone for the work to follow, one might divide the group using a more creative approach. Various techniques energize the process and lead to more interesting interactions among group participants.

One activity for dividing the large group involves candy. For the training seminar, with twenty-one participants, the worker may purchase twenty-one pieces of candy divided equally among three different kinds. These candies are thrown into a large hat or bag that is placed in the middle of the circle formed by the large group. The group members are then instructed to come up, close their eyes, and reach into the hat or bag and select one item. All of the participants who share the same candy selection are assigned to the same small group. An alternative approach might be for the worker to escort the group members individually to the hat or bag, while the group members close their eyes, select candies, and then return to their positions. Even in using this approach, the worker must consider many issues. The selection of candy seems benign enough; everyone likes it. If you are dealing with young adults or even older adults, choosing candies helps pull for a "playful" healthy child part that is useful in activities. In addition, the candy provides some immediate oral gratification that can be important in reducing anxiety and even perhaps in soliciting feelings of being nurtured by the worker. However, the worker might have to consider that a member of the group might be a diabetic or might have a religious orientation that restricts diet to particular foods. Without the worker considering these variables, someone would be left out, seen as different, or feel rejected.

If this exercise were done in the beginning of the group, when people have little trust with each other and high dependency on the worker, members might feel safe. However, here, too, the worker must be conscious of the particular characteristics of the membership. If escorting members to the hat or bag, for example, the worker must consider whether or not to touch the member. Generally, taking the hand of a group member in this type of exercise is relatively safe; however, if the worker and members are of opposite sexes, and if the members are of certain religions, touching might be prohibited. It could be useful for the worker to ask ahead, "I'm taking you to the hat. Is it okay if I take your hand?" This shows respect for the member's preference and also allows the less trusting members to exercise some degree of control. If they indicate that they are uncomfortable with the touching, or if the worker senses a hesitancy or ambivalence, the worker can suggest, "Okay, just follow my voice." Minimizing the differences among members and focusing on the group activity is important at this point to begin building the cohesion of the group. Obviously, it is necessary for the worker to know the population well enough to address as many variables as possible even when planning the small-group selection part of the activity.

Sometimes the large group is not divided into smaller groups immediately. Instead of dividing the group in the beginning of the large-group sessions, the worker may choose to maintain the large group at first and wait until the middle phase to break down the group into smaller units. Once the large group enters middles, where trust and cohesion is high in the group, the worker might be less concerned with issues related to these factors but still needs to be conscious of group members' religious or cultural differences and requirements. As a result of increased trust and cohesion in middles, the selection process for the small groups can be open to greater creativity. For example, the worker might escort the first member to the hat or bag and then that member is asked to escort a second member, and so on. This process increases bonding between members as dependency on the worker decreases, which is characteristic of middles.

At times, the selection of candidates for a particular small group needs to be based on more specific criteria primarily related to purpose or task. An example of this comes from a teen camp setting in which the adolescent campers face issues around cultural differences. The worker's purpose is to help a large group of approximately fifty new campers on their first day build intimate and cooperative relationships that will assist them in having a positive summer experience. To achieve this, the worker breaks down the larger group into small groups of five to ten campers who are asked to complete a structured group exercise designed specifically to address matters of cultural differences and similarities. The campers in this situation are specifically chosen to reflect as diverse a composition as is possible in terms of race, ethnicity, age, and gender. The goal in this purposeful selection is to minimize difference by exposing similarity. As noted earlier in this chapter, structured exercises are often particularly useful in beginnings as a way of addressing issues that may be threatening before trust is established.

This camp activity begins when each small group is given a general set of instructions about how the exercise will proceed. They first are asked to choose a secretary who will be responsible for recording all deliberations and, later, for reporting back to the larger group regarding the discussion. All members of the small groups are then asked to share with the other members of their small group three things from the cultural background of their current families that they would like to retain once they establish their own families and three things they would reject in establishing their own families. The worker needs to provide some examples of areas in which the group members may focus their discussions. These may include discussing attitudes about race and ethnicity, sexuality, adolescence, child rearing, education, drug and alcohol use, family responsibilities and loyalties, independence of family members, appearance and dress, censorship, expression of feelings, and customs regarding holiday celebrations, food, the arts, and religion.

The worker's suggestions for focusing the discussion need to be geared to the specifics of the population served. If this exercise were done in a senior center, perhaps the worker would have to be concerned about different cultural practices as they relate to aging and death, issues which would be significant for an older population. In the teen camp setting, however, where campers are likely to spend two to four weeks together, it is necessary to move quickly to the issues that concern adolescents and getting along. Once the directions have been given, the small groups begin their process.

As with all group activities, the amount of time allowed for the exercise depends upon the general availability of time within the entire program, the level of frustration tolerance of the population, and the receptivity of group members to the completion of the task. In this process, the worker may periodically check in with the groups to see where they are in relationship to their readiness to return to the larger group. Throughout the small-group process, the worker moves from group to group facilitating the work, helping to increase participation by the group members, and keeping the groups focused on the task. The worker must also be available to each group for their specific concerns.

After the small groups complete their sessions, the large group reconvenes for a report on the work. At this time, the worker's skills in reaching for commonality, clarification, and exploration, and development of key themes come into play. Group members other than the secretaries are encouraged to participate and support the secretary in representing their small group in the larger group discussion. This open, free-flowing exchange fosters a sense of groupness and contributes to a feeling of being a member of a team. It is only through the use of the small group, in what otherwise is a large, alienating, and unmanageable setting, that campers can feel a sense of belonging. Clearly the initial selection process involved in breaking down a larger group into smaller working groups needs as much consideration as the selection of the composition of small groups in general.

Conclusion

In this chapter, we have explored ways in which programs can be used to (1) elicit feelings, (2) provide alternate means of expression, (3) problem solve, (4) enhance and develop socialization skills, and (5) allow for mastery and thereby development or increase of self-esteem. In all cases, the nature of the program must be geared to the cultural, developmental, and environmental needs and common problems that bring the participants together. Most importantly, however, the choice of program and how it is successfully implemented is determined by the worker's capacity for inspiration, imagination, improvisation, and skill. In order to be creative, the worker must remain open to intellectual, emotional, and cultural enrichment in her or his own life. The worker's openness to new experiences can indicate permission for clients to expand themselves as well. The successful use of programs, as with any tool in social work, relies on the worker's ability to remain fresh, enthusiastic, and invested.

Table 8.1 Baseball Group

Members' Needs	Group Needs	Group Phase Issues
Coed Adolescents		Beginnings
1. Physical exercise	1. To heighten self-esteem	– Worker in direct and active role
2. Socialization	2. To increase capacity for intimacy	– Creation of emotionally and physically safe environment
3. Mastery	3. To assist in the solidification of sense of self re: identity, sexuality, and independence	– Trust versus mistrust – Approach-avoidance

continued ...

Table 8.1 *Continued*

Members' Needs	Group Needs	Group Phase Issues
Coed Adolescents		*Beginnings*
4. Peer approval and affiliation	As above	
5. Resolution of identity issues		
6. Exploration of sexuality issues		
7. Resolution of dependence versus independence		

Factors	Coed Adolescents' Group	Ego-impaired Adolescents' Group
1. Power roles	1. Worker establishes rules for conducting game – worker chooses team captains and directs them to choose team members and possibly batting order	1. Worker establishes rules of conduct – increase worker–member ratio – worker chooses team members and assigns positions and batting order
2. Group environment	2. Regulation-size baseball field – standard safety equipment – include a softball	2. Regulation-size baseball field – standard safety equipment
3. Tension levels	3. Worker serves as umpire – usual roles	3. Worker serves as umpire – usual rules with modification
4. Frustration tolerance	4. Option to shorten game – adjust strikes, balls, and outs to allow everyone a turn at bat	4. Shorten game

continued . . .

Table 8.1 Continued

Factors	Coed Adolescents' Group	Ego-impaired Adolescents' Group
	– worker engages waiting batters and individuals with special needs	
5. Degree of intimacy	5. Bonding occurs spontaneously	5. Pregame "getting to know you" exercise essential
6. Availability of experiences	6. Players may rotate positions based on captain decisions	

Members' Needs	Group Goals	Group Phase Issues
Ego-impaired Adolescents		Middles
1. Same as above	Same as above	– Worker less active
		– Development of leadership within the group
		– Developing cohesiveness
		– Increased sense of group empowerment
		– Trying on new roles
		– Conflict resolution
		– Confrontation
		– Increased socialization skills and mastery permit intimacy and problem solving
		– Increased risk-taking
		– Active decision making

continued . . .

Table 8.1 *Continued*

Members' Needs	Group Goals	Group Phase Issues
Ego-impaired Adolescents		*Middles*
2. Increase frustration tolerance		
3. Enhance ability to cope with external and internal stress		
4. Establish clear boundaries		
5. More structure	Same as above	
6. Emphasis on cooperation rather than competition		

Factors	Coed Adolescents' Group	Ego-impaired Adolescents' Group
1. Power roles	1. Members choose team captains	1. Worker chooses team captains who choose teams – worker assigns batting order and position – worker acts as umpire – members take turns pitching
2. Group environment	2. Same	2. Same
3. Tension levels	3. Members elect or take turns from session to session being umpire	3. Same
4. Frustration tolerance	4. Games played full 7 or 9 innings	4. Shorten game time as needed – modify adjustment of strikes, balls, and outs to move closer to standard rules

continued ...

Table 8.1 *Continued*

Factors	Coed Adolescents' Group	Ego-impaired Adolescents' Group
		– worker involved with waiting batters and members with special needs
5. Degree of intimacy	5. Worker helps group focus on its responsibility to resolve disputes and problem solve	5. Worker encourages problem solving—worker encourages team spirit and cheering, "talking it up," congratulating each other for good plays and effort
6. Availability of experiences	6. Greater flexibility in playing various positions—greater flexibility and spontaneity in changing playing positions and team roles	6. Encouragement of sportsmanship and cheering of opponents—members encouraged to try different positions

Members' Needs	Group Goals	Group Phase Issues
		Endings
Same as above		– Worker's role again more active
		– Regression to earlier forms of behavior
		a) decrease in trust
		b) increase in dependency on worker

continued . . .

Table 8.1 Continued

Members' Needs	Group Goals	Group Phase Issues
		Endings
		– Loss themes surface – Evaluation – Separation/ individuation from group

Factors	Coed Adolescents' Group	Ego-impaired Adolescents' Group
1. Power roles	1. Worker holds group to end on time	1. Worker holds group to end on time – worker more active
2. Group environment	2. Same	2. Same
3. Tension levels	3. Worker more active in helping group settle disputes as conflict increases – group problem-solving skills regress – worker active in helping members verbalize feelings about endings to lessen acting-out	3. Same
4. Frustration tolerance	4. Worker clarifies expression of feelings regarding loss and ending	4. Worker more active in supporting the completion of tasks
5. Degree of intimacy	5. Planning of championship games, playoffs, and/or party	5. Worker helps group express loss – group plans its final game/party

continued ...

Table 8.1 *Continued*

Factors	Coed Adolescents' Group	Ego-impaired Adolescents' Group
6. Availability of new experiences	6. Worker helps group plan future activities	6. Worker helps group plan new activities

Table 8.2 Community Center—Storytelling

Members' Needs	Group Needs	Group Phase Issues
Senior Citizens		*Beginnings*
1. Dealing with loss	1. Aid in reminiscence	– Worker in direct and active role
2. Adaptation to change	2. Strengthen ego function	– Creation of emotionally and physically safe environment
a) social		
b) emotional		
c) physical		
3. Dependence versus independence	3. Develop mastery	Trust versus mistrust
4. Life review	4. Resolve psychic conflicts	
5. Socialization	5. Address issues of loss	
	6. Decrease isolation	
Preschoolers		*Beginnings*
1. Mastery	1. To enhance emotional development	– Approach-avoidance
2. Expression of feeling through play	2. Assist in communication skills	
3. Development of social skills	3. To teach problem solving, sharing, cooperation, and impulse control	
4. Development of sense of self		

continued . . .

Table 8.2 Continued

Factors	Senior Citizens	Preschoolers
1. Power roles	1. Worker directs and chooses engagement materials and exercises – worker actively solicits participation – worker contracts to allow maximum participation from members	1. Same – worker utilizes physical to control acting-out a) holding a hand b) helping a child to a seat c) removing child from room – worker establishes norms by modeling acceptable behavior – co-leadership needed for more than 5 minutes
2. Group environment	2. Comfortable seating and lighting – good accessibility – round table option – nonintrusive warm-up exercises	2. Small room—child proof with few distractions – quiet room to provide low stimulation
3. Tension levels	3. Worker selects nonthreatening engagement material	3. Same
4. Frustration tolerance	4. Worker ensures fairness in equal opportunity to speak	4. Same – shortened sessions – use of short stories
5. Degree of intimacy	5. Worker selects material to heighten shared historical experiences	5. Touching—primarily to direct and calm children

continued . . .

Table 8.2 Continued

Factors	Senior Citizens	Preschoolers
6. Availability of new experiences	6. Focus on old experiences, reminiscences	6. Children have opportunity to meet other children

Members' Needs	Group Goals	Group Phase Issues
		Middles
		– Worker less active – Development of leadership within the group – Empowerment of members – Increased cohesiveness – Trying on new roles – Confrontation – Increased socialization skills and mastery, permit intensity, and allow problem solving – Increased risk-taking – Increased decision making

Factors	Senior Citizens	Preschoolers
1. Power roles	1. Members select materials or topics – worker less active in directing discussion – members more active in directing discussion	1. Worker actively encourages withdrawn children to participate – children more active in selection of material

continued . . .

Table 8.2 *Continued*

Factors	Senior Citizens	Preschoolers
2. Group environment	2. Comfortable seating and lighting – good accessibility – round table option – nonintrusive warm-up exercises	2. Worker and children may sit on floor together
3. Tension level	3. Worker selects more provocative material – worker addresses more conflictual elements in stories	3. Same
4. Frustration tolerance	4. Worker encourages members to deal with conflict – worker increases level of provocative material	4. Worker may increase number of sessions and length of stories – worker encourages children to deal with conflict – worker delays gratification
5. Degree of intimacy	5. Worker solicits feelings about shared historical experiences and their relationship to the here and now	5. Greater exchange of physical expression of feeling—worker may hug children and children worker. Children may sit on worker's lap, sit with arms around each other
6. Availability of new experiences	6. Worker challenges members to participate in new ways	6. Children encouraged to act out the stories assigned to different roles

Members' Needs	Group Goals	Group Phase Issues
		Endings
		– Worker becomes more directive – Regression to earlier forms of behavior a) decrease in trust

continued . . .

Table 8.2 Continued

Members' Needs	Group Goals	Group Phase Issues
		Endings
		b) increase in dependency on worker
		– Loss and evaluation
		– Helping group to move on
		– Separation/ individuation

Factors	Senior Citizens	Preschoolers
1. Power roles	1. Worker holds the group to end on time	1. Worker holds the group to end on time
2. Group environment	2. Same	2. Same
3. Tension level	3. Worker more active in settling disputes and resolving old conflicts as they surface	3. Worker more active in settling disputes and resolving old conflicts as they surface
4. Frustration tolerance	4. Worker selects stories dealing with loss or endings – task of party planning sets the stage for the discussion of feelings	4. Selection of stories dealing with loss or endings by the worker – themes of growth and change – task of planning party sets the stage for the discussion of feelings
5. Degree of intimacy	5. Worker clarifies and solicits expressions of loss and ending – worker encourages evaluation of group activity	5. Worker helps children let go (physical clinging is common) – worker clarifies and solicits feelings about endings

continued ...

Table 8.2 *Continued*

Factors	Senior Citizens	Preschoolers
		– worker encourages evaluation of group activities
6. Availability of new experiences	6. Worker helps group plan new experiences	6. Worker helps group plan new experiences – transition objects utilized to assist in the separation, i.e., booklet of stories for each child to take home

9   CONFRONTING ACTING-OUT BEHAVIOR AND POWERFUL LATENT THEMES

He who learns must suffer and even in our sleep pain that cannot forget falls drop by drop upon the heart, and in our own despair, against our will, comes wisdom to us by the awful grace of God.

Aeschylus
Agamemnon (485 BCE)

Introduction

Practitioners have long struggled to deal with clients whose behavior seems to be disruptive to group process. The angry client, the client who challenges the worker and the group, the verbally abusive client, and the negative leader who constantly devalues the group experiences create an atmosphere of intimidation and often a sense of helplessness and powerlessness of the group that interferes with the work of the group. Similarly, in perhaps a more subtle way, clients avoid painful but necessary exploration by withdrawing, monopolizing, ruminating and obsessing, intellectualizing, minimizing, rationalizing, and by demonstrating a multitude of other defensive behaviors. Workers, too, have difficulty confronting certain problematic material, those areas that may stir countertransferential issues for them with members or other workers as these influence group process. Workers may avoid difficult topics by focusing only on positive subjects or by problem solving rather than exploring difficult or painful material. They also may collude with clients by focusing on minutiae or details, by intellectualizing rather than approaching emotional content, and by educating about the process rather than really engaging in the process, thus keeping away from areas that neither clients nor workers wish to address.

Throughout this text we have stated that workers must first tune in to what they are feeling, identify it, and then make the cognitive connection between the present feeling and the historical reference. In this way, elements are identified so that they are no longer unconscious blocks to the process. The next step is to trust that the countertransferential issue is a response to external stimuli and to turn the workers' interventions into skilled interventions rather than knee-jerk responses. In particular, in situations that involve confrontation or conflict or emotional intensity, workers are responsible for being aware of their own dynamics and their influence on the confrontative process. If workers are generally unaware of the impact of certain feelings, they will be unable to recognize the significance of the absence of specific material.

For instance, in a bereavement group, a worker not conscious of his or her own feelings of abandonment and anger in the grieving process might not help the group to address these very important issues. The group might instead focus solely on the sadness, just one element related to the loss, possibly inhibiting the healing process. In such groups, the worker might explore the underlying feelings of rage at being abandoned and some of the guilt associated with feelings of relief after a prolonged dying process. Also the worker needs to consider that some group members may have unresolved issues related to the deceased that could be sources of guilt and need to be expressed.

The worker's understanding of the relationships among the members of the group in the confrontative process is also necessary. As does the worker, the members react to each other, to the group as a whole, and to the worker(s). These reactions also have a historical context. An intimidating group member may trigger among other group members historical associations with abuse. In certain circumstances, scapegoating may be an expression of some of these transferential feelings. At least two possible transferential scenarios are common in these situations. In the first, the group members ally with each other to scapegoat the perceived abuser in an attempt to overpower or expel the individual. In the second instance, the group members ally with the perceived abuser as one group member assumes the historical role of victim and is scapegoated by the entire group.

The fact that group members may be of different races, ethnicities, sexual orientations, genders, and ages influences the process of confrontation as well. In certain cultures, for instance, women may be expected to be more passive and indirect about expressing feelings. Men, too, may be indirect about expressing deeply felt emotions, considering these expressions as signs of weakness. Recognizing the variety of experience from cultural, gender, and age perspectives, the worker applies the techniques of confrontation differently. For example, in work with an older adults' group, the worker's use of familiar and non-offensive language would facilitate the confrontation. With teens, however, it would be acceptable to confront using street language. Also the group may use the differences among them to avoid intimacy. The underlying issues of difference, which may include prejudice and racism, must be confronted and consciously identified in order to achieve the common goals of the group. Where behavior is hostile between members, the worker must be able to help the group to differentiate between constructive expression of anger and destructive assaults.

Powerful Angry Feelings

The next piece examines confrontation between members and its meaning for a group. The excerpt comes from a group to help persons with AIDS cope with the strains of their illnesses. The group has been meeting for over a month with co-leaders, Bob and Alexis. Group members Harry and Michael have been arguing for a while. Harry thinks Michael is too depressed all the time, "too negative," and that the group should be more upbeat and dwell less on the "dark side" of having AIDS:

Michael:	(after a long monologue about how depressed he feels today) So I just feel stuck. I don't know what step I can take . . . Everything I think of has a problem attached to it.
Harry:	Are you going to be like this every week?
Michael:	Fuck off, will ya? I've got a right to talk.
Harry:	Watch it, pal. And you don't have the right to depress everybody. That's not what this group is for. You can't do that here every week.
Michael:	Who the fuck do you think you are? Telling me what I can say, what I can do here. Give me a break. You listen, pal. Last night, I got myself out of bed to have dinner with a friend. And I started feeling bad. And I ran to the bathroom. But just as I was pulling my pants down, I lost control and shat all over the floor. And I sat there and cried. And then I cleaned up my shit and went back to the table and didn't say a word. (yelling) So don't you fucking tell me what I can and can't do here. I don't have anywhere else to do it . . . pal!
Harry:	Oh, excuse me. You're a goddamn martyr. I forgot. (Harry and Michael are screaming at each other. They speak simultaneously, neither listening to the other.)
Michael:	Oh, kiss my ass. Fuck you! You sit there like Buddha, only fatter. And all you do is judge. And (mimicking) "Let's keep things light . . . No bad vibes, please." Well, check in with me after your first spinal tap. Christ, I hate your fucking guts!!
Harry:	And I'm getting pretty tired of that mouth of yours. Nobody talks to me like that. Did you hear that? Huh? Answer me, faggot. Did you hear that? I asked you a fucking question. Can you shut that hole of yours for two seconds?
Alexis:	(screaming to make herself heard) Stop! Stop! This is not productive. (The group members quiet down.)

At first glance, one is impressed with the level of anger that seems totally dissociated from anything other than the relationship between Michael and Harry. Michael is constantly complaining, and Harry does not want to hear it. The real issue, however, as in all strong confrontations, runs much deeper. When a worker sees emotions expressed with such intensity, an underlying meaning always exists, one that should be detected upon examining the emotional needs of the population. The theme permeating this discussion focuses on issues related to the loss of control. The group members are people with AIDS, a disease with the potential to rob those infected of their independence, their health, their freedom, their loved ones, and, finally, of their lives. Feelings of powerlessness and the accompanying rage must be expressed. As Michael says, he is stuck and, in this sense, helpless. He has lost control, both figuratively and literally, through his inability to control his bowels. Harry says that he is furious. The object of Harry's anger is Michael for representing Harry's fear of the loss of power and control.

In any confrontation, the task for the worker is to allow intense feelings to surface to the degree that the expression can be cathartic and yet to maintain sufficient control to permit healing. Premature intervention prevents the group from effectively experiencing what must be felt. In addition, moving too quickly to stop the interaction gives the group the message that it cannot survive intense emotions and that honesty is inappropriate for discussion here. In this group in particular, but in other groups as well, members need to wrestle with problems with their full intensity and know that even if they cannot control the entire situation, they are still functioning and alive. Fighting is a sign of vigor and life.

If the worker waits too long to intervene, the potential exists for the confrontation to be nonproductive and sometimes even destructive. In such instances, the group becomes so polarized that there can never be a return to comfortable and open communication. Group members may feel too frightened to return once they have experienced the loss of control in the group. Antagonists may be ashamed of the raw way in which they have challenged each other. Others may be afraid that they will be expected to engage in such open self-disclosure before they are ready. The environment can become unsafe.

The worker in the excerpt might have intervened after Harry's response about Michael's playing the martyr. We recognize that this exchange occurred so quickly and with such fury that it might have been impossible for Alexis to move in any more quickly than she did. An appropriate intervention would simply be to call for a cessation of the yelling, ask that everyone calm down sufficiently to talk, and bring in the rest of the group regarding the thematic content. An intervention might be, "You are both so angry at these issues of control we have to grapple with here." The follow-up question to the group might be, "Is this something only Harry and Michael are struggling with?"

Confrontation in Beginnings

The following vignette is taken from a session of an alternative-to-incarceration program for parole violators. The group members are African-American and Latino males, twenty to thirty years of age, from a low socioeconomic class. A number of the men are rather physically intimidating and verbally aggressive, and several have a history of physical violence. The worker is Caucasian, middle class, and in his very early twenties. He is soft-spoken, highly verbal and articulate, appears genuine, and possesses a good sense of humor. The group is called the "anger management group." Although the members already know each other and the worker from other groups in the program, this is the first session for this particular group. At the point where we enter the session, the group has just finished developing group guidelines, and one member has asked permission to leave the room to go to the bathroom. The worker has nodded, expressing his approval, and the member has left. The group then erupts into a heated discussion:

Eduardo:	Yo, I got something to say, and I'll say it again when Freddie gets back, but we shouldn't have to go to the bathroom in the middle of the group. I don't see why he had to leave.
Dan:	That's right. If you're here, you're here. It's only an hour. There shouldn't be nobody that has to leave.
Eli:	Yeah, man, he could be walking back from the bathroom, and if someone sees him, they could write him up for not being where he's supposed to be, right here in this group.
Dan:	There ain't no reason why anyone should have to leave. You can hang on for an hour.
Mike:	Sometimes you just got to take a piss, man.
Dan:	You can fuckin' hold it!
Julio:	Yo, fuck that, man. What if you're feeling sick, and you have to take a shit?
Eduardo:	(looking at the worker) Well, there's emergency situations . . .
Worker:	Well, I can't control when you have to go to the bathroom. We're all adults, and I assume that you'll only leave if you have to.
Dan:	That's right. Like the man said, we're all adults so we should all know that we have to be here for an hour and go to the bathroom before we come.
Jack:	Yo, sometimes you can't control that shit.
Angel:	Jack, yo, don't be tellin' me that if you were going on a trip to Central Park that you wouldn't take a piss before you go, because y'all know there ain't no bathroom anywhere around there.
Eduardo:	We gotta make a rule about it. We should add it up there. (points to the newsprint with group guidelines written on it)

(Freddie walks back into the room)

Worker:	Freddie, you started quite a conversation when you left. Does anyone want to fill him in on what we were talking about?

Eli:	Yeah, man. We were just saying that there's no reason to be leaving the group in the middle. Everyone should go to the bathroom before they come here. Because, you know, we could be gettin' into it here, and a brother could get up and leave and get out of dealing with his shit.
Julio:	If we're gettin' into it like that, I'd shit in my pants before leaving. We all gotta deal with our anger. You could just avoid it by leaving . . . you get mad and then leave and when you get back you're cool, but you didn't deal with it.
Eli:	It's like Ken said—we're adults; we should be able to go to the bathroom before we come.

In confronting the powerful feelings expressed in this piece, one first must consider issues related to group phase—in this case, beginnings. The group struggles with contractual issues of rule establishment, setting of boundaries and limits, and the identification of norms and goals. Also apparent is the initial testing of the leader and the members' attempts to establish their roles in relation to each other and to the worker. The dynamics of trust versus mistrust and the need for safety in the group, also beginning phase issues, get played out on at least two different levels. Members grapple with internal issues of whether they can trust themselves to contain their own impulses—"Sometimes you can't control that shit"–and on an external level of whether they can trust others, the leader specifically, to contain the group within its limits: (to the worker) ". . . we shouldn't have to go to the bathroom in the middle of the group." Eduardo, by speaking to the worker in this way, starts the questioning of the worker's ability to control the group. In effect, he is saying, "What's the matter with you? You can't trust us. We avoid dealing with expressions of feeling." The group follows up, and Eduardo concludes the discussion with, "We've got to make a rule," again expressing the feeling that the worker must tighten the rules and take more control.

Immediately apparent in this piece is the intensity of the anger expressed in a group identified as an anger management group. The whole group, in its discussion of leaving for the bathroom, focuses on an extended metaphor related to impulse control and appropriate versus inappropriate expressions of feeling. Control over one's bathroom behavior is not unlike control over one's anger. At times, each is on the verge of explosion. Socially acceptable and socially unacceptable releases of tension exist.

The discussion of rules and limits is especially significant for this group, whose members have already violated the rules in the larger society, of which this group is a microcosm. Group members also deal with the very strong feelings of powerlessness they experience in their larger communities and with the feelings of powerlessness because they are not in charge of their own problematic impulses. The force of the language, evidenced by the vulgarity, further expresses their rage and is an outward posturing that defends against inner feelings of inadequacy and vulnerability. The demand on the part of the members for a rule regarding the use of the bathroom is a cry for help to manage the terrors of unleashed feelings. Additionally, it is the healthy part of themselves that pleads for assistance in staying with feelings, "dealing with this shit."

The worker in this vignette faces a number of questions: how can he help the members to consider him as authentic considering the differences between them and him? If they experience him as inauthentic, how will they be able to trust him? How will his handling of the rules of the group help or hinder this process? The beginning issue of the necessity for the group members to believe that the worker will be able to manage the group members' needs, which at times may threaten to overwhelm the members and the worker, is accentuated in this group in which everything is so intense. Like a balloon about to burst, feelings in this group are trapped just below the already-stressed surface. Explosion feels inevitable. How will the worker manage this tension so that nobody is hurt?

This worker's tasks are similar to those for all workers in beginning groups: he must establish himself as leader with authority, compassion, and a quality of nonjudgmental acceptance. What is significant in this group, however, is the special need for conveying these qualities. For people feeling out of control, it is extraordinarily important for the worker to communicate strength and power. Since this worker is not physically imposing, he must gain their respect through other means. Also, for a group in which members have felt themselves stigmatized by social conditions of poverty, racism, and lack of education, the issue of establishing a nonjudgmental atmosphere in the group is essential to its success. The worker must use the group experience to avoid duplicating and reinforcing negative self-images that the group members experience in the larger community.

It seems that the worker in this piece begins the process of developing trust in a positive way. At first, he simply nods permission for a group member to use the bathroom, acknowledging his own authority in granting permission but treating the group member respectfully. Second, he allows the group members to express themselves more fully, comfortably accepting the intensity of affect and language, thereby communicating the message that he will listen and is willing to allow them to have a role in controlling their own meeting. The fact that this young worker is able to listen to the group members and not become ruffled by the intensity of the emotions expressed communicates a quiet strength to which group members respond. Third, he intervenes by saying, "We're all adults," communicating equality and respect for the judgment and autonomy of members, and then, "I assume that you'll only leave if you have to," communicating a more subtle message that the contract calls for leaving "only if you have to."

When Freddie returns from the bathroom, the worker once again establishes the terms of the contract: when there is any issue, it needs to be discussed, and when a member is missing and returns, he needs to be included in what has transpired in his absence, particularly if it pertains to him. By saying, "You started quite a conversation when you left," the worker brings Freddie back into the group. The second part of the worker's statement, "Does anyone want to fill him in on what we were talking about," establishes the responsibility of the group members to communicate specifically what has occurred. Communicating the responsibility of the group members is important because it gives the group to the members, emphasizing that it is their group and not the worker's group, again communicating the worker's comfort in his position of authority—such ease that he does not have to exercise power in a dictatorial fashion. It is impressive that a soft-spoken young man can appear so powerful and as a source of strength for group members who are physically far more imposing than he but psychologically so very fragile.

Although the worker appears to have executed the tasks for confrontation in the beginning group phase effectively, other approaches also might have been used, depending primarily on different styles or personalities of workers. A worker might, for example, use humor to invite discussion: after the bathroom conversation, the worker might remark, "Sounds like our head's been in the toilet," or "This is some deep shit we're into." More nonverbal approaches also are effective sometimes. A raised eyebrow and a cocked head may suggest, "What do you think about that?" or "That's interesting!" enabling the discussion to proceed without interruption. The worker could elect more actively to invite judgment by directly asking the members for their opinions: "Do you all agree with what _____ is saying?" or "What do you think about what's happening here?" This intervention would certainly be an option if this group were more passive or reticent in sharing feelings. Another interventive technique might be to use direct process interpretation. An example of this is for the worker to say: "Here we are meeting in this anger management group for the first time, and we're talking about our inability to control our bathroom habits. I wonder if there is any connection to controlling our anger." Certain risks are inherent in any of these interventive styles. Above all, workers must function in a place that for them is ego-syntonic and maintains their integrity. No one right way to intervene exists, but whatever the approach in confronting difficult material, the goal should be to stimulate process and engage members.

Tips on Confronting

When a worker is debating whether or not to confront a group, it is generally a signal to step back and assess. The worker must examine what he or she is feeling, define what is the dominant issue, and anticipate possible group responses to any proposed intervention. This preparation accomplishes several important tasks. Stepping back gives the worker distance from the relatively strong personal emotions about the current issue in the group, which helps the worker eliminate any countertransferential partiality that he or she may be feeling, and subsequently enables the worker to make an intervention free from contamination. For example, if the group sees the worker as confronting them in order to defend what they see as the "favorite member," the worker's confrontation loses validity and can be countertherapeutic. Confronting with objectivity requires skill. A worker might be angry with the group, disappointed, or feeling as though he or she has failed in his or her work with the group. These feelings, although quite natural for workers to experience, need to be removed, as much as possible, from the confrontations or the group will be unable to trust, perceiving the intervention as serving the worker's needs rather than benefiting the group.

An element of exposure always is attached to confronting, which makes group members feel more vulnerable. Heightened vulnerability will likely demand protective measures from group members in the form of defensive posturing, a natural response to perceived danger. Even when the confrontation is directed at one group member, the others tend also to protect themselves, lest they too find themselves under assault. It is therefore imperative for the worker to make any confrontation as nonthreatening and non-assaultive as possible to ensure that the group as a whole or the individual group member will remain open enough to work with the feedback, be self-reflective, and then return to the work of the group. The confrontative process, even when the confrontation is mild, at first momentarily interrupts the interaction among members, making the individuals move to a self-reflective stance. The worker's responsibility is twofold: first, to allow the self-exploration that necessitates withdrawal and, second, to help the group members reengage with each other.

It is crucial to keep the confrontation simple and to the point. The worker needs to state clearly and succinctly what the issue is without getting lost in examples, specifics, or theories about why the confrontation is happening. The confrontation should be an objective statement that reflects some form of behavior or series of events such as, "It seems that every time someone brings up the issue of loss, the group changes the topic," or "I've noticed that each time Michele describes her mother's worsening health, the group gets very quiet." The confrontation needs to be nonjudgmental and simply reflective: "John, I noticed that each time Sue mentions her father, you seem angry," or "Has anyone else been noticing that several people have been coming to group late almost every week, and we haven't been talking about it?"

Sometimes the worker will be required to confront in a more powerfully direct way. Such situations generally are ones where the group has a strong, aggressive response to one member, or where the group as a whole is actively locked in some form of self-destructive behavior, such as refusing to contain or set limits on acting out, or constantly rejecting new members or members who challenge some powerful group collusion or resistance. The worker's confrontation of the group or group members must always be direct, to the point, not personally invested, nonjudgmental, and clear.

When the group is engaged in an intense exchange, a member with difficulty containing impulses may need to be refocused by the worker if the group is unwilling or unable to do so. The worker may need to confront the behavior directly: "Sarah, I understand this is very difficult, but I need to remind you that you can't threaten anyone physically in group. Please sit down and say what you feel." This direct response to Sarah's behavior accomplishes several tasks at once. First, it allows other group members to feel safer in knowing that physical acting out will not be tolerated. Second, it recognizes Sarah's level of anxiety, validating the intensity of Sarah's feelings. Sarah also, in the long run, will feel safer knowing that when she is out of control, someone will help her to regain control. Other group members will get this message as well and eventually may learn to confront behavior in and out of the group in a manner similar to that of the worker. Third, it redirects the entire group to the terms of the contract; that is, this is a place to *talk* about all feelings, which is how we manage emotions, rather than a place in which we act out feelings. This lesson is helpful within the group and models behavior that hopefully will be helpful in other life situations.

When the group is not working but entrenched in resistance, the worker also may need to confront that resistance: "It seems since Carole left the group three weeks ago, the group has been avoiding dealing with her absence," or "Since last week's difficult session, people have been very quiet." The confrontation can take the form of a question, an observation, or a demand, but it always must be balanced with objectivity and caring.

The purpose of confrontation is to help free the group or an individual member from something that prevents them from moving forward in their lives; it is not to prove that someone is right or that someone else is wrong. If the confrontation is tempered in tone and intensity, presented clearly, directly, and without judgment or interpretation, the worker is inviting the group to sit back and look at itself. In addition, this form of confronting by the worker models for the group members how to confront others and establish healthier relationships both in and out of the group.

Another important element in confronting is timing. As with any intervention, the worker needs to allow sufficient time for processing of feelings, thoughts, and observations. As tempting as it might be to confront the group, a subgroup, or an individual member when, at five minutes before the end of a session, the worker sees the issue clearly, it is best to restrain the urge and wait until the following week. It helps for the worker to remember that the issue will still be there the next week, and the worker will then have the opportunity to explore it. If the confrontation occurs with inadequate time to process it, members are left feeling exposed and vulnerable, without the opportunity for supportive exploration and reality testing, and the following week the group will feel unsafe and likely will be distant.

Workers should observe a note of caution: often when a group is in the throes of a prolonged difficult time, the worker and the group must struggle to tolerate lack of clarity and nonresolution. Often at times like this, a worker begins to see something clearly that demands a confrontation and is tempted to blurt it out and say, "Aha, I have it!" As understandable as is the worker's enthusiasm about the discovery, he or she must exercise restraint to prevent the bluntness from being experienced as assaultive. It is important to remember that although the worker may be processing a thought or intellectual observation mentally, when she delivers it, she is having an impact on another person in an area that is generally sensitive. The last thing a worker wants is to confront in such a way as to cause a psychic tsunami in the group that will take weeks or months to recover from. There is an old saying: "One does not use a hatchet to remove a fly from the forehead of a friend." Everything is in the delivery.

Confrontations in the beginning phase, as noted elsewhere in this text, are generally rare, primarily because the worker is attempting to achieve a safe and stable environment, and effective confrontations require a level of trust. In the middle stage, where trust and safety are secured and where a sufficient degree of cohesiveness has developed, confrontation is a common and necessary mode of intervention. If the group and worker experience little confrontation and conflict, something is wrong and *that* must be confronted. For example, in one group, a worker watched as group members, in the middle phase of their group, avoided any challenges for thirty minutes, accepted rude behavior previously challenged in group, and agreed with each other even when disagreement was obvious. Finally, in a playful way, the worker commented, ". . . what a lovely, polite, and proper group we [have] tonight."

The worker may be frightened that if she or he confronts, she or he will be rejected or will make people angry and the group will self-destruct or fail. Most important, workers need to remember that it is their job to push the group to work and if they do not—if they become invested in maintaining "peace" and avoiding conflict and confrontation—they *ensure* the failure of the group and do a disservice to those who have trusted them to help. The worker in private practice must particularly heed this issue, as the fear of loss of the group can be tied to the loss of income for the worker, which can further prevent the worker from feeling free to challenge and confront the group. Private practice necessitates supervision of some form to ensure worker objectivity that can be easily lost in the isolation of private practice where conferences, presentations, and even informal discussion of one's work are not part of a weekly ritual requirement as they are in agency life.

Avoiding Confrontation

Whether in a private practice or in agency practice, workers often have difficulty maintaining their objectivity. Often in an attempt to avoid confronting painful feelings, people become involved in subtle and elaborate forms of self-deception. Generally the failure of relationships that had sustained the person in the self-deception motivates that person to seek help. The worker's purpose in a group is to create a healthy environment that will not support or foster continued illusions. Workers and members, however, can often unconsciously conspire to deny threatening feelings. This collusion between group members and worker(s) serves to promote the illusion that everything is under control. In particular, in the face of overwhelming traumas, both workers and members may need to create a world (group) with more order and in which there is a more equitable distribution of hardship than exists in reality. If the universe is out of control, at least the group is not, and, for that time shared together, all is safe. However comforting a false sense of order may be, the price for the group's avoidance of real feelings is a failure to meet its goal. The workers' responsibility, however problematic, is to struggle to identify their parts in any attempt by the group to avoid confronting difficult material.

A session from a group for HIV-positive late adolescents and young adults illustrates some issues for workers in the process of confrontation. This group is the intervention component of a longitudinal research study being conducted in major cities across the United States. The intervention consists of three parts (modules), each one consisting of twelve sessions completed over a three-month period with a three-month waiting period between modules. The purpose of the group is to help HIV-positive young people live healthier lives by addressing safer sex practices, drug and alcohol use, and stress reduction. The group has eight members, ages nineteen to twenty-three.

The incident related below occurred in the beginning of the seventh session. During the previous session, members had opened up in what one worker, Keith, described as "an unprecedented manner," talking about the group as a "second family." They had all shared ways in which the group was important to them and articulated a commitment to "be there for each other." At this session, however, there was an unmistakable tension. Three members were absent, and group members were being very short and sarcastic with one another. It became clear that anxiety was felt about the inevitable end of the group. The mention of the word research sparked this discussion:

> *Keith*:   It sounds like people are unclear about how long this group is going for. Should we review how the program works?

(group generally agrees)

> *Keith*:   The group is broken into three modules. We started the first module in February and then finished it in April. Then we had the summer off, and now we're exactly halfway through the second one. In December, we'll finish this module, have three months off, and begin the third module in March.
> *Norma*:   Why does it have to be broken up like that?
> *Ricki (co-facilitator)*:   Because ABC is a research study, the schedule of the group has to coincide with the schedule of the study. That way you can be interviewed between modules. (Participants are interviewed eight times during the course of the study.)
> *Lola*:   But this group isn't research.
> *Ricki*:   No, not really, but it has to fit into the parameters of the study.
> *Katie*:   So it is research.

Joel:	And we're just guinea pigs?
Thomas:	So once ABC is over and you got all the information you need out of us, then you just abandon us? Then you just decide to stop the group?
Norma:	I never thought of this group as research. I thought it was like a place where we could all feel good to come.
Thomas:	I come to this group because it's like a family to me, and suddenly, I'm in a laboratory.
Joel:	It's like everything else—you just take this HIV-positive kid, do something nice for him, and then dump him.
Thomas:	My whole fucking life. Why should this be any different?
Keith:	The word research really seems to have upset people.
Katie:	It's because that's not what this group is. We know ABC is research, but this group is different.
Joel:	It's really hard for me to get to know people, and I feel like I know people in this group, and I can talk. I don't want to go to another group when this is over. Why can't this one keep going?
Thomas:	It's like, why bother to get to know anyone else. They'll just abandon you anyway.
Lola:	Can't you find a way to keep ABC going?

After expressing their anxiety about the time-limited nature of the group, the members began to discuss whether or not they were capable of keeping the group alive after ABC was officially finished. In the discussion that ensued, many questions addressed why Keith and Ricki could not continue to run the group after the third module was completed. The workers encouraged the group to explore why they felt they could not do it on their own. The members facilitated the rest of the discussion with the workers nearly silent throughout. At the end of the session, Keith asked what had just happened. Lola said, "Yeah, we just ran the group."

Self-deception and mutual deception can continue to exist only so long as the deception is not spoken about. In this group, as the worker states in his own words, the "inadvertent" use of the word research sparks this particular confrontation with a painful reality that all, including the workers, are hesitant to address.

It is clear from the worker's comments regarding the session previous to the one excerpted here that the group has been struggling with issues of intimacy and loss, dynamics common to a population living with a life-threatening illness. In that session, members referred to the group as their "second family." The workers' knowledge about this population tells them that often the families of these group members abandon the seriously ill person. The comment about the group as a "second family" signals the group's importance to the members, but may also signal the unconscious fear the members have of again being abandoned by those upon whom they depend.

Even if the workers are unable to pick up on the subtle messages regarding family in the earlier session, the reactions in the current meeting signal even more clearly the members' fears of abandonment, intimacy, and loss—the group reconvenes with some members absent and others, who risk coming, distant in their exchanges. As the workers note, "People were being short and very sarcastic with one another." This description by the workers indicates that they register the contradiction between the intimacy of the last group meeting and the distancing of the current group meeting, yet this contradiction is not consciously identified. The behavior of the group is rather telling, yet neither worker comments on it. The workers' difficulties in identifying the blatant avoidant behavior by the group members (i.e., the absences and the hostility apparent in the members' exchanges) could possibly indicate that both workers were also avoiding confronting those painful issues.

What is important to note here is not so much the workers' missing the opportunity to explore the themes presented early in the group process but rather that the workers were unable to tune into and trust what they were feeling. Not having the benefit of using their psychic radar, the workers were caught off guard by the angry response of group members to the seemingly innocent word "research." It is equally important to note that the group gives the workers many opportunities to understand what is happening, and a skilled worker eventually will be able to hear the group's message and intervene appropriately. Such is the case in this vignette.

In the excerpt, Lola confronts the issue of dehumanization that she feels as a research subject—"But this group isn't research"—and Ricki, the worker, continues to half-heartedly deny, "No, not really, but it has to fit into the parameters of the study." Katie is quick to confront the worker again: "So it *is* research." The group follows Katie's comment with expressions of anger and disbelief, feelings of being deceived and abandoned, and finally an overwhelming sense of impending loss. The workers and the agency are like everyone else in their lives, not to be trusted. Perhaps, they conclude, their instincts were correct—never get close, never let anyone in.

Eventually, the workers are able to help the group members express their rage at the limited control they have not only in the group but in their lives, which leads the members to struggle to persuade the workers to continue the group. Although the members realize in this process that they cannot stop the impending loss of the group, they come to understand that they can still have a significant measure of control in their lives both in and out of the group. The workers help the members feel some sense of control by allowing the initial confrontation, by accepting and validating their feelings, and ultimately, by stepping back and allowing the group members to take control of the interactive process in the group. By having the skill and courage to step back and trust the group, the workers were able to offset the feelings of dehumanization experienced by the group members. However soothing this process might be to the workers and members, the reality of the struggle these members will face remains, and that reality needs to continue to be recognized in the group.

Workers who face these most difficult situations in group must not be too hard on themselves when they need, at times, to avoid their own feelings of helplessness and grief. It is essential for workers to recognize the power of the work they do and to respect the level of demand and difficulty inherent in it. As workers are accepting of the limitations of group members, so too must they be accepting of their own limitations. It is only with an open and accepting heart that the worker can truly engage with the group in a joint attempt to confront the challenges before them both.

Workers' Confrontation with Self

Workers confront extraordinary suffering and a sense of powerlessness in their struggles to meet the needs of various deeply scarred and troubled populations. Thus far, this chapter has discussed techniques for confronting group members around issues of importance, but has not focused on the feelings generated for workers who are in the midst of intense human tragedy. A chapter on confrontation would be lacking if it did not include some discussion about workers, about how hard it is for them to confront such intense need and to feel so limited in being able to help.

The following piece was written by a student worker, Joseph Garrambone, who describes in vivid detail the worker's struggles to prepare for a creative arts group in a clinic serving poor and mentally ill people living in Single Room Occupancy (SRO) housing. What is most striking about this piece is that Garrambone was suffering from his own life-threatening illness at the time of his writing and yet could so sensitively appreciate the needs of others. Garrambone died shortly after completing his placement, but leaves us this legacy. Although everyone can recognize through his writing what an exceptional person Garrambone was, he is by no means unique in the courageous way social workers commit themselves to working with the struggles of the human condition.

O'Malley stood like a sentinel at the top of the stairs leaning on the wall. He looked like an old fisherman, knit hat pulled down above the ears. A scraggly beard covered his face; his pants were too short, hovering above his tired sneakers. He looked tired, too, somewhat dazed. "Good morning, O'Malley. How are you? I want you to meet Joe. He's gonna be working with us till May," chirped the social worker who was showing me around. O'Malley shook my hand lifelessly, mumbling something about, "We need more help." Help; what kind of help was O'Malley talking about?

Conditions in the hotel are deplorable. He didn't look like he got enough to eat. What did my group have to do with this? The dank smell of the SRO hotel had already numbed my sense of smell, but I thought I smelled alcohol on his breath. Would my group address the fact that it was 9:30 a.m., and O'Malley had already begun deadening himself to this world? He barely moved as he spoke. The hotel was dimly lighted, giving it a sense of lifelessness like the look in O'Malley's eyes. He was the first of many I was to meet on our rounds, people living in a world I couldn't comprehend, hesitated to judge. To me they were existing in a place where the operative word was nothing—nothing to hope for, nothing to look forward to, nothing to do . . .

It feels to me like CPR [cardiopulmonary resuscitation]. I'm trying to breathe some life into these people. I agree. I want to do this. So my mind keeps returning to that hotel. What can we give them? Keep it simple; keep it light. They are low-functioning and psychotic. Keep it simple, make it joyous, give them something to brighten their world. When my supervisor initially asked me what kinds of things I had in mind, I said, "Well, I don't want to make moccasins." Seeing their world firsthand, I wished we could make moccasins. At least then, they would have a pair.

I would like to paint the hotel. I would like to clean their rooms, open their windows, literally and figuratively. Can we open the windows? Can we let the light in? Can we infuse life? Can this be the purpose of a group?

We'll bring them to the center. The room is light and airy. I'll fill it with plants and posters and music. I'm desperate: I fear they've stopped breathing. Take a deep breath, Joe. Calm down. I feel such a sense of urgency. Is this about me or them? Can I allow myself to see the squalor, smell it, sit with it?

Tina wears a skirt and blouse, a baseball hat and dark glasses. If I couldn't see the flesh of her legs, I wouldn't be sure there was anyone in there. She sits motionless, reading a magazine, clutching her pocketbook to her. "I'm waiting for coffee," says Jimmy, who looks collapsed into a chair in the "community room" at the SRO. A large coffee urn is grumbling in the corner. There is a pile of sugar packets on a filthy table, no cups, no milk. "I like to work with my hands, yes," says Jimmy in a voice that comes from a body he doesn't seem to inhabit. "I like clay," he says. I don't know how old he or Tina is; age seems irrelevant. I can't tell if Tina is white or fair-black; race seems irrelevant. The "community room" is decorated with enormous paintings—the March Hare scurrying away, the Red Queen. I refuse to look at them all. I fear I'll see the Mad Hatter, and he will mock me. I feel like Alice. At times I feel big, big enough to be of help, then small, ineffectual.

Tina and Jimmy don't relate to each other. Can I get them to relate in the group? Marta enters gushing greetings in Spanish to my colleague. They kiss and hug, a kiss on each cheek. I am introduced. Marta clutches my hand, doesn't let go. "Mucho gusto," I say. This launches her into a barrage of Spanish too fast for me. I think of Jose who may join the group. He speaks Spanish too, but he's deaf.

What have I gotten myself into? Will Marta let go of my hand? Can I get my hand free gracefully?

Okay, breathe. So we have this group, six to ten low-functioning, slightly psychotic, depressed, in some cases, alcoholic clients of varying ages, probably thirty to sixty years old. Anyone from the SROs who are interested can join. Most have some experience with groups, many while institutionalized. "I did that once," says Jeremiah, a black man in his sixties. "I did it at Bronx State." Alma comes to the door; she looks frail and scared. She nods at me shyly when we are introduced. She is looking past me, not at me. She speaks quietly and haltingly. She disappears into a room that looks like the bowels of chaos and despair.

She returns with a little yellow camera which she opens the back of. "I . . . I don't know how to rewind . . . I mean rewind this. I, I uh, want to, I took some pictures . . . want to . . . get them. Can't rewind them." My colleague, "Oh, Alma, you shouldn't have opened the camera—the film wasn't rewound. It may have ruined the pictures." She hands me the camera. It takes me awhile, but I figure out how to close the camera, rewind the film, and slowly and carefully explain to Alma how to do it, praying that if there is a God, she or he intercedes and these pictures aren't ruined. It feels so important. I want her to have them. I want her to have something. I want to be able to give her something. I feel foolish, helpless. I want this group to work. I explain about the group. She seems interested. "But I . . . I, I don't know how to do things. I . . . I . . . it's hard for me."

"That's okay, we'll teach you—we'll learn together how to do things. We'll have fun."

Alma looks frightened. She stands separate from us. She looks as though she is trying to imagine it. "We'll have fun." She repeats it twice. We'll have fun.

10 USING HUMOR IN GROUPS

When old folks laugh, they free the world.
They turn slowly, slyly knowing
the best and worst
of remembering.
Saliva glistens in
the corners of their mouths,
their heads wobble
on brittle necks, but
their laps
are filled with memories.
When old folks laugh, they consider the promise
of dear painless death, and generously
forgive life for happening
to them.

Maya Angelou
"Old Folks Laugh" (1990)[1]

The ability to laugh at oneself in the face of adversity has long served humanity in its fight to sustain psychic balance during times of crisis. It is well known that oppressed peoples have commonly used humor to express their shared understanding of their plight. Humor also is used often as a coping mechanism to deal with emotionally charged issues. One need only view popular television hospital dramas where desperate situations are combined with a large dose of gallows humor. Humor can effectively disarm the entrenched, enable the terrified to confront their fears, ease the vulnerability associated with newness, and minimize events that feel overwhelming. Humor can be an effective mechanism to explore, facilitate, engage, support, challenge, and empower group members. There is also no better antidote for worker burnout, often an occupational hazard, than the ability to laugh at oneself.

The Absurdity of Suffering

In groups, frequently members will tell horrific tales of abuse and degradation as if they were relating a sequence from a television sitcom. For example, in a mixed group of men and women who shared histories of abusive family relationships, a forty-three-year-old Italian man, Joe, was recounting a "funny story" from his childhood about his older brother, Vincent, and their father. Joe reported how Vincent, who as an adolescent had constantly challenged his stern disciplinarian of a father, had again arrived home after curfew one evening. As Vincent quietly entered the back door, which was adjacent to the cellar stairs, his father pulled the door back and punched the startled boy in the face with such force that Vincent fell down the basement stairs and lay still at the bottom. Joe, who was hiding and watching, became terrified and ran down the stairs screaming, "My brother's dead; my brother's dead!" As Joe reached Vincent and leaned over him, crying, Vincent whispered, "Shh, shh. I'm okay, but if he thinks I'm dead, he'll feel guilty and won't hit me again." At this moment in Joe's story, Joe and the other group members were howling with laughter at how "crazy it was growing up," but yet how many "good memories" they had.

We Can Either Laugh or Cry

Humor has a way of cropping up in what may seem to be the most unusual circumstances in groups and can be used by workers as a tool to address some of the most difficult material. The following piece demonstrates how one worker attempts to use humor to help both himself and his terminally ill group members confront their complex feelings about multiple losses associated with their illnesses. The group meets in a hospital. In the author's own words, "nowhere was the indomitability of the human spirit . . . more evident and more humbling than among those who had sustained permanent mental impairment resulting from the neurological damage done by their malignancy or by the surgical procedure to remove it."

The purpose of this group was to help prepare members to leave the hospital and return home. These severely ill people had endured long inpatient stays, often up to eighteen months, filled with painful and difficult procedures, yet they remained terminal and would be discharged home ultimately to return and die. Although the hospital stays were initially alienating, most patients had come to feel safe in the hospital and dependent upon the staff, developing intimate and trusting relationships with them. The group members, and to some degree the worker also, struggled to separate themselves from the familiar safety of the hospital and the group in order to return to a life of which they were once a part but in which they now felt lost. Note the odd juxtaposition of termination from the group, discharge from the hospital, and the ending of life.

The group is composed of seven members, all of whom happen to be Jewish and in their sixties or older. The worker, Max, is also Jewish and in his late fifties. The following excerpt comes from a group session held three meetings prior to the anticipated termination of the group. Mr. Schwartz, a sixty-five-year-old member of the group, who is recovering from the removal of a malignant brain tumor, has returned to the group after a weekend visit to his home. He has a harrowing tale to tell his peers in hopes that they can be of help:

Mr. Schwartz:	I wasn't home two hours before a friend of my wife had the gall and insensitivity to ask if my mental faculties were impaired by my treatments! Was I confused, she wanted to know!
Mrs. Bern:	(a wry chuckle) Oy! So help me, God . . . the same thing happened by me!
Max:	His wife's friend asked you the same questions? (laughter around the room)
Mrs. Cohen:	Uh! He's making with the jokes again. Max's a regular kibitzer. We all know that by now.
Mr. Davidson:	Why not? We could use a little laughter in our lives.
Mrs. Emmet:	It's supposed to be good medicine. Even for cancer. This . . . whatsisname said so. Cousins. Norman Cousins.
Max:	(prompting) You know my philosophy . . .
All:	(in unison) We can either laugh or cry at life. The former is recommended.
Max:	Mr. Schwartz looks as if he's itching to tell us more.
Mr. Schwartz:	And how! The woman didn't stop there . . . you know, with the prying into the condition of my head. She ran down a list of questions. She wonders also if I had radiation and chemo after surgery; did I feel different than before; could she see the scar . . . A regular ghoul, this person. Feh!
Mr. Davidson:	(disgustedly) People are ignorant bastards! If it's to do with the brain—a disease, a growth, whatever—right away they think you're not normal no more.
Mrs. Bern:	(interrupting) Like that Nicholson fella in *Cuckoo's Nest*. Remember that picture? The big shots who ran the asylum wanted him to be nuts, so he was nuts. That's it! Awful!
Max:	And frightening. (to group) What do you suppose Mrs. B. is getting at? What parallel is she drawing with *Cuckoo's Nest?*
Mr. Schwartz:	Being seen as a freak. Or even a mad dog, or something.
Max:	Yes. It's scary when you suddenly find yourself being treated as something to be shunned, or pitied, at best. You feel suddenly alone and defenseless.
Mr. Davidson:	You don't know what fear is until your own family—never mind a stranger—treats you like you're on leave from the booby barracks. A nut house.
Mrs. Bern:	Your own family doesn't know the difference between a cancer hospital and a mental hospital? They should have their heads examined. (laughter throughout the room)

Mrs. Cohen:	(to Max) God willing you'll never have to know what it's like.
Max:	God willing. But don't kid yourself; I know what it's like to have everyone think you're a nut, as mishugah. Only I didn't have the excuse of a brain tumor. (more laughs)
Mrs. Emmet:	What'll we do without you, Mendel (Max's Yiddish name)?
Max:	Without me or without the hospital . . . the doctors and nurses?
Mr. Davidson:	Without you and them. Go out into a world that we no longer belong to? Where we don't fit anymore?
Max:	Do you all still feel that way after what you've been through together in this group?
Mrs. Cohen:	A little. I'm a little apprehensive. I don't have family . . . Maybe I'm better off, after what I've heard here. But even with the training in managing with daily living and all that, it'll be hard. Different. Strange even.
Max:	What about you, Mrs. Frank? What do you have to say about it?
Mrs. Frank:	I was just listening and thinking . . . I'm eighty-three years old, second oldest here, I think. I've been through so many changes in my life—beginning with fleeing from Russia with my parents, from pogroms, the loss of my parents, then husband, my prince, now my health—what's one more change?
Mr. Davidson:	She's right. I changed jobs at least twelve times and wives three times. Isn't that what we're preparing for, another change? So it isn't easy. So what's new?
Max:	Anybody else?
Mr. Schwartz:	It's easy for him to say. He hasn't been through what I've just been through over the weekend. I'm telling you, I couldn't wait to get back here. I felt like a refugee from my own home. I don't look forward to going back there.

When we look closely at this piece of interaction, we can see how it clearly demonstrates the mutuality of the group and the worker. Here the group helps the worker move beyond his fears, and he, in return, is then able to help them come to a better place with their fears and pain. Humor is the vehicle that guides this process.

Max's first humorous comment, "His wife's friend asked you the same question?" follows Mr. Schwartz's painful expression of rage and loss—rage at being viewed as "less than" and loss at being made to feel like an outsider who is no longer part of life. It appears that Max is anxious about feeling and addressing this level of pain and uses his humor to allay his own anxiety, shifting to the joke rather than staying with the deeply troubling emotional content of Mr. Schwartz's remarks. The worker's intervention causes Mr. Schwartz's feelings to be left behind temporarily as the group's focus moves to reassuring Max (and themselves) that he is known, accepted, and needed, "He's making with the jokes again . . . we all know by now. . . We could use a little laughter in our lives . . . it's good medicine." The group members show their acceptance of Max's fear and express their appreciation for him and his ability to make them laugh.

This might act to reaffirm the worker's own life force and purpose, thereby offsetting his own death terror. The worker is then able to move the group back to its work with one last attempt to hold the group (and himself) together, "You know my philosophy . . ." The group's response to Max's intervention (in unison) concretely reassures both him and them that they are indeed whole, not less than, and that they are able to return to work. The worker's next intervention, "Mr. Schwartz looks like he's itching to tell us more," gently reinvites Mr. Schwartz to continue—they are fortified and can deal again with the real issues.

The group returns to its work, again expressing feelings of anger, loss, and fear. The worker is now able to help them to go deeper, touching feelings of isolation and vulnerability: "You feel alone and defenseless." The fear of loss of control, loss of mind, and loss of family support expressed by Mr. Davidson triggers another move by the group and the worker away from the pain, once again using humor as the vehicle: "Your family . . . they should have their heads examined"; and Max: "I know what it's like to have everyone think you're a nut, as *mishugah* [Yiddish for "crazy"]. Only I don't have . . . a brain tumor." Tenderly, Mrs. Emmet calls the worker by his Yiddish name, Mendel, acknowledging that he is one of them, a part of them that they love. He is, perhaps, the part of them that will go on after they have gone, that will remember them. They are all together, safe again for a moment, out of the pain and feeling loved. Max, this time, returns quickly to the theme of loss, moving the focus to the loss of their hospital family. The group courageously continues the journey, accepting the reality of their losses and the new limitations of whatever life they have yet. The hospital, the group, and "Mendel" will be there for them to return to when they can no longer sustain the struggle.

The relief of humor creates a sense of the group's struggle to approach and deal with painful work and its need to pull back and regroup in order to continue. It is as if the group is breathing, in–out, in–out, the living pulse of a group working.

I Am What I Am

As noted earlier, humor can be effective in reaching out to many different populations. A short vignette taken from a first meeting of a group of nine-to thirteen-year-old children of substance abusers, who are being treated in an outpatient mental health facility, illustrates a quite different approach to using humor. As the worker reports, the children are particularly disadvantaged, experiencing both social and economic marginalization. All members have started to manifest relational problems with family members, school personnel, and peers. The worker is a forty-two-year-old Caucasian male. The group members are of various races and ethnicities:

Worker:	Okay, let's get started. Some of you seem to know each other already. Let's all get to know each other by just going around the circle, saying your name, your age, and what school you're from. (to Erika) Will you start?
Erika:	(with firmness and a touch of alarm) No.
Worker:	Oh, okay. (to Reuben, who is on the other side) How about you? (Reuben shakes his head, no.) Okay. Who wants to start? (No one answers, and the worker pauses.)
Alisha:	Not *me*.
Worker:	(Pause) No one wants to start? (still no reply) I guess I'll have to have to start then. I'm Len, and I'm ... (thinking) ... twelve years old. (exclamations from the group) I am twelve. I just started to lose my hair very early ... (the group members laugh), and I'm from Washington School. (turning to Nathaniel who is seated to the worker's right) And you are?
Nathaniel:	I'm, uh, Nathaniel.
Worker:	Good. And you are how old?
Nathaniel:	Thirteen.
Worker:	And you go to what school?
Nathaniel:	Prospect School.
Worker:	Thanks, Nathaniel.
Casita:	I'm Casita, and I'm eleven years old and go to Prospect also.

The use of humor in this excerpt is a technique specifically related to engagement, a task for all groups in beginnings, made particularly problematic by the level of mistrust experienced by these children. They are in a setting totally foreign to them, one that has been assigned to them because of their failures in life, at home, in school, and with peers. They feel no honor in being chosen to participate in this group. The children are ashamed of their own perceived indiscretions and those of their substance-abusing parents; they understand themselves to be unacceptable in some way, as they have been stigmatized by many in authority in all other areas of their experience. At the very least, talking about themselves is scary.

The worker in this piece is sensitive to all of these issues and proceeds with the introductions in the most limited way, asking for nonthreatening concrete facts about the children—their names, ages, and schools—rather than asking invasive questions about home life or feelings. But it is still too frightening for any of these youngsters to be the one to start the responses. The silence is palpable, adding to the level of discomfort. The simple questions feel almost like a cross-examination: the worker acting as prosecutor instead of friendly advocate, the children armed against the expected assault.

The atmosphere is emotionally charged until the worker, as a last resort in reaching out to the children, elects to introduce himself, a balding, forty-two-year-old man, as one of them, a twelve-year-old boy. The absurdity of Len being twelve years old creates a new sort of atmosphere in the circle. The laughter destroys the grim foreboding mood. Perhaps this goofy guy is not so threatening, particularly when he adds the comment about his own vulnerability, his thinning hair: "I am twelve. I just started to lose my hair very early." People with the capacity to make fun of themselves are clearly not as intimidating as those who regard themselves very seriously. Once the laughter has been shared among the group members, the session can continue, and the children are freed up to begin to introduce themselves. Although Nathaniel does so timidly, the others, modeling themselves after Len and Nathaniel, follow suit. The humor breaks the ice, and the children start to become engaged.

The worker could have approached this introductory session in a number of other ways: identifying his own feelings of nervousness or apprehension about being in this situation for the first time and asking whether they too felt uncertain; or using a planned nonverbal activity with drawing or game playing to help the children get to know each other; or helping the children develop guidelines for the group and introducing the children in the course of this process. In this particular case, the humor used by the worker was clearly effective. Again, there is no absolute right way to proceed, but whatever the approach, it must consider, above all, these children's need for protection, trust, and safety.

Getting the Message Through

In the beginning phase of a group's development, a worker has many tasks. As illustrated in the children's group described above, the worker may use humor as a tool in the contracting process. Another task for beginnings is for the worker to model behavior that sets the acceptable norms and establishes a method of working. Humor can be useful in this pursuit as well. In order to foster the norm of self-reflection, for example, the worker might openly comment on her or his own behavior or feelings, thus communicating to the group the message that self-reflection is an acceptable and desirable technique in the group's work. When confronting a group member, the worker needs to model healthy confrontation, demonstrating the values of respect, acceptance, and objectivity that set the standard for the work in which the group will engage.

Every action that workers take models and sends messages to the group. Often, nonverbal expressions of surprise, acknowledgment, and playful questioning are effective ways of modeling the technique of further inquiry.

A simple gesture, rather than a lengthy intellectualized exchange, can add a human element to an otherwise clinically accurate but sterile environment. So, too, during the beginning phase, a worker may use humor as an effective way of relating and working in the group. The worker must be comfortable and appropriate with the use of humor, being cautious not to be sarcastic or to be seen as making fun of the group or its members. Sarcastic humor, with its natural element of hostility, can be more damaging than healing. Feedback that is difficult to hear must be delicately delivered, especially in the beginning phase. Humor often serves as the "spoonful of sugar" that makes the medicine go down.

One example of this use of humor comes from a long-term group for both male and female adults who have issues of depression, poor object relationships, and low self-esteem. As with all of her groups, but particularly with this population, the worker here noted early the need to establish a trusting and caring environment, believing that only in such a supportive and safe environment would these fragile people be able to receive painful but necessary feedback. It is vital to the group's work to expose the dysfunctional aspects of a member's behavior or the parts of the self about which they may have shame. These insights, however, are often experienced as wounds and assaults, unless they are offered within the safe confines of an emotionally accepting environment.

From the beginning phase of this group, the worker used humor to lighten difficult feelings. Using herself as a model, she openly laughed if she made an error in speech, scheduling, or so forth. This behavior illustrated for the group that it was okay to make mistakes, to look foolish, and to be human. It also modeled acceptance of oneself and one's shortcomings. This style was gradually incorporated into the group, and the members established the norm of being able to laugh at themselves and each other when they "slipped up." Over time, nonverbal expressions (a favorite technique of the worker) became accepted ways of challenging (raised eyebrows or furrowed forehead), soliciting more information (beckoning with the finger to indicate "come further"), and supporting (smiling softly). Often the group would joke by inventing hand signals, such as pointing behind someone to indicate that what they were saying was historically based.

Another acceptable style of confrontation involving humor developed as the group grew more trusting. Once a pattern of dysfunctional behavior was identified for a member, it was recognized openly each time that it occurred. This approach of conscious and continued recognition and identification enabled the member to understand his or her role in the problematic interaction. Eventually, if the pattern persisted, members often gave it a name. The purpose of naming this behavior, another technique the worker modeled, was to make the behavior more acceptable, less alien, and therefore less threatening. For example, one member, Charlotte, had a history of severe competitive sibling rivalry with her twin brother. She would repeatedly report angry counterproductive confrontations with men, both at work and in social situations.

Once the group helped her to identify her transferential response to men, everyone began to call it her "Frankie" response (her twin brother's name). The group also began to identify whoever the male was in the altercation as Frankie. Often Charlotte would come into the group in a rage, reporting how her boyfriend, boss, or colleague did something "unfair" or "hostile" to her and how wounded she was by this. When it became clear that her response was related to more than the concrete incident, invariably another group member would say, "Was this guy's name Frankie?" Frequently, the laughter that followed would stop the intensity for a moment, breaking through Charlotte's entrenchment and helping her step outside the event. It was only then that she could see the reenactment of her sibling issue and how it stopped her from relating effectively in the present situation.

In the same group, another female member, Janet, told the group about how furious she became when she felt mistreated at work. Having difficulty expressing her anger directly, Janet generally acted out these feelings in some passive-aggressive way. During the reported incident, Janet went to her desk and logged on to the Internet and spent hours "surfing" rather than working. The group more generally identified this passive-aggressive response as "surfing." Thereafter, whenever Janet reported similar incidents without insight into her behavior, one or more members of the group would make some reference to surfing: "Looks like Janet's going surfing today." This playful way of identifying her acting-out made her more able to take responsibility for the impact she had on others.

Eventually, this humorous style of imparting insight came into the here and now in the group. Janet was angry and out of touch with her feelings in a group session one week. The following week, she came in late, eating an ice cream cone in open defiance of a group rule. The group tried unsuccessfully to explore the actions, meeting with stern denial and resistance. It was only when another member commented that the "surf was high today" that Janet was able to recognize her behavior and laugh at how out of touch she sometimes can be. This allowed for a very caring and honest exchange about how the group had inadvertently hurt her the past week and how she had been unable to express the pain. This prompted other members to share, for the first time, how they each defend against pain and to recount previous episodes in the group that demonstrated these defensive actions.

Laughing through Our Tears

Sometimes the overwhelming feelings of distress at the situations of life simply need to be alleviated by recognizing the absurdity of it all. Sharing these experiences with others who are in a similar place and laughing together with them sometimes make it possible to return to the difficulties with a renewed sense of the ability to cope.

In a discussion among family caregivers, who felt totally burned-out from the emotional and physical strains of looking after their very ill loved ones, the following exchange took place:

Linda: I can't believe it. I had some day yesterday! I went to see my mother at her apartment in Long Beach near the ocean. I've been back and forth there three times in the last week since her most recent surgery. I've rescheduled my work responsibilities each time. I had to go yesterday to pick up my aunt who has been staying with my mom all week since the last operation. My mother's greeting to me was that she had been thinking how nice it would be to just swim out to sea and kill herself instead of going through treatments. Great! When my dad was alive, when he was sick at the end, he also had some thoughts about swimming out there and getting lost.

Anyway, my mother and aunt are like oil and water. The week was a disaster. They're ready to kill each other about half the time, and they really love each other but can't seem to communicate. Well, my aunt gets into the car and gives my husband and me an earful about how difficult the week was and how she felt like swimming out into the ocean and ending it all herself. After she got out of the car, I said to my husband, "What's with that friggin' beach?" (The whole group is roaring with laughter.) Then, I get home and call my mom to let her know we've arrived, and she starts in with a conversation about how she's been thinking about Kevorkian and wondering about the option of assisted suicide. Now she wants another thing of me, to help kill her? (The group is laughing hysterically.)

Worker: Yet another job for Linda! (chuckling)

Joan: I know exactly what she means. It never stops, the demands. Some days I can't even go to the bathroom without some interruption—the nurse calling, the pharmacy showing up, the aide calling in sick when I have to go to work. But I got a real laugh, the tables were turned, when I finally said I was going to focus on me a little and not on all these people who need me for everything. My mother's dying of uterine cancer, and I haven't been to the gynecologist, because I haven't the time or energy or perhaps the inclination, to check on me for nearly two years. I finally make an appointment to see someone new, which makes me crazy and nervous anyway, and the guy comes into the examining room—picture me with my feet in the stirrups—and his fly is wide open. It wasn't anything. He just wasn't aware of it. He's leaning over me and I'm trying my damnedest not to look directly into his pants, but it's pretty difficult to do. (Again the group is laughing uproariously.) Anyhow, it's finally over, and I'm dressed, and he's in the hallway with his back to me, talking to one of his partners who is alerting him about the zipper, and I see him, from the back, trying feverishly to zip himself. It's not working at all. I thought this must be a gynecologist's worst nightmare. The finale was when he showed up to talk with me in the office room wearing one of those long lab coats.

Worker: Those coats cover a multitude of sins. (group laughs) But really, how'd you do with the results?

Joan: I'm okay, thank God, but it really felt good to have this guy in a compromising position. The doctors always seem so superior, especially these guys who've been treating our family through this disaster. I thought maybe he got a little of his own medicine. (more laughter)

Millie: Sweet revenge . . .

Worker: It's seems so hard dealing with these things—the emotional issues in having a really ill loved one, the difficulty even of dealing with the medical community, the ceaseless demands and the lack of time and energy, especially for yourselves. And what about fun?

Vivian: Fun has been basically off the agenda for the last six months since my folks came to live with us so we could take care of them. We don't go out unless the nurse's aide is in the house. We have help but not quite full-time, so even going to the movies according to the film schedule is often impossible. But this Sunday, we really had a terrific outing (said sarcastically). A friend had complimentary field box seats to go to a Mets home game.

Linda: But Sunday, it was pouring.

Vivian: You got it! It was raining off and on all morning, and we kept on calling to find out whether they were canceling. But no, the game was definitely on. We bundled up with our umbrellas, our son, and his friend, and sloshed over to Shea Stadium. The parking was fantastic. No one else had decided to go. These were the best seats in the whole stadium; I had never sat so close. We could see every detail of the three times they took the tarp off the field and then put it back in place. (rueful laughter) We got to spend lots of money at the concession stand, mostly on hot chocolates, because we were all freezing, and we also stood around in a bar with the kids and the rest of the very few baseball fans attending the game. This was the only place we could keep warm.

We were determined to stay and have fun at the game! After two and a half hours, they put us out of our misery and sent us home, also very enjoyable in Sunday rainstorm traffic. We were going to stop at the supermarket and get some real amusement out of the day with food shopping, but from the cold, I had to go to the bathroom so badly, I was going to have a serious flooding problem if we didn't get home directly. Too bad to miss Foodtown. (The group is again laughing so hard, some can hardly catch their breaths.)

Millie: (chuckling) From now on we're going to have to call this story "Vivian's Day Out"!

This group session focuses on the multitude of demands the group members encounter as caregivers to very ill relatives. The humor in their exchange provides relief from the overwhelming burden of caregiving and also allows for catharsis. Through the anecdotes, group members experience support, validation, and mutual aid, enabling them to go forward without being immobilized by the intensity of their suffering. One role of the worker is to validate the use of the humor as an acceptable means to deal with the absurdity of the level of demands on group members that their situations create for them.

The first comment of the worker is delivered with a chuckle: "Yet another job for Linda!" Along with giving permission for laughter and decreasing the sense of guilt these women are experiencing for being unable to meet the demands, this remark acknowledges the absurdity of Linda being asked to perform still another impossible task. Once this validation is accomplished and the group members are freed from the immobilization, the worker attempts to guide the group back to the work of the session. The worker's initial response to Joan's story about the trip to the gynecologist is to join in on the humor of the doctor's situation: "Those lab coats hide a multitude of sins." While this comment seems innocuous enough and in the spirit of the exchange, it also addresses some underlying issues—the anger felt toward medical providers on whom these women are so dependent, the feeling that doctors often are not forthcoming and hide information or feelings from patients and families, and the desire for the women to be in a position of having more control in their situations. The next part of the worker's intervention is to address the real issue of Joan's visit to the doctor, the fact that her mother is dying of uterine cancer and Joan has anxieties about her own health: "But really, how'd you do with the results?" In all of the laughter, Joan needs to feel the concern of others about the results of the examination. Part of the purpose in this group is to help the caregivers focus on some of their own needs while they minister to others.

In her final comment in this excerpt, the worker specifically identifies the issues the members have been addressing in their stories. This process clarifies the issues and puts them in perspective, so that the group members can continue their work. By noting that these are difficult struggles for the group, she normalizes their experience and lends them support. Over all, the session ends with a considerable sense of camaraderie that all of these women will be there for each other as a source of support and sharing. The use of humor has served as a cathartic release that permits the group to move forward in their struggles.

Note

1   From *I Shall Not Be Moved* by Maya Angelou. Copyright © 1990 by Maya Angelou. Reprinted by permission of Random House.

11 DIVERSITY AND THE USE OF SELF

> We need to give each other the space to grow, to be ourselves, to exercise our diversity. We need to give each other space so that we may both give and receive such beautiful things as ideas, openness, dignity, joy, healing and inclusion.
>
> Max de Pree
> *Leadership is an Art* (2004)

Diversity or variation among people in terms of race, age, ethnicity, culture, sexual orientation, gender, socioeconomic class, and a host of other features impacts group functioning in both positive and negative ways. On the one hand, differences among people should be celebrated as a source of enriching insights, each group member bringing a somewhat unique perspective to the group experience based in part on the differences among them. On the other hand, great diversity in a group can be a source of misunderstanding and suspicion with group members unable to overcome their differences sufficiently to come together to work on a common problem and shared goals. Finding that balance that both utilizes those differences to enhance the group's collective common experience and, at the same time, diminishes the sense of separateness, is essential to a successful group. The central question is "Can we be so different from one another and yet able to understand one another, appreciate each other's pain, each other's longing, each other's hopes?"

Group members may have feelings of wariness and uncertainty as they approach those other members who at first seem dissimilar from themselves; they also may have strong responses to workers who, too, feel unfamiliar. In the beginning encounter, members go through a sort of sizing-up period, observing the more blatant characteristics of difference. Are the other group members and the worker old/young, male/female, white/people of color? Is her smile inviting? Does he seem aloof? Shortly after the observations comes a second level, a delicate dance of inquiry in which the questions of identification of others become slightly more intimate: are you from this area too? Have you ever been here before? In a parents' group, the questions may be more pointed: "How old are your kids?" "Do they go to this school?" In a support group for cancer survivors, members may ask, "how long have you been coming here?" or "does someone always come with you?" The purpose of the sizing-up stage (observation and the initial inquiry) is to find basic connection and a comfort zone of commonality.

The second stage, what we refer to as the "testing stage," involves a deeper level of communication. The questions and statements may be more personal. "When did you start drinking or how many years have you been a widow?" The purpose, at this point, is for members to test the waters to see whether it is safe to get closer and to start work on the issues that have brought them together. The questions here relate directly to the group members' common needs.

The third stage, what we call "settling in," involves an increased level of exposure of self and occurs concurrently with the end of the beginnings phase of the group. Diversity may now, ideally, become less intrusive to the bonding process. The focus in this stage is on the common characteristics rather than on the dissimilarities, but the abundance of different perspectives enhances the process. Now, the purpose is to let the deeper work begin.

Group workers may experience uneasiness in working with a population that appears unknown and even intimidating, simply because it is different from them in some odd way. A young worker may struggle to address aged group members, a straight worker may feel uncomfortable working with a group in which the members are gay, and workers, too, face the issues of diversity in a gingerly manner. Their tentativeness parallels that of the group members as they pass through the periods of sizing up, testing, and, finally, settling in to do the group's work. We believe, however, that the worker must take responsibility from the beginning for bridging differences, that differences between workers and group members can be overcome by a worker who nonjudgmentally accepts the group members, who remains open and sensitive to the ways in which they experience life, who respects difference, and who is honest and aware of his or her own issues regarding these differences.

Also, as with all exploration of members' needs, the worker must consider how the particular characteristics of any population have an impact on the participation of members in the group, how people from a culture in which there is a strong tradition of not discussing private matters with others are likely to feel uneasy in sharing in groups, how older women may tend to defer to older men in a group discussion rather than expressing their own thoughts, how latency-age children may be more comfortable in expressing themselves in groups with other youngsters of the same gender. Clearly, factors related to diversity influence group process. Understanding these variables without stereotyping populations is key to the success of the worker in reaching common goals. Lastly, it is important to note that people from several somewhat distinct populations may find themselves in the same group. It is often true that subgroups will form based on common characteristics, complicating the process even more. As we have suggested in every preceding chapter, and particularly in Chapter 3 on latent and manifest content, the task of the worker remains the same, to identify what is happening on the surface and to use this information to reach for deeper levels of meaning underneath with the goal of meaningful discussion and, in turn, achievement of group purpose.

Differences and Sameness: The Use of Self

Throughout this text, we have often referred to ascriptive characteristics of the worker in relation to the group. This section focuses on the issue of the group worker as different from or similar to the group members with regard to race, ethnicity, gender, age, sexual orientation, and presenting problem. Is it more effective for group members to work with someone similar than with a worker who is different from them? This issue comes up repeatedly in planning various groups. Should a group for substance abusers be led by a recovering worker? Should a group for gay men have a gay worker? Should a group of African-American children have an African-American worker? These issues are complicated and go to the gut of who we are and how we identify ourselves.

Nevertheless, we recognize that there may be good reasons for considering the background of the worker in staffing particular groups. Justifications for having workers of similar backgrounds to their clients, in certain groups, include the following.

1. Such workers have greater familiarity with the issues and the ways in which people address them.
2. Such workers may provide positive role modeling that offers alternatives to members for problem solving, positive lifestyle choices, and assistance with identity development.
3. Such workers may provide members with an initial feeling of safety and lessen the threat associated with difference, thereby increasing the sense for members that they are understood.
4. The presence of such workers creates a greater potential for the earlier development of positive transference.

Difficulties with workers who are similar to their clients include the following.

1. It is possible that the worker's overidentification with the client will reduce objectivity, move the process too quickly toward problem resolution, and negate individual differences.
2. Clients may resent the worker for being similar but not being in the same situation.
3. The reduced exposure to difference allows for the maintenance of stereotypic attitudes.
4. Workers may disclose prematurely or inappropriately.
5. Members have difficulty believing that someone like themselves is capable of helping them.

In certain circumstances and in an ideal world, one might recommend a worker similar to his or her clients, but in reality one seldom has all the options one might desire. Young workers most commonly deal with elderly nursing home patients. Caucasian workers most often deal with people of color. Cancer support groups are not necessarily led by workers who have the disease. Workers need to discuss the differences openly and be willing to explore the meaning of those differences for clients. The differences exist whether or not they are addressed. If they are left unexamined, these issues, like many latent themes, are bound to cause difficulties and obstruct the work of the group. When the worker is asked how he or she can understand without having experienced the situation of another person (what it is like to be old or black or ill), he or she must respond to the question honestly. "I don't know what it is like, but perhaps you could tell us what it's like for you. If we can listen to each other, we might understand." As other questions arise naturally in the course of group discussion, workers may focus on the feelings of the group members regarding the worker and the fantasies they may have as to the worker's ability to be helpful. The worker must respond without defensiveness, reassuring the group but not dismissing their concerns.

Are You One of Us?

A complicated situation involving similarities and differences is illustrated in the following excerpt from a group in a unit for people who are multiply disabled within an agency serving persons with physical and emotional disabilities. The clients, who are developmentally disabled, have some physical impairments and secondary psychiatric diagnoses. They are in the third meeting with their worker, Russ, who must use a wheelchair due to cerebral palsy:

Fred:	What are you going to do for me? What will the group do for me?
Russ:	What do you want the group to do for you?
Donald:	Why are you in the wheelchair, Russ?
Mick:	Hey, Russ, how did you get in the wheelchair?
Russ:	Do you want to know how I got in the wheelchair? (Mick nods.)
Lee:	Yeah, tell us about it.
Russ:	Well, when I was born, there was damage to my nervous system that affects the muscles in my arms and legs. I have what they call CP—cerebral palsy. Ever hear of it?
Lee:	Oh, yeah, I know what it is. That's when the muscles don't work right and do what you want. You can't walk or run or play games and you have to be in a wheelchair.
Russ:	Yes, that's right, but there are things that I can do. I can read. I can play some games. I can write a little bit.
Mick:	Can you sing?

Russ:	A little. (Mick begins to sing verses from "Let Me Call You Sweetheart." When he finishes, everyone applauds.) That was good, Mick. You're a good singer.
Lee:	Did you ever see the Jerry Lewis telethon? They get a lot of money for people in wheelchairs. Did you see it? How long is it on?
Russ:	Yes, Lee, I've seen it. It's on for a long time—twenty-one hours.
Mick:	Have you ever seen the whole thing?
Russ:	No, it's too long. I have to go to sleep.
Fred:	Did you ever see it? They get a lot of money for people in wheelchairs.
Russ:	They sure do, but as I told you, I don't have muscular dystrophy. I have cerebral palsy. Muscular dystrophy is different.

The interesting point about this process is the difficulty this group and worker have simultaneously with similarity and difference. Russ is in a wheelchair, stigmatized in many situations by his physical limitations, a young man unable to do many of the things associated with being masculine and youthful. He is supposed to be the helping person in this group but appears to the members to be much like themselves and limited in his capacities. As for most clients, the idealized notion of the helper is one in which the worker is all-powerful, all-knowing, and problem-free. Russ presents a different picture. The questions the group members ask about what Russ is able to do physically and why he is confined to a wheelchair really center on whether he is able to assist them. These underlying questions are typical of those asked by other groups in other contexts as part of the beginning phase. If Russ is limited as they are and still able to help them, this is a source of empowerment for group members.

Russ shares many of his clients' difficulties as a member of an often stigmatized group and by being limited in his physical independence. Yet he is still quite different from the group members. Russ's emotional health, social skills, and intellectual capacity, as well as his role as a helping professional, distinguish him from his clients. Russ struggles with the issue of communicating information on a level suitable to his clients' comprehension. Any worker might have this difficulty because of the concrete nature of the members' communication skills and their limited intellectual abilities. Russ's problem is complicated by the direct way in which the group members confront him and his concern about the appropriate degree of self-disclosure. Russ also experiences the discomfort of having to discuss something personal and hard to explain. In the process record, we see how easily group members open the discussion of Russ's wheelchair and the reasons for his need to use it. Partly because they are similar to Russ, group members enter into this discussion in a natural way. We also suspect that the uninhibited quality in their directness arises from the fact that they are not as heavily defended as other populations might be.

Russ is quite skillfully making information available to the group members so that they can know who he is and what his limitations are (beginning phase issues). He does not over-personalize: "Well, when I was born, there was damage to my nervous system which affects the muscles in my arms and legs. I have what they call CP—cerebral palsy. Ever hear of it?" Rather, he moves the group to a point of engaging them concerning the issues. In a concrete way, he defines what he can offer them: support for Mick ("You're a good singer"), emphasis of what he can do ("read, play some games, and write a little bit"), and a clear comprehensible way of imparting information ("Muscular dystrophy is not cerebral palsy"). Russ might have also addressed the meaning for them of the differences between himself and themselves, what they felt about him, and what conditions were like for them. Last, and probably most importantly, Russ lets the group members know that this is a place to talk about feelings and ideas in an open way, that all issues (including questions about himself) are acceptable. Although Russ does not reach for feelings as much as he might have by asking the members how they felt about having a worker with cerebral palsy or if they were worried about such a worker being able to help them, he creates the sort of atmosphere that leads to more exploration.

Use of Self

Our intention throughout this book is to help workers gain an awareness of the use of self in all groups (but particularly as it pertains here to issues of diversity), which is key to working with transference and countertransference issues and helps to unlock the underlying meanings, themes, concerns, and needs of the group. By use of self, we mean the process by which the worker identifies personal internal responses to the external stimuli created by the group. While tuning in to his or her own feelings, the worker must also pass this subjective emotional content through a cognitive filter composed of knowledge about the population, its needs, and group dynamics in general.

A very different style of handling beginnings is illustrated in the following poignant example. It is taken from the initial session of a mothers' group for Latina prisoners. The group is led by a Latina social worker, in some central ways demographically similar to the group members and in some ways not. She is a newcomer to the agency and the group, who is herself a mother of three children, from four to nineteen years old. The group members are in prison for various crimes ranging from minor offenses to drug trafficking and murder. However, the worker has been instructed not to inquire about the nature of their crimes or sentencing. She has not met with the group members individually prior to this group session. The women have been told about the group by a favorably regarded counselor who has been organizing Latinas in the prison.

Although they attend this group voluntarily, the members know that group participation is regarded as rehabilitative and is noted positively on their prison records. The group is conducted in Spanish. As the members enter the room, the worker introduces herself to each one. The worker reminds the group, particularly a few latecomers who have overslept because the previous evening was "late night," how important it is to be on time for the sessions. She briefly explains that the group is for talking about their "interpersonal relationships" with their children and family and "any problems" encountered with their children with respect to their incarceration.

Evelyn, Nilda, Connie, Ana, and Maria: (almost immediately and nearly in unison) We want to talk about our children who don't really know where we are.

Ana: I am worried about my nine-year-old son, who is having problems.

Worker: Could you go into more detail about the problems?

Ana: My son wants to know when I am coming home from "school" so that I can pick him up like the other mothers do.

Worker: Do any others of you have children who think that you are away at school?

Nilda: My five-year-old daughter also thinks I am away at school. Many times when she speaks with me on the telephone, she asks me if I've done all of my homework, because if I do it, I'll get good marks and be able to come home.

(Several group members express concern over not telling their children the truth.)

Worker: Why don't you tell the truth?

Nilda and Ana: When the children are young, it could harm them to know the truth. (Other members indicate that they are in agreement.)

Connie: I wouldn't tell my three younger children, who are three, nine, and eleven years old, but my older five children, who are eighteen to twenty-seven years old, know. The older ones understand and won't think badly of me.

Worker: Why do you think the children will think badly of you?

Evelyn: You know like it is. TV shows things their way, and kids get their ideas in their heads.

Worker: Could you explain more about these ideas?

(Group is silent.)

Worker: Are you talking about prison life?

Evelyn: Yes, you know how they are always showing people behind bars, and how we are supposed to be like animals.

Worker: Is this the only fear you have in telling the children the truth?

(Group is silent.)

Ana: My son, in a way, knows, because one day when he was leaving he saw a prisoner in handcuffs leaving the building. When I spoke to him on the phone, he asked me if they put handcuffs on me. I didn't know what to tell him, so I changed the conversation.

Worker: I will also be working with some of your children, but I will not tell them anything you don't want me to tell them. It is important for you to be able to tell your children about your being in prison.

Maria: I want to tell my son, but I just don't know how to go about it.

Worker: The purpose of my being here and forming this group is to help you—to help you gain insight into coping with problems that arise between you and your children and family.

Evelyn: Why are you here? Why do you want to help us? Aren't you afraid to come into a prison?

Worker: Why should I be afraid of you? I don't go by the TV and the movies. I'm not going to judge you. You've already been judged and sentenced by the law. My concern is with you as people, as human beings who need my help and hopefully can benefit from my help. Also, with helping your children adjust to and understand their separation from their mothers.

(Group is silent.)

Ana: I'm glad that you care enough to help. Most people don't care about us, and I need a lot of help, especially with my son.

(Group members smile. Another social worker interrupts the group at this point to call the women to "brunch.")

Worker: I just want to remind you to be on time, because we have a set limit on our time together. Also, think about issues relating to yourselves and your children for our next meeting.

What is striking about this piece is the absence of the formal introduction and the immediacy of the entry into group issues. The setting itself is formal, authoritarian, and hierarchical, yet something in this group feels nurturing, friendly, and accepting. Part of the magic here is not readily available to the reader. Although the tone, warmth, and genuineness of the worker, a little older than her clients, are difficult to convey on the written page, certain factors are easier to analyze and many of these relate to the inherent commonalities between worker and group.

The discussion is in Spanish and the worker is herself a Latina, which certainly makes these women feel more comfortable. The worker and clients address each other by their first names, creating less distance between them and stripping away some of the authority issues usually present in this setting. The clients are given some structure to guide the beginning discussion: "We are going to talk about interpersonal relationships with family and children and any problems you have encountered with respect to your incarceration." However, the framework is rather broad and allows clients to respond as they choose, revealing as little or as much as they wish about their personal selves. A recognition of vulnerabilities and an understanding of special exposure issues for these women partially govern the worker's decision to avoid individual introductions and specific questions about the past. It is also likely that some of the worker's initial fears or anxieties about this population are preventing her from being more specific. As time goes on and trust is developed, such discussions will flow naturally.

Throughout this piece, the worker also avoids pursuing "feeling" issues. She asks for "more details," clarification as in "why do you think the children will think badly of you" or more explanations about "ideas," but she never requests the clients' feelings about the material they present. At this point, it seems appropriate to be less intrusive. However, it is also probably true that the group—in the person of Evelyn, who challenges her, "Aren't you afraid to come into the prison?"—has accurately identified the source of the worker's avoidant behavior. The issue is that, on some level, the worker is afraid. Earlier in the discussion, Evelyn is provocative when she mentions that prisoners are shown "behind bars" and "like animals." Although the manifest content concerns the image the children may get of prison life, the latent material is part of a testing pattern by Evelyn. If Evelyn conjures up a picture of wild animals, shackled, shaved, foaming at the mouth (a projection of her own low self-esteem), will the worker be frightened away? Is the worker strong enough to deal with the intensity of their emotions and the degradation of their lives?

The group seems to accurately perceive the worker's initial fears. These fears are evidenced, in part, by her avoidance of feeling content. The worker flees to the safety of the contract in response to Ana's description of her son's concerns and her own fears about addressing these concerns: "My son, in a way, knows, because one day when he was leaving he saw a prisoner in handcuffs leaving the building. When I spoke to him on the phone, he asked me if they put handcuffs on me. I didn't know what to tell him, so I changed the conversation." The worker responds with: "I will also be working with your children . . ." Despite the worker's inability to address the powerful feeling element in this discussion, in some way the group acknowledges her strength in dealing directly with Evelyn about being "afraid." They may not buy her response, but they get the message that she is there to stay.

The worker continually returns to her purpose for being there, reinforcing the terms of the contract, the structure, and her desire to be helpful, "The purpose of my being here and forming this group is to help you—to help you gain insight into coping with problems that arise between you and your children and family." And later, "I just want to remind you to be on time, because we have a set limit on our time together. Also, think about issues relating to yourselves and your children for our next meeting." The message this worker conveys to the group is that even if she is afraid, she will continue to be there for them, to hold the group together, and to confront the issues that frighten both worker and group. The worker has a strong, self-assured quality that makes her seem to have everything in control even if this is not true internally.

The process offers many opportunities for greater discussion of feelings. When Nilda tells the story of her five-year-old daughter, who thinks Nilda is away at school rather than in prison, the worker might have queried, "How does that feel for you?" and followed with a request for other members to share their feelings. The worker does not pursue this course at this point or elsewhere in the excerpt. Some might believe that she should, not necessarily on an in-depth level but surely in an introductory way.

When a worker addresses feelings, the result may be an increased intimacy among group members that creates cohesiveness, a movement toward the real substance of the group, which leads to catharsis and a focus on what will later become the work of the group. Exploration of feelings at the onset of a group establishes the norm that this group is for addressing feeling issues. But when exploration proceeds prematurely, before trust is developed, such questions may result in defensive behaviors that close off communication. In this excerpt, if the worker (very new and somewhat scared herself) had plunged into the feeling area too dramatically, she might have deterred clients from expressing themselves. The environment is one of suspiciousness, forced interaction, and lack of privacy or confidentiality, and both worker and clients feel unsure of themselves in it. Therefore, it is wise for the worker to respect both her own limitations and those of the setting and proceed with a conservative approach.

In summary, this worker utilizes a number of beginning skills. She contracts with the group by helping them establish beginning norms, find a comfortable structure, and identify goals. By sharing concerns, the group is also helped to recognize common needs and to make connections with each other. Although this group gets to some issues, the discussion helps allay anxieties for both the worker and client. However, much of the real content of beginnings-intimacy, trust, testing—remains latent.

Are We Too Diverse To Trust?

The following vignette takes place in a group for transgender, gay, lesbian, and bisexual people in which members are of several different ethnic, class, and racial backgrounds. The group will be meeting to discuss their feelings and concerns about gender. The group meets weekly with the aid of two facilitators, both of whom are Caucasian and identify as heterosexual. The following interaction takes place during the first session where members are speaking about trans-phobia and how it occurs in the job-hunting process.

> *Ava (a white 30-year-old female)*:   Well, I noticed the class differences in the jobs I apply to. I'm originally from the suburbs and there are jobs I'll walk into and it's, well, "ghetto"—there's girls in the back room snapping their fingers (does her imitation using motions and accent) and they're clocking me. I just can't be around that—it's so ghetto, I'm just not like that. Also, if one of them sees I'm trans, it's really over for me.

> *Diego (a black/Latino 27-year-old male)*:   I have something to say (to Ava—I'm actually really offended by what you said. I take offense to the way you are speaking about people of color, and about using the work "ghetto." I don't think it has to do with you identifying as trans, and I don't think what you said had to do with your feelings about trying to find a job. I don't feel comfortable listening to that.

> *Jesus (an African-American 27-year-old bisexual male)*:   I'm confused.

> *Ava (defensively)*:   Well, what would you have liked me to say?

> *Diego*:   I dunno, I guess I would rather that in this group, we just talk about how we feel, but not make comments about other people or other types of people.

> *Connie (a Caucasian 34-year-old co-facilitator)*:   Hmmmm . . . okay, so what you're saying is that the word "ghetto" made you feel uncomfortable?

> *Diego*:   Yeah, and just the way she was talking about the experience—it's like she wasn't talking about herself anymore, but about these people of color.

> *Connie*:   Hmmm . . . I dunno. I guess I just didn't see it that way—I saw it as her way of trying to describe trying to get a job. (She then goes into how she is Caucasian but from the city and how people never expect her to have African-American friends . . . Diego's face is clearly shocked and he seems angry that Connie is "taking sides.")

> *Donna (a Caucasian 26-year-old female student facilitator)*:   Well, I think what's most important here is recognizing that both have differing opinions, neither of which is more valid than the other—and this is actually really helpful because I imagine we will have different opinions on a lot of things brought up in this group, and (to Diego) I really appreciate the fact that you were able to let us know that something

	made you uncomfortable. That is how we will learn from each other.
Connie:	Though at the same time, it is not easy for people to speak up, so we also have to keep that in mind.

As noted previously in the chapter on beginnings, the primary issue in a developing group is the struggle to establish trust. In order for the group to work effectively, there must exist a level of trust that will enable members to confront and explore sensitive issues. The task of trust building is made even more difficult when there is a high level of diversity in group composition. Members and workers often bond more readily when there exists greater homogeneity with regard to such variables as race, ethnicity, class, and gender. However, high levels of homogeneity can also act as a deterrent, particularly in the middle phase of a group, when the group task involves the in-depth exploration and confrontation of often nuanced differences.

In the above example we see multiple differences in the population of the group. The diversity in this group involves race (black, white, and Latino), economic class (middle, working, and lower), and gender identification, (male, female, transgender, gender-nonconforming, and gender-questioning). The commonalities of the members are age, young adulthood, and the degree of conflict all members experience in negotiating their worlds.

When Ava, a Caucasian thirty-year-old transgender woman, verbalizes her fears and discomfort while looking for a job she addresses all the issues of diversity that are present in the group. "I noticed the class differences . . . I'm originally from the suburbs . . . other employees are 'ghetto' . . . If one of them sees I'm trans, it's really over for me." In this statement Ava verbalizes the various levels of difference and mistrust she experiences. On every level—class, race, and gender—she feels unsafe. She is different and frightened. Is this also an expression of how she feels in this very mixed group?

Diego, a black Latino bisexual male, confronts her stereotyping "people of color." He denies her concerns regarding her being transgender. Jesus, a gay Puerto Rican male, expresses the confusion of the entire group. Things are mixed up—literally and figuratively. What is everyone really talking about?

The group's discussion is on the "concrete" differences among members. The focus on race, class, ethnicity, and gender becomes a vehicle for the group members to proclaim their lack of safety, their feelings of mistrust, and their feelings of vulnerability in this new and unknown environment. The level of diversity allows the group members to play out the fears that are present in the beginning stage of all groups. The challenge for the worker is to acknowledge the differences, validate the trepidation, and support the expression of all concerns without becoming overly involved in specifics, all the while building the contract and providing structure and safety. It is a difficult task to balance these powerful group dynamics.

We see in Connie's response to Diego her struggle with separating her own feelings about race and class from what is happening within the group. Rather than validating Diego's expression of discomfort with Ava's remarks, Connie permits her own identification with Ava's issues to prevail: I just didn't see it that way ... A more effective response would be, "It seems that these are sensitive topics and the challenge for us will be to express honestly our fears, while understanding the impact of our comments on others inside and outside of the group. So, Diego, it sounds like you're pointing out the essence of the difficulty that we are trying to address in this group, that we are all different, come from different places and are all trying to negotiate with a world which sees us as different from them."

Conclusion

This chapter has dealt with the significance of diversity in group process. In some groups, the members have various ascriptive characteristics which are different from each other. In some groups, it is the worker who appears quite dissimilar in background from the members. In other groups, the similarities between members and workers aid in the ability of the group to develop trust and connection rapidly but can hinder deeper exploration.

As noted previously in this chapter, issues related to diversity are most pronounced in the early stages of group development. In the beginning phase of a group there is little trust, negligible commonality, and significant unknown factors. In addition to multiple issues of vulnerability in new situations, there is the added dynamic of being with others who are different. The diverse composition of group members magnifies the trust issue and challenges the group's ability to become cohesive. Subgrouping as a defensive protective measure may develop and further hinder the bonding process. When feeling threatened or vulnerable, humans tend to stay with that which is familiar to them.

In order for the group to move forward, early trust and safety issues must be sufficiently resolved. When there is enough safety established the group can begin to explore the depth of their purpose together. As the safety develops the power of diversity diminishes. Common ground among members develops and the differences fade. In all human interaction, when something threatens, when conflict arises, or when challenges are mounted, fear surfaces again and the instinctive response is to withdraw to a safer place in order to reduce stress and increase survival potential. Regression to earlier behavior and thinking can occur in order to protect the individual by creating a familiar "safe place," which does not include people of different backgrounds. Regression in a group that is dealing with the middle phase issues of confrontation and conflict or with the termination phase issues of loss and separation will also often take the form of subgrouping alliances re-forming or old stereotypes returning.

Whatever the case, whether in beginning, middle, or termination phases, the worker's responsibility is to respect the differences and to support building on the commonalities that move the group to its shared goals.

12 SPECIAL PRACTICE ISSUES

I want, by understanding myself, to understand others. I want to be all
that I am capable of becoming . . . This all sounds so strenuous and serious.
But now that I have wrestled with it, it's no longer so. I feel happy—deep
down. All is well.

Katherine Mansfield
Journal (1922)

We have discussed concepts that generally apply to most groups. This chapter
focuses on issues that apply more particularly to situations that warrant special
consideration. The discussion is admittedly a potpourri that centers on ways
to modify the use of self to meet the challenges of distinctive group structures,
transferential elements in groups, work with other professionals in groups, and
difficulties presented by individual clients as they interact with other group
members.

Special Structures

Many groups do not have stable predictable memberships and do not meet on
an ongoing long-term basis that might allow for the development of
relationships among members and between members and the worker. Some
groups are open-ended; that is, members can join at any point in the life of
the group and may terminate at any point. Such a group may be available to
any clients of the agency, as in a parenting group for all parents whose children
attend a particular school. Or it may be restricted only to clients meeting
certain criteria, as in a discharge planning group on a psychiatric inpatient unit
for patients who are within a few weeks of leaving. Other groups may be open
to registration for a limited period. In some groups for battered women, for
example, the worker permits new members to join for a three-week period
at the beginning of a fifteen-week cycle, closes the group to new members for
the next twelve weeks, and reopens the group at the end of the fifteen weeks.
Because the discussions in such a group are extremely intimate, comings and
goings of members after the third week may disrupt the process of creating
trust. The open period at the end of the cycle allows new members to be
integrated once other group members feel more secure.

In certain settings, most commonly hospitals, participants in a group may meet with the group only once during their hospital stays. These single-session groups possess distinctive structures and present unique problems that require the worker's use of particular techniques. In short-term (particularly single-session) groups, the structural requirements demand the worker's more active, directive, and focused leadership. Open-ended groups may either continuously and randomly change membership or have planned introduction and termination of members. The worker must help these groups to have a sense of continuity. In a heart surgery group, for instance, the patients may vary from week to week. The worker will introduce the purposes of the group at each session, define the group structure, provide information, and limit the group to its immediate focus while allowing for a future focus on further group participation for patients who may need to talk more. Because no member returns, the worker, in effect, carries the group norms. If some members have attended a session before, the worker will engage these people in transmitting the norms and relating to the previous meetings. In open-ended groups with a planned introduction of new members—for example, some substance-abuse groups—the worker will prepare the group and the newcomer for entry. In this case, the group transmits the norms while the worker's role is more active in facilitating the discussion of feelings.

The lack of predictability and the erratic nature of the discussions—sometimes focused, sometimes intimate, sometimes disjointed, sometimes distant—in groups that totally change from week to week can be unnerving for the worker. One session may have nearly perfect chemistry while the next may seem totally without merit. What makes these groups so difficult for the worker is that, unlike groups with a consistent membership core, the former have no possibility for retrieval or repair. Particularly for novice workers, work with these sorts of groups seems to be an awesome responsibility.

It is helpful for a worker in a changing group to think about the group in a somewhat different fashion from a more traditional long-term group. By visualizing each meeting as a total group experience, moving from beginning engagement issues to problem-solving middle issues and finally to future-directed ending issues, the worker can maintain his or her focus. It is essential that he or she has clear, well-defined, achievable goals for each session.

The worker also must master a new sense of timing, not staying too long on any one phase but encouraging the entire sequence to be realized. The primary problem regarding timing that sometimes trips up inexperienced workers is that, in their desire to fully engage clients and develop trust, they spend too much time in beginnings. In reality, clients will become engaged in the session with less effort on the worker's part by simply moving into the work and sensing the worker's command of the situation. That sense of command makes members feel at ease and trusting.

Also, in single-session groups, most members enter with fairly clear expectations ("I am here to talk about my operation . . ."). They have come to the group with specific objectives. The skilled worker knows and understands those objectives as an expression of need on two levels: first, the concrete needs; and second, the need for validation, support, mutuality, and catharsis. The greatest asset the worker brings to the session is his or her thorough preparation regarding the population and its needs.

Another special group structure requiring a particular approach is seen in milieu therapy. The setting may be a day treatment program, a residence, or a school. Every aspect of the clients' activities while at the agency is geared to treatment goals. One such setting is a therapeutic nursery for developmentally delayed children who are thought to be at risk for abuse. Mothers will be helped to master parenting skills, and their preschoolers will participate in an educational program. Both will spend weekdays at the nursery. As part of the plan, the mothers will work alongside the teachers and the social workers in the children's classrooms. They will be taught to prepare nutritious lunch meals for their families, working closely with the professional staff in the kitchen, and will share many informal moments with workers during coffee breaks and similar encounters throughout the day. The mothers also will have formal meetings with a worker both individually and in group. Any interactions between workers and parents, parents and other parents, parents and children, workers and children, and children and other children are open to examination as part of the therapeutic process. Both the formal and informal exchanges provide opportunities for learning and growth.

The primary challenge for the worker is to maintain a balance between using himself or herself less formally and remaining a therapeutic agent. Although the entire setting is therapeutic, the formal, small-group, parent meetings are in some ways different from the other programs. In these groups, the primary task is to explore behavior and its origins in depth. During the rest of the day's activities, conflicts may arise and also will be examined but with more of a problem-solving or educative focus and less discussion of etiology. Once the problem is solved or the behavior identified, the clients will return to their tasks.

Certain environmental manipulation can be used to draw distinctions between the formal and informal. By setting aside a space and an arrangement of chairs and tables in an area reserved for the formal meetings, the worker can establish a separation from other client activities. When conducting the group, the worker may set some limits not ordinarily required in the rest of the program (for instance, no eating or drinking during sessions). Discussions arising in the course of the day that are appropriate to the group meetings should be identified as such: "That sounds like something you might want to discuss with the group later . . ." This intervention is useful as part of establishing the contract for the group, setting limits, and helping clients to prioritize. It establishes some of the differences between the more and less formal aspects of the treatment. The worker may refer to comments made earlier in the day (provided that these comments were not made to the worker in confidence) and elicit responses during the group. By listening to the informal communications throughout the day, the worker can prepare for the emergence of critical themes in the group meeting. Important issues will reveal themselves many times in a variety of veiled and open communications.

Co-therapy

In many agencies, co-therapy is the usual method of choice. Successful co-therapy, which can be a wonderful experience for workers and clients alike, includes many of the following elements:

1. workers modeling expression of feelings and problem solving;
2. workers contributing different perspectives;
3. workers modeling healthy conflict resolution;
4. workers providing the group a greater range of transferential material;
5. co-workers of opposite sexes demonstrating mutual respect and an equal distribution of power;
6. workers more effectively controlling potentially explosive situations and recognizing individual need (in large groups or in work with difficult populations);
7. workers providing continuity for the group in the event of one of the worker's absence or agency crisis situations that force a worker to leave the session;
8. workers providing each other with support when working with emotionally charged material;
9. more experienced workers offering training to less experienced workers;
10. workers providing a check and balance for each other;
11. workers providing stimulation and challenge to each other.

Despite the abundance of literature concerning co-therapy, certain problematic issues remain for which few solutions have been offered. These include difficulties with status differences between the workers, inability to resolve personality and stylistic differences, some workers' use of the group as an arena in which to express interpersonal issues, the failure of communication between the workers, difficulties with role definitions for workers, workers involving themselves with subgroups and alliances with clients, unproductive competition between workers, and problems between professionals with different training.

The decision to use co-therapy has been discussed in Chapter 7. Much of the decision relates to agency imperatives and population needs. Ideally, once these factors have been considered and co-therapy has been elected as appropriate for the group, the worker can embark on the proper choice of a partner. Selecting the appropriate co-worker should include finding someone with shared values, someone willing to set aside time for planning and processing meetings, and someone open to the examination of his or her work. Similar styles of training are not necessary, provided both share a commitment to working through differences. An intangible element of choosing a co-worker is that both persons feel positive about each other. To assess the compatibility of their potential relationship, workers must have an opportunity to meet and become familiar with each other beforehand.

The selection process described above occurs only in ideal situations; in most circumstances, selection of a partner occurs without worker input. It becomes necessary to find ways to work out differences. Regardless of the degree of input in choosing a partner, each worker has control over his or her own participation in the co-therapy process. They each must take responsibility for confronting problematic issues between workers, seeking alternate solutions, and making time to review and demanding that co-workers make time as well. Additionally, each co-worker must take responsibility for holding to the focus of discussion in examination of the process.

To maximize the effectiveness of working together, both workers need to agree to a few ground rules. Meeting prior to the group session and setting up goals and strategies are essential. This discussion should include a review of the previous session to determine where the group was when it last met and to tune in to unresolved themes that may reappear in future meetings. At this conference, the workers may also discuss ways to reach out to certain group members, focus on particular problem areas or sources of conflict, and deal with clients who may be out of control or in need of special attention. The pre-session conference should review the processing of the past session. After each session, it is helpful for the co-workers to review the events of the session. By examining the process of group interaction and analyzing themes together, the workers can come to some understanding of what has taken place and what interventions should be planned for the future. In addition, workers should use this time to explore their relationship and its meaning to the group experience. By investigating and identifying their feelings regarding each other during the session, workers can discover the parallel processes in the group and note obstacles to working effectively. All of this discussion assists in assessment of whether the goals of the session have been met. The use of the documenting tool suggested in Chapter 3 may give co-workers a quick means of understanding the session and force a certain degree of cooperation. Meetings before or after group sessions need not take inordinate amounts of time provided that both workers keep to the focus.

Another means of helping co-workers work with their group is for a third party to supervise the co-workers together. The right supervisor often can see something that the workers miss and provide a safe atmosphere in which to air differences and test reality. Third-party supervision is most effective when workers are of equal status and of similar training; otherwise, turf issues tend to interfere. When co-workers have different status or training, supervision may be conducted by a more senior clinical person and done in groups for co-worker training.

A Cooperative Effort

We have chosen a few examples of the successful and unsuccessful use of co-therapy. The first excerpt illustrates co-therapy in a job-training group for late adolescents. The director of the program, Rachel, is leaving the agency. The workers, Orlando and Norma, work cooperatively to help the group identify their feelings about the termination:

Orlando:	Alma, Rachel has agreed to adjust your schedule so you can get to work by 9:30. (At the mention of Rachel's name, Carla starts to make a clicking noise that usually indicates annoyance.)
Norma:	(to Carla) Can you put words to that sound you just made when Orlando was talking?
Carla:	(lowering her head and responding adamantly) No!
Tírese:	Carla is pissed off because Rachel told us that soon we have to start group meetings with Larry and Kevin so that they can learn about the program for when she's not here.
Orlando:	It sounds like it's difficult for you guys to hear about Rachel's departure. (A brief silence follows, accompanied by lowering and nodding of heads.)
Norma:	(breaking the silence after a few moments) Not only do you have to deal with saying good-bye to Rachel but also accepting these new people in her place.
Raymond:	That guy, Larry, man . . . I don't know about him. I went to him for a job, and he never came through for me.
Tírese :	And Kevin, he's dingy; he always be laughin' at nothin' funny!
Norma:	(as other group members offer agreement with Tírese) It sounds to me like you guys are saying these new guys won't be able to take Rachel's place. What made Rachel's work with you so special?
Raymond:	Things just going to be out of control with Larry here.
Tírese:	Yup!
Orlando:	So when Norma asked you what made Rachel's work with you so special, you're saying it was that she helped keep things in control?

Orlando and Norma are able to bounce off each other, picking up and exploring issues each has raised. Norma initially recognizes Carla's nonverbal communication and its relation to Orlando's mention of Rachel in his interaction with Alma: "Can you put words to that sound you just made when Orlando was talking?" Norma's intervention leads the group to the identification of the problem, which Orlando attempts to explore further with a follow-up comment: "It sounds like it's difficult for you guys to hear about

Rachel's departure." When the group fails to respond to Orlando, Norma takes the issue one step further by breaking down the problem into its parts. Perhaps the issue relates also to getting used to "new people." Together, Orlando and Norma have opened up communication, and the group members have begun to address their feelings. In the final lines of the vignette, Orlando clarifies, connecting the group members' responses with Norma's question. Throughout, Orlando and Norma are a team.

The next piece stands in contrast to the preceding piece, the workers being very much in sync with each other regarding the goals, purposes, and structure of the group. A community center children's cartooning class, co-led by an art teacher and a social worker, shows workers at odds with each other and unable to resolve their differences. The art teacher, Sandy, is fixed on her goal of teaching cartooning skills to the children. Meanwhile the cartooning is secondary for the social worker, Nancy, who is most interested in helping the youngsters develop socialization skills. One must remember that in task-oriented groups, the function is twofold: to accomplish specific tasks (in this case, learning cartooning) and to be ego-enhancing (in this case, developing socialization skills and a sense of mastery). This group is defined by the agency as a cartooning class, and the teacher is a permanent staff member who has been with the agency for a number of years, while the social worker is a newcomer and considerably younger than the teacher. Therefore, a given relationship places the teacher in a higher status position:

(Sandy draws a cartoon of Donald Duck on the blackboard, and six children begin to copy the cartoon.)

Sandy:	Okay, is everybody clear on how to do Donald?
Joanie:	I'm not doing that. It's too hard. Can I do something else?
Heather:	This is boring. Do I have to do this?
Nancy:	Now, people, you know that rule number one here is that everybody has fun. If you aren't having fun drawing Donald, then it's okay to draw something else as long as you don't disturb anyone who wants to do the project.
Heather:	Okay, I'm going to draw a big castle and put my mommy and my daddy right in this window.
Joanie:	I'm doing a castle, too, with this big door, and here's a butterfly over here and a big mountain . . .
Sandy:	Girls, what's this? Why aren't you drawing Donald?
Joanie:	'Cuz we don't want to. We're doing this castle with . . .
Sandy:	Well, you have to do Donald, or else just give me your pencil, and just put your head down on the table for the rest of class. I can't have you doing what the class isn't doing.
Heather:	Why not? It's boring. I don't want to.
Sandy:	Now that's enough. Give me your pencil right now and you just sit there. This is a cartooning class, and everybody has to learn cartooning. I never heard such nonsense.

Nancy:	Girls, do you think you could . . .
Joanie:	I'm not giving her my pencil. It's mine!
Sandy:	Now give it to me, Joanie. Come on now. Give it to me right now! (Joanie hangs on to the pencil. Sandy grabs it, and the two engage in a tug-of-war for it. Heather, who has given up her pencil, puts her thumb in her mouth and her head down on the table and begins to cry.)
Joanie:	How come we could draw what we wanted before and now we can't?
Nancy:	So many people haven't been doing the lesson that Sandy's feelings are probably hurt. (The girls appear to accept this explanation. Heather does not participate in the drawing for the rest of the class, but Joanie resumes work on the project after a while.)

The excerpt clearly depicts a problematic relationship between the two workers. As stated in our introduction, the workers have different goals for the group; they play out a power struggle that reflects these differences and places the youngsters in the middle of the battle. Had the workers agreed to a planning session in which workers' roles, group purpose, and contract had been defined, no doubt they would have had fewer difficulties. Since this did not occur, the differences were acted out, and the group suffered.

As the problems arose during the session, the workers still had the opportunity to resolve the issues without sacrificing the group experience for the members. In fact, the workers could have used the opportunity to demonstrate problem-solving skills. Neither Nancy nor Sandy seems ready to encourage the children to learn problem solving. We believe that responsibility for working out the differences rested first with Nancy, the social worker. Nancy's first intervention supports drawing something other than the cartoon, provided that the youngsters do not disturb each other. However, this rule does not seem to have been agreed upon by the children and Sandy. This immediately undermines Sandy's position and sets the scene for the ensuing conflict. Sandy is concerned about upholding what she understands to be the rule (that all children must be working on the same project), but part of the anger she expresses toward the children is really a reaction to Nancy's overriding her. Both Nancy and Sandy are invested in maintaining power, and both rob the children of those things for which the group was intended. Nancy sets up the children for punishment by encouraging them to break the rules, and Sandy insists, without any compromise, that everyone conform. They make it impossible for anyone to win.

When the problem first arose with Heather's expression of boredom, Nancy might have said, "What seems so boring to you?" thereby exploring Heather's feelings. She then might have opened it up to the group as a whole, "What do others think?" Finally, she might have said, "Sandy, the group seems to have mixed feelings about the project. How might we work this out?"

engaging the co-worker in problem solving and modeling a cooperative way of settling differences. By involving them in the process, the worker empowers the children so that asserting themselves in an oppositional way becomes less necessary. Clearly many ways exist to accommodate Sandy's desire to have all the children work on a single project and Nancy's desire to give them more freedom. Perhaps it would have been more acceptable to the children to learn to cartoon Donald if they had been given a choice of two or more characters or if they had been allowed to place the Donald character in a scene of their choice. The workers' relationship, rather than the issue of drawing Donald or not, was the source of the problem. Improving that relationship must be the source of the solution.

Parallel Process

Often the difficulties between co-workers manifest themselves through parallel processes within the group. When misunderstandings between workers are not confronted either in a private meeting or in the group session, members are likely to sense the difficulty. The workers unintentionally encourage covert communication rather than open exchange by modeling covert behavior for clients.

A case in point involves a new social worker, Bonnie, and a seasoned worker, Sara. They are co-leading a women's support group in a mental health clinic. Sara has been with the group for several years and is also treating several of the members individually. As time has passed, Sara's responsibilities in the agency have increased, and as Bonnie has observed, her interest in work with the group has declined. Sara is often late for the group, engages in personal telephone conversations in the group room after some members have already gathered, and comes and goes while the group is in session to attend to other agency business. She tells Bonnie that she has little time for discussing or reviewing the sessions and praises Bonnie for her intelligence, excellent approach to the group, and general ability. Although Bonnie has many questions about Sara's handling of certain situations and although Bonnie is furious about Sara's lateness, telephoning, and disruptive comings and goings during the group, Bonnie is fond of Sara on a personal level. Sara's laudatory appraisal of Bonnie's work and the warmth she displays toward Bonnie interfere with Bonnie's ability to challenge Sara about her behavior.

Circumstances become further complicated when group members start to respond nonverbally to Sara's lack of availability in the group. They chuckle when she seems to be getting up for the third or fourth time to leave the group. Bonnie has difficulty addressing the source of the laughter and pretends that nothing is really occurring. During a meeting in which Sara has left the room several times, one group member, Paula, begins to tell a particularly sad story about how hard things have become for her at home. The core of the tearful account centers on the fact that Paula's important relationships are undependable, that people are constantly coming into and going out of her life, and that those who remain do not defend her. The story bears an almost uncanny resemblance to what seems to be happening to Paula in the group. Sara, who had been Paula's long-term worker, is coming and going, and Bonnie is failing to defend the rights of the group members to consistently available attention.

The group members rally around Paula. Bonnie, who knows that Sara has said that she does not have time to see Paula individually, volunteers to treat Paula herself. By volunteering without consulting Sara, Bonnie expresses her anger at Sara and plays out the competitive feelings about who is the better worker: she demonstrates her genuine interest in Paula and her problems. It is even unclear whether individual sessions are an appropriate treatment plan for Paula, but the offer of individual treatment has less to do with Paula than with the relationship between Sara and Bonnie. Talking about the issues between them and addressing the needs of the group certainly would be more productive. The two workers have sufficient rapport to work together effectively if they can overcome the hurdle to communication. Also, the group session can be used to address the latent content. Bonnie could reach out to the members and explore the meaning of the laughter when Sara leaves the session or help Paula express more directly to Sara the feelings of abandonment, loss, and sadness related to Sara's coming and going.

Working out Irreconcilable Differences

In certain groups, the differences between co-workers are of a profound nature and concern fundamental value issues that are not easy to discuss. The following process excerpt is from a mental health clinic group for violent adolescent boys who have had truancy and criminal records. The co-workers are Matt, who has been working with the boys for a little over a year, and Tim, who has been with the group for approximately two months.

John: (loudly bragging) Hey, I had a great week! For Halloween weekend, we went over to this synagogue, and we caused so much trouble that some of their patrol guys held me for a while to scare us off. It was fucking fantastic! We threw whole egg cartons at the Jews as they were comin' out of the synagogue! We got them so bad, the rabbi chased us down the street screamin'!

Danny: That's great! I wish I could've seen it. (Drew is smoking constantly throughout, flicking lit matches onto the table; Rick looks sullen and withdrawn; and Victor seems nervously silent. John's voice becomes louder and his manner more menacing as he relates his story.)

Tim: What do you guys think about what John is saying? People in this room seem angry about things. What's going on with the matches, Drew?

Matt:	(encouraging the boisterousness and laughing with the boys) So tell us more about it, John . . . (By this time, the group is so noisy that it is difficult to hear what is being said.)
John:	I'm going to get even with those guys for holding me in their car. We'll bomb one of their synagogues or just mess it up real bad.
Tim:	Victor, what do you think about John's plans to bomb synagogues?
Victor:	Oh, not much, to tell you the truth.
John:	(angrily) Hey, what's your problem, Tim? You like Jews or what? (howling) Hey, Rick, why you sitting there like a big baby sulking? Oh, I know, you're not getting any! (The boys all start laughing, and Danny jumps up onto the table. Tim tries to get Danny to sit down, but Danny remains in place. Matt is laughing too.)
Tim:	I guess talking about sex makes this group pretty noisy and wild. Maybe we could calm down so that we could really listen to each other.

(The group members, still very chaotic and loud, start in on a lengthy discussion of the vilification of women, of their pride in violent assaults on women. They describe their sexual conquests in lurid detail, gleefully recalling incidents of rape.)

Matt:	Is rape appropriate behavior?
Tim:	Would it be okay for someone to rape your mothers or your sisters?
John and Danny:	No way, but these women are okay 'cause they're niggers, spics, and kikes.
Matt:	Tim has a point. What is he trying to get you guys to see?
John:	Tim, I bet you have something to say about fags, too.
Danny:	(challenge) Yeah!
John:	You guys know how you get AIDS? I'll tell you. Just touch a fag or let him screw you up your ass, and you've got AIDS. All fags should die!
Danny:	(shouting) Yeah! They brought AIDS to America, and they should die now!
Tim:	Hey, wait you guys. You've got some wrong information about AIDS and about gay men. You catch AIDS by having sex with someone—anyone—who is infected, or by sharing needles with someone who is infected. Anyone can get AIDS. When you guys use needles together, you're at risk. Being homophobic, anti-Semitic, or racist is contemptible. It makes life unlivable for all of us.
John:	Tim, are you a fag?
Tim:	John, what would it mean to you if I were gay?

John:	Jesus, if you are gay, I'd fuckin' . . . I'd get the hell out of here. You've touched me before. You might have given me AIDS!! (He jumps up from his chair, and the other group members start to jump up and yell at each other.)
Matt:	Now guys, come on.
John:	Look, Tim, just say what you are!
Tim:	What I am is evident to all of you, John. I'm the guy you've talked to and shared stuff with for the last couple of months now.
Danny:	God damn it, Tim, are you straight or are you gay?
Tim:	What if I were straight, Danny? What would that mean to you? Stop screaming and answer my question, Danny.
Danny:	If you're straight, then you'd be okay. If you're a faggot, then you'll give us all AIDS!!!
Tim:	Didn't you listen to me earlier when I talked about how people get AIDS?
John:	(screaming) You are a faggot! (Matt is quiet throughout this exchange. He has mentioned his wife on many occasions and is now displaying his wedding band to remind the group of his sexual orientation. The boys are very wild. Everyone seems to be standing, scrambling over the tables and away from Tim. The noise is oppressive.)
Danny:	Just say you're straight, damn it, Tim, and this'll stop.
Tim:	No, Danny, you have to accept me without knowing any more. What have I been to you in these meetings? Let's talk about that, not some boring fantasy about my private life, which, I can promise you, will remain private.

The discussion continues for about forty minutes longer with the boys taunting Tim throughout by yelling each time they brush against him that they are going to get AIDS from the "faggot." A game of Ping-Pong in which Rick is teamed with Tim results in Rick's receiving similar treatment from John and Danny. Matt makes no attempt to intervene but, just as the group is ending, comments offhandedly that Tim has been trying to teach them about prejudice and that they have all flunked the test.

In a meeting between Matt and Tim afterward, Matt chastises Tim for not having asserted that he was "straight." Matt says that the boys are at a time of troubled sexual identity, they need strong male models, and the abuse directed at Tim was well deserved since he was responsible for stirring "instinctual conflicts." Tim, who is a gay man, is infuriated at being asked to "betray his identity" and say that he is straight in order to kowtow to what he sees as blind prejudice and hate. Would Matt respond to questions about private matters regarding himself and his wife, or would he ask the group why these questions were important to them? Tim wants desperately to help the boys with their issues but also to remain true to himself.

Tim also recognizes that Matt has widely advertised his heterosexual orientation and believes that Matt's lack of intervention is indicative of Matt's own homophobic feelings. He believes that his right to privacy should have been supported by Matt in the confrontation with the boys. Tim is also afraid of being hurt by the boys who are physically more powerful than he and seem completely out of control. Matt is also frightened since he knows that some of the stories told by the adolescents about their capacity for violence are not hyperbole. Matt has difficulty with what he experiences as Tim's self-righteous approach as evidenced in Tim's speech about the contemptibility of homophobia, anti-Semitism, and racism.

The lecture has no positive effect on the boys. When the adolescents first become out of control, Tim identifies their issue as sexuality. Matt believes this is not the primary issue at all. Matt is apparently afraid of antagonizing the boys and fails to intervene to correctly identify the wildness as part of their aggression and a reflection of problems with impulse control and tolerance for difference. Matt's failure to intervene helps Tim to set himself up for the scapegoating that follows. Tim is so invested in his own issue, which becomes a group issue, that he misses the opportunity to help the members find alternate ways to express fear and anger. The two workers are tentative toward each other and feel threatened by their clients. They respond to each other with suspicion and anger. Their relationship parallels what is occurring in the group between members and workers as well as members and other members. We can also postulate that this relationship parallels their relationships in the world outside of the group.

What, if anything, could be done to help these two men to reconcile their differences and allow them to work more effectively with this difficult population? We suspect, in part, that some of the answers lie in the cognitive rather than the affective approach to the problems. By using concrete tools with the boys, both workers will feel safer in the work and will be supportive of each other as they struggle to understand their clients. Matt and Tim need to talk about their differences, but even more so, they need to plan how they will work cooperatively. What should they do when the boys make racist or ethnic slurs? What structures can be put in place to prevent the sort of chaos that took over this meeting? Together, how will the workers deal with adolescents when one boy stands on the table and everyone is yelling at once? Specifically, how can John or Danny be helped to develop some internal controls that prevent them from hurting others and give them sufficient self-esteem so that they do not strike out in blind hatred against anyone who is different from them?

The workers must know, before the session, who will handle disruptive youngsters and how. For instance, will Tim or Matt remove a boy from the meeting room for a cooling-off period? Or will the boys who are out of control be asked to leave until the following week? Setting strict limits that are reinforced by both workers will contribute to a safer environment because the boys will experience the workers as being in control. The rules should be enforceable and reasonable, communicating caring as well as structure to the adolescents.

Both Tim and Matt know what to expect from the adolescents and surely can prepare for certain contingencies, but they can also prepare for the inevitable surprises. They can practice ways of following up on questions, explorations, and latent and manifest content. They can set clear priorities and goals for each meeting. Tim must confront Matt about what he feels is Matt's homophobic reaction, and Matt must confront Tim about his self-righteous quality, but their discussion should not be limited to the sharing of feelings. It should relate to a plan for intervention with the group.

Of course, the relationship between the co-workers might have been quite different if considerations of compatibility had been explored in the preplanning phase of the group. Perhaps Tim or Matt might have worked more comfortably with a female co-worker, and perhaps this might have been beneficial for the group. In any event, given the workers who were selected, there should have been an opportunity to meet, discuss philosophical and stylistic issues, and develop strategy regarding the group.

Dealing with Problematic Situations

This text addresses general issues dealing with groups. Some special situations—work with difficult individual behavior, work with scapegoating, and work with explosive incidents—are phenomena that occur regularly in the course of group work. These are worthy of special consideration. Although these situations are really no more significant than others we have already mentioned, they are experienced by workers as somehow more problematic. We suspect that this difficulty is caused by the fact that these situations are likely to trigger powerful countertransferential feelings having to do with fear, anger, and loss.

The first piece for review uses a record-of-service format (Schwartz and Zalba, 1972). It is taken from a newspaper group for post-hospitalized psychiatric patients. The issue centers on helping an individual in the group to stay reality-oriented. The novice worker, in particular, may be put off by bizarre behaviors. In this case, Alice's hallucinations are both a distraction and a source of discomfort for the group and the worker:

> 2/16—I was explaining contract and discussing question when I heard someone to my right (Alice) say something. I asked "What did you say? I'm sorry I didn't quite hear you." She stared blankly at me. The group just watched. I was surprised, and the group noticed it. I realized Alice was hallucinating. This behavior continued through the meeting, but I failed to deal with it there because of my embarrassment.
>
> 12/23—While discussing how we would manage group time, I asked the group what they thought we could include in our meeting

[contracting]. Several people offered suggestions. I listened and also noticed Alice staring into space. I said, "Alice, what do you think?" [reaching for feelings, making her part of the group]. She said, "I'm sorry, Miss Phyllis, I wasn't listening. What were we talking about?" I said that we were offering suggestions about what to do in our meetings [refocusing] and, since she was a member of the group, maybe she'd like to help us with an idea [identifying her as belonging to the group, engaging, and focusing]. She said she really didn't know, but she liked the way we discussed things. I asked the group for a response, and they spoke some more [reaching for feedback, opening avenues of communication]. Alice stayed with the discussion.

1/7—While discussing hospitalization, I noticed Alice having a conversation with her voices. I said, "Alice, join us in reality" [bringing her into the here and now, confronting]. She said, "Oh, yes," and was back. I said, "Now tell me, Alice, which world was better?" She said, "Well, Miss Phyllis, I think I like the other." The group laughed, and we spoke about how each preferred to escape from reality as it was so often painful [identifying the problem, using humor to dilute intensity, reaching for commonality].

2/4—Sam asked Alice what she would be doing on the newspaper, and Alice said she didn't know. It was hard for her to concentrate. I asked the group and Alice if we could be of help [reaching for mutuality, reaching for cohesiveness]. The group offered various ideas. I suggested that perhaps there was something she liked a lot [partializing]. She said, "Yes, poetry. I enjoy some beautiful poems." I said I wondered if anyone else besides Alice liked poetry [reaching for commonality]. Most members said yes. I suggested, "Perhaps, Alice, you could share your favorite poems with us in the newspaper" [concretely giving her a part in the group]. She said, "Yes, I could copy them down, and we could print them." The group agreed.

My manner of calling Alice back to reality developed over time. I began saying such things as "Alice, are you with us? Alice, come on back. I know it might be nicer where you are, but this is reality, and we need you." The group picked this up and began using the same method.

2/18—Sam was having trouble finding an end to his article. We asked for the group's help. Alice was whispering to her voices. Sam said, "Come on, Alice, help us out. Talk to us. We're real."

The worker in this piece skillfully moves from an identification of the problem to a confrontation of the behavior, then to involving the group in the process, and finally, to modeling problem-solving skills. The group is finally able to incorporate these skills and become the therapeutic agent. The group is empowered. The method used can be transferred to many other situations involving members whose behavior is unusual, troubling, or disruptive to group process.

Scapegoating

Another problematic situation that interferes with the group's growth and sometimes makes workers uncomfortable is scapegoating. Scapegoating is a reciprocal process in which group members see some unacceptable part of themselves in one group member. Often the group member may feed into the process by acting provocatively.

Scapegoating occurs with all populations and in all circumstances, but it is probably evidenced most blatantly in work with youngsters. In our work with children, we all have seen an individual ridiculed for being different from the others. The child wearing eyeglasses identified as "four eyes," the slow child called "retard," and the overweight child nicknamed "fatso" are common to nearly every classroom and schoolyard. In certain groups, we see children of different cultures, different physical and intellectual abilities, and different races ostracized. The need to conform and belong—to be acceptable to peers—and the fear of the unfamiliar are so strong as to promote hurtful behavior. The scapegoat, believing on some internal level that to be different means to be unacceptable, may interact in a way that causes further separation from others. The group worker's task is to help create a norm that not only accepts difference but also recognizes its potential for enrichment. Variety is not rejected but rather welcomed. In response to name calling or other negative behaviors, the worker might say, "Could someone explain what's happening here? It seems people are uneasy about difference." The worker also might address the scapegoat, "I wonder how it feels to you to be called . . ." And, to the group, "Has anybody ever felt similarly?"

This type of exchange will often suffice to address the scapegoating and help the group to overcome it, but it will be successful only if the scapegoat rejects the role of the abused. Such an ongoing problem is addressed by the following process record. The excerpt is from a women's support group in a day treatment program. The workers, Iris and Marsha, have a long history with this group and are very familiar with these clients:

Theresa:	Everyone always picks on me.
Louise:	Oh, be quiet, Theresa.
Theresa:	I don't see what the big deal is about putting my feet up. I have swollen feet, and the doctor said I should put my feet up.
Andrea:	It happened in the other group.
Theresa:	I asked Diane if I could get a chair for my feet, and she said okay.
Louise:	This is Women's Group, Theresa. You're talking about something from Children's Group. It belongs in Children's Group, not here, so drop it.
Iris:	Louise, how would you like someone doing this to you?
Theresa:	I knew I shouldn't have come in today. My feet are swollen, and I can't even put them up.

Nanette:	She's out of line. The rule is that you're not supposed to bring issues from one group into another.
Theresa:	I don't see why everyone is picking on me. That's it. I'm leaving. (Theresa heads for the door. Marsha and Iris also get up. Marsha blocks the door.)
Iris:	Wait a minute, Theresa. You always do this, Theresa. You run away. You are going to stay in the group and deal with it this time.
Theresa:	No. I don't need this. I'm leaving. (Marsha spreads her arms wide, blocking the door.)
Iris:	Come back and sit down. You run when things get difficult, but you're not going to this time.
Theresa:	Why does everyone pick on me? I shouldn't have come in today. And now my blood pressure's probably way up.
Marsha:	This is not a big deal, Theresa. It may seem that way, but this is really not a big deal.

This incident seems like an isolated one in the history of this group. How often does a member have a health problem that necessitates elevating her feet, and why should the group object so vehemently to her doing so? The history of the group, however, reveals a pattern in which Theresa constantly presents situations that demand special attention. Her insatiable neediness is frightening to other members, who also experience their own deprivation and powerlessness in having their needs met. Theresa uses the swollen feet as a means of gaining attention, albeit in a negative way, and perpetuating her role as a needy, neglected member. No doubt, this stance is reflective of Theresa's role in her primary family and in other relationships. The ability to eventually receive feedback about how she is experienced by others may be helpful to all concerned.

The first response of Iris to the group's attack on Theresa, "Louise, how would you like someone doing this to you?" seems to be a classic attempt by a worker to protect the scapegoat. The defense of Theresa is also, we suspect, a response to her comment that a worker in the other group was sympathetic to her need: Diane had gotten Theresa a chair. Iris also wants to be appreciated. When Theresa heads for the door, apparently a pattern of behavior, the co-workers join to address the problem. Marsha nonverbally sets limits by blocking Theresa's passage. Iris identifies Theresa's pattern of behavior and makes a demand for work: "Wait a minute, Theresa. You always do this, Theresa. You run away. You are going to stay in the group and deal with it this time." Blocking the door is a potentially problematic method of dealing with a person desiring to leave. These workers have adopted this plan of action beforehand with knowledge of this population and a fully established relationship with this group. Clearly, this approach is inadvisable unless a context of a relationship exists. Even then, such an approach must be thoroughly evaluated.

Theresa continues to test the limits, and the workers hold fast to their demand for work. Marsha's final statement that this is not a "big deal" both reality tests and diffuses some of the intensity and allows Theresa to reenter the group. Once Theresa has returned to the group, workers have an opportunity to help the group examine their parts in the incident.

Other ways of dealing with the scapegoating of Theresa might have been useful. The workers could have intervened sooner to stop the escalation of the confrontation between Theresa and other group members by exploring their feelings: "Hold it a minute. What's happening here? How come we all sound so angry?" By identifying the anger in the room and allowing each to confront the others about their contributions to the difficulty, the workers could have helped members receive feedback. The workers, too, could have expressed their views about what was happening: "Yes, it is true that Theresa does this frequently [validating the group's perception], but what Theresa feels about your response to her is also true [validating Theresa's feelings]. This sort of intervention leads to problem solving and the opening of lines of communication. The worker identifies the problem as belonging to the group, and no good guy or bad guy can emerge as a victor or victim.

Conclusion

This chapter has dealt broadly with a variety of practice issues that focus on the worker's use of self in different practice situations. We can only give a taste of the myriad of complicated structural collegial and transferential issues that come into play in groups. Our approaches to what we have included are also admittedly limited. The complexity of the human condition, the diversity of experience, and the infinite number of extraordinary variables weave a different tapestry each time. The worker as weaver helps the group bring out its colors, rich textures and threads, to create a magnificent panorama. Of utmost importance in whatever scenario is analyzed is the monitoring of the worker's countertransferential responses in the light of an appropriate assessment of members' needs. All problems in group process need to be approached with the same basic tools. Regardless of population, phase, or circumstance, the methodology remains the same. The worker should not become lost in the specifics.

Reference

Schwartz, W. and Zalba, S., Eds. *The Practice of Group Work*. New York: Columbia University Press, 1972.

APPENDIX: GLOSSARY OF GROUP GAMES AND EXERCISES

We have explored the use of some conventional activities in work with people of various ages and circumstances. To enable readers to use specific activities to address the phase issues, we have developed a short glossary of phase-appropriate games and exercises. Our intent is not to limit the worker to the items listed but to offer this glossary as a starting place from which to develop population-and phase-appropriate activities. We hope that the descriptions and applicability of the games can be a ready resource to start the group worker on the path to a more creative use of program. Some of the games and exercises come from our shared experiences, and we are not necessarily able to credit our sources. Others have been gleaned from readings included in our bibliography.

Activities for Use in Beginnings

All of the following activities deal with engagement, trust, or approach-avoidance issues common to beginnings.

Desert Island

Members are asked to introduce themselves and to state three things they might take along on a trip to a desert island. The list should be fairly specific and reflect the interests and activities of each group member. With each member's participation, the worker may ask for a little more information to help the group member be more specific. For instance, if a person says that he will bring music to the island, the worker should ask what type of music and about the member's favorite musician, composer, or song. Members may also elect to take other people with them on the fantasy trip, and the worker should also ask about which people they might take.

Throughout the exercise, the worker should ask group members to concentrate on what is being said. The worker should make connections among members, noting similar comments by group members and joking about similarities and differences: "So you're bringing food, and you're bringing a CD player. We can have a party!" After the introduction of all the members, members should be asked to write their names on slips of paper and place them in a common pot. Then, each member should pull one slip from the pot, identify the person whose name is on the slip, and tell one thing about that individual that was learned during the desert island exercise. Individuals struggling to remember should be helped to do so in order to keep the activity as nonthreatening as possible.

Population

Appropriate with all populations. Particularly good for training groups.

Therapeutic Values

This exercise enables members to share information in an easy nonthreatening way. As a result of sharing information, members get to know each other and quickly begin to develop a sense of connectedness and group cohesion. Due to the low level of risk involved, vulnerability is decreased and trust develops. The exercise creates a playful feel that contributes to a sense of safety and that encourages creativity.

The Introduction Circle

Group members are seated in a circle. The worker explains that the group members are going to play a game of introductions. The worker asks the person immediately to his right to state her name and something related to the group purpose, such as why the person chose to come to the group. In addition to answering this question, the member should be asked another question directly related to the content of the group such as, in a mother's group, what are the ages and sexes of her children. In a hospital discharge group, the question may focus on how long the person has been hospitalized and where the person expects to go immediately after discharge. These questions should be of a concrete nature and relate to the purpose of the sessions.

Once the first member has been introduced and shared her information, the next person is asked to do the same. An additional responsibility for the second person is to state the first name of the person preceding him. The third person then introduces herself in the same manner as the previous two. She must state the name of her two predecessors along with her own. The game proceeds with each group member introducing herself or himself, answering the questions, and stating the names of all those introduced before. If any group member has difficulty with the names, the others in the group are invited to help in the process. Once all of the members have been introduced, the worker takes a turn at reviewing everyone's name.

Population

Groups may be of any age, but should not be too large. This exercise is not appropriate for very young children or persons with memory impairment.

Therapeutic Values

This exercise is particularly helpful in early beginnings to identify the contractual issues, why individuals are there, what they hope to achieve in the group, and what concrete information needs to be shared before beginning together. Remembering the names of fellow group members establishes the beginning of cohesion and some intimacy in the group. The ability to remember the names adds a feeling of mastery for group members, and the encouragement for members to help in this process adds further to the establishment of groupness and mutual aid. In general, this game can foster a friendly, familiar, and cooperative atmosphere where the initial resistance typical of beginnings is minimized. For training groups, it may be helpful to combine the "Desert Island" exercise with the "Introduction Circle."

Throw a Sock

A ball or a rolled-up pair of socks is tossed among group members who are standing in a circle. When a group member receives the ball, he must answer some nonthreatening question about himself. In the first round, members may be asked to state their names; in the second round, grade in school or place of birth; and so on, with the questions becoming only slightly more intimate as is comfortably tolerated by the group. Following the activity, the worker may make connections among the comments.

Population

Any population, but particularly valuable for populations with severe trust issues or with difficulty in expressing themselves verbally.

Therapeutic Values

In this exercise, the process of the "go-around" creates a sense of order, structure, and predictability, all of which address the issues of trust and safety inherent in the beginning phase of a group. At the same time, the random selection, associated with choosing which member to throw the sock to, adds an element of fun and excitement to the beginning phase. Information is easily shared, enabling members to feel connected to each other and free to continuing building the cohesive structure of the group.

Group Mural or Poem

This activity requires a large blackboard or sheet of newsprint and chalk, crayons, or markers for the mural. A large blackboard or pad is needed for the poem. The exercise proceeds with the worker suggesting a theme for a group mural or poem on which everyone will work together. Members of a parenting group, for example, may be asked to make a mural or poem about the hardest things they experience in being the parents of adolescents. For the mural, group members may either draw for themselves or ask other group members who are more secure in drawing to draw on their behalf. In the case of the poem, if no group member is willing to initiate the process, the worker may offer an initial line, and each member may be asked to contribute some free association or image which comes to mind. In either the mural or poem, however, everyone must contribute ideas. Pictures or thoughts can be symbolic. With large groups, the group can be divided into two or more smaller subgroups, each making its own mural or poem, or one subgroup simply may have a discussion about the theme. After fifteen minutes or so, the small groups should be brought together to discuss the meaning of their drawing or poem.

Population

Appropriate to most populations, but the worker must modify the theme accordingly. Useful in beginnings with short-term groups when time is a factor in engaging the members.

Therapeutic Values

This activity develops an almost immediate sense of mutuality and belonging among group members. Because the activity uses mediums other than verbal expression of feelings, it encourages creative expression even in members who are nonverbal or who are hesitant to verbalize their feelings. By using the group mural or group poem, the worker provides a vehicle for the expression of powerful and deeply personal feelings in the safety of a creative expression rather than a personal one. The necessary distance from self provided by the mural or poem is particularly useful in beginning phases or in later phases with highly vulnerable populations. In the middle phase, when a group is stuck, somehow unable to discuss conflictual issues, this exercise may open up difficult material to allow for exploration.

Two Pieces of Paper

Group members each receive two pieces of paper. On one piece (A), they are asked to write down something that they would like to give up. On the other piece of paper (B), they are asked to indicate why they would like to give up A. The A and B papers are collected in separate piles and the responses in each pile are jumbled. An A response is drawn and read aloud and then a B response is drawn and read aloud until all the A and B responses are drawn and read. In one group, a member may say that she wishes to give up smoking because her husband says kissing her is like licking an ashtray. Another member may say she wishes to give up her marriage because her husband is a louse. When the papers are randomly selected from the two piles, a member gets the A item, giving up a marriage, and the B item, her husband says kissing her is like licking an ashtray. Afterward members are asked to talk more about the exercise and those things they wish to give up and why.

Population

This may be used with various populations.

Therapeutic Values

This exercise is highly effective in helping members reduce initial anxiety associated with fears of exposure and risk in the beginning phase of a group. The game can be useful as an icebreaker. In the hilarity that usually occurs in playing, members experience a lightheartedness and a sense that the group can be fun. Members feel connected in the process of enjoying the exchanges as well as in the sharing of information regarding their needs in a nonthreatening manner. For the worker, the topics that are introduced in the group may provide beginning clues concerning members' issues.

Hog Call

With any size group, make a line facing the worker. Ask members to stand shoulder to shoulder so that the oldest person is to the worker's left and the youngest to the worker's right. During the process of determining ages, the worker should encourage laughter. Ask the youngest person to file around and walk to the other end of the line so that the youngest ends up facing the oldest person in the group. Opposites are asked to shake hands. The members are told that each pair is to select a matching set of words or sounds, for example, shoe–foot, peanut–butter, buzz–ball, whiskey–sour, salt–pepper. Each member of the pair chooses one of the words as his own name. Each pair is asked to announce their names to the entire group, allowing everyone to share. This process generally produces lots of laughter.

Each line is then told to move to the opposite side of the room or field. All participants are blindfolded and told to find their word partners by shouting (if outdoors) or whispering (if indoors) their partner's chosen name. Before starting, the worker mixes up each line so that partners are not directly opposite each other and instructs people to put their hands out in front of them as "bumpers" to avoid walking into each other or other things. Once partners find each other, they are permitted to remove the blindfolds and are asked to share their names, where they are from, and other things about themselves that may be pertinent to their participation in the group. After five to ten minutes, the entire group comes together, and each member of each pair introduces his partner to the group.

Population

Useful with most populations, but special caution is needed regarding trust and the use of blindfolds with certain groups.

Therapeutic Values

This exercise helps decrease the initial anxiety and mistrust associated with the beginning phase of a group. Group members are quickly engaged with each other, act cooperatively around a mutual task, take responsibility in caring for and protecting each other, and also challenge each other and the group. Early bonding is created by the necessity of working together as dyads and then, in a larger context, by being required to introduce one's partner to the entire group.

Funny Face

The worker divides the group into smaller groups of five to seven people seated in a circle. At the signal, everyone in the circle tries to make the others smile. All eyes must stay open, and no touching is permitted. Whoever laughs or even smiles is eliminated. Everyone else continues until two people, the regional champs, remain in each group. The worker encourages applause and celebration. The regional champs then go against the other regional champs in a "face-off."

Population

Primarily used with children and young teens and can also be effective in group training.

Therapeutic Values

This game encourages spontaneity, unselfconscious participation, fun, and healthy competition while simultaneously reducing defensiveness. Younger populations particularly benefit from the ability to express their feelings of anxiety and fear in a nonverbal manner (making faces) that traditionally they are told not to do. Videotaping of this exercise provides the additional benefit of group members seeing themselves and having the opportunity to laugh at themselves in an open and accepting environment.

People to People

Members pair up and stand in a circle facing the worker who is in the middle. The worker sets a beat by clapping or snapping her fingers and chanting "people to people." Everyone joins in. Once everyone is caught up in the rhythm, the worker substitutes a body part for the word "people" in the chant. For example, the worker says "elbow to elbow" or "knee to knee." The rhythm continues throughout. As members repeat the chant, they assume whatever position is called for. Members continue matching body parts until the worker chants "people to people," the signal for everyone to find a new partner. The worker participates in the scramble for a partner. Whoever remains without a partner moves to the center of the circle and becomes the new leader.

Population

Children, adolescents, and young adult populations and training groups. Due to the physical aspects of this game, caution should be used with populations who have physical trauma, touching, or boundary issues.

Therapeutic Values

This exercise is highly effective in addressing the initial defensiveness in the beginning phase of a group. The worker's initiation of the exercise sets the stage for risk-taking when members see the worker in the center of the circle and then scrambling to find a partner. Sharing with one another by assuming various silly positions develops a level of intimacy and bonding necessary for a group to begin working together. This activity also offers an opportunity for everyone to assume a leadership role and a position of power. Unlike other activities of this kind, the loss of one's partner in this game does not result in banishment from the circle or in the loss of power. Since the activity does not require any highly skilled physical movements, risk and exposure are at a minimum, essential to the needs of members in the beginning phase of a group. This activity also can be used in middles when there is a higher level of trust and intimacy. In both phases, but particularly in beginnings, the worker should choose body parts that do not offer so much intimacy as to sacrifice safety.

Mirror Game

Divide the group into pairs with partners facing each other. One partner is secretly given a topic by the worker. In slow motion and in silence, that partner must act out the topic. The other partner must mimic the motions. Suggested topics include shaving, combing hair, eating lunch, and getting ready for bed. Depending on population and phase, members may select their own topics or be completely spontaneous.

Population

Any population, but especially valuable for children with poor skills in listening to others.

Therapeutic Values

This exercise demands concentration, attention, and focus. The activity of mimicking another develops close observation skills and enhances intimacy. Because this close contact is achieved in a structured manner, the risk factor is reduced, and creativity and sharing are enhanced—all important factors in building cohesiveness in the beginning phase of a group.

Tiger—Man—Gun

The group is divided into two teams. Members of each team conference and decide whether the team should be a tiger, a man, or a gun. The worker counts to three, and each team assumes its appropriate position representing the selection. The tiger wins over the man, the man over the gun, and the gun over the tiger. Each win is worth a certain number of points. The team to reach the highest number of points after a specified time period or a set score first is the winner. Winning can involve prizes appropriate to the population. Second-place prizes help lessen feelings about the loss.

Population

Children with various diagnostic categories.

Therapeutic Values

Requirements for minimal skill and the need to work cooperatively effectively create a sense of safety by lessening the feelings of vulnerability associated with beginnings. The worker demands that members make decisions but with the help of others, so the individual member is less exposed. This joint decision-making enhances a beginning sense of cohesiveness and a sense of mutuality in the group. The low-risk competitive element between teams gives permission for group members to openly compete, channels some aggressive impulses into socially acceptable avenues, and allows for fun and discharge of energy.

Activities for Use in Middles

The middle phase activities are all concerned with problem solving, decision making, the creation of group cohesion and intimacy, and the shifting and flexibility of roles.

The Rubber Band

The group is divided into teams and told that they are going to participate in a contest. Instructions are that both teams represent groups in a rural community that has mistakenly received a delivery of thousands of boxes of rubber bands. The teams must develop lists of things that can be done with the rubber bands. The team with the longest list is the winner. Members are encouraged to be as creative as they can be. After twenty minutes or so, the whole group reconvenes, and the lists are read aloud and compared.

Population

Recommended for use in recreational groups for all ages and in training groups in work environments for different populations.

Therapeutic Values

This activity, generally used in the middle phase of group development, can also be used in beginnings. Working together in teams helps develop trust in the group as well as an increased sense of group cohesion. The risk factor is low, as the task is not personal and does not produce nor exacerbate any vulnerable feelings. Cooperative effort is demanded if the members are to solve the problem, and this effort contributes to the enhancement of budding cooperative problem-solving skills, which adds to a sense of empowerment and mastery.

Red Light, Green Light

In "Red Light, Green Light," one child, the game leader, is chosen to stand twenty to twenty-five feet away from the others who are lined up facing the leader. The leader turns her back to the other children and recites, at whatever speed the child chooses, the verse, "Red Light, Green Light, One, Two, Three." While the leader is facing away, the other children run forward to tag the leader before the leader turns back to face them. If the leader, on turning back to the group, sees children moving, she instructs those children to return to the starting point. They must do so. The children attempt to advance without being seen, and the game proceeds until someone has reached and tagged the leader and has run back to the starting line without being tagged in return by the leader. The person tagging the leader and returning to the starting position without being tagged back becomes the new leader.

Population

Young children

Therapeutic Values

Children learn to give and take directions, work cooperatively, be fair, confront, and problem solve.

Giant Steps

In "Giant Steps," the children stand in the same configuration as in "Red Light, Green Light"—facing the leader and moving toward him. The children are permitted to advance by taking giant, baby, and umbrella steps in accordance with the instructions of the leader. A giant step is made by taking the largest possible step, a baby step by placing one's feet heel to toe, and an umbrella step by stepping forward and twirling around. Each child, in turn, requests directions from the leader who tells the child how many of each step the child may take toward the leader. The child repeats the instructions but must precede the directions with the words "May I?" Failure to repeat the directions correctly with the request "May I?" requires that the participant return to the starting point.

The leader may respond to the question "May I?" in either the negative or the affirmative. If the answer is "Yes, you may," the child proceeds with the directions, taking two umbrella steps and one giant step, for example. If the answer is "No, you may not," new directions are offered, and the procedure follows anew. The object is to reach the leader first and thereby become the new leader. The game resumes from the beginning. In both "Red Light, Green Light" and "Giant Steps," the worker may manipulate the leadership role to allow children with poor self-esteem to be placed in the position of leader. An alternative is for the worker to assume the leader's position to model appropriate leadership behavior and to ensure fairness.

Population

Young children

Therapeutic Values

These games help children to become structured, follow directions, enjoy some spirit of competition, and learn to share activities with peers.

Indian Chief

In order to play "Indian Chief," all the children but one are seated in a circle. One child is sent out of the room; then the worker chooses another child to be the Indian chief. This child starts an action that the others in the circle must mimic, patting his head or clapping his hands, for example. The child who has been waiting outside is then called back into the room and, by observing the actions of the group as they change from one motion to another in accordance with the chief's actions, must determine who has been selected as the chief. After three incorrect guesses, the Indian chief identifies herself or himself and leaves the room, and the game starts over again with a new Indian chief. If the guess is correct, the child doing the guessing may be permitted to leave the room once more. The worker has the option of choosing another person to guess in the next round.

Population

Young children

Therapeutic Values

The opportunities for allowing more withdrawn youngsters to take on leadership roles in each of the three previous games make them particularly useful in the middle phase when the development of role flexibility is an important task. Caution should be used by the worker in selection of a leader. Usually it is best for the worker to be the leader in all of these games at first, modeling fairness, acting in a nonpunitive way, limiting frustration for the children, and generally demonstrating appropriate social behavior. Children benefit from the structuring and learn cooperation and how to give and take directions. The ability to tolerate frustration and contain anxiety is often a part of the developmental tasks associated with preparation for the latency period and adolescence.

In the middle phase of group development, members are required to risk more, relate at an increased level of intimacy with other members, and to challenge each other as well as themselves in order to maximize their growth potential. These challenges of the middle phase can easily trigger the developmental challenges of latency and adolescence, increasing anxiety and pushing the limits of impulse control. The structured format and the clarity of roles, once established, in these games provide a stimulating but relatively safe environment for members to engage in the struggle of their individual developmental tasks and the demands of a group in the middle phase.

Wearing the Sign

Group members have a sign, which they have not seen beforehand, pinned to their backs by the worker. They must guess what the sign says by questioning the other group members. All questions must have a yes or no answer. The sign may have the name of a famous personality or an object or an emotion. The category depends on what the worker wishes to achieve with the game.

Population

Useful with considerable variations for all populations

Therapeutic Values

This activity is generally used in the middle phase of group development where cohesion is more developed and a higher level of trust has been achieved.

Cohesion and trust are necessary if members are to risk being in the vulnerable position in a group, unaware of what is on the sign on their backs, although others in the group have this information. To find out what is on the sign, the members must depend on their own communication skills and the honesty of others in replying to the questions. This intimate process can stimulate a good deal of exchange and is most beneficial to populations who have difficulty interacting. The activity may stimulate reminiscence for older persons, placing names of well-known personalities from their youth on the signs. It also may be used to help adolescents identify feelings as part of a psychotherapeutic process.

Thermometer

The worker begins the exercise by designating one side of the room as "hot" or "yes" and the other side as "cold" or "no." The worker presents issues that he has identified as salient for the population, but begins the exercise with relatively benign questions. In an adolescent group, one question might be whether they like heavy metal music and another might be whether they like baggy jeans. The worker then asks members to take positions in the room nearer or farther from either wall reflective of their opinions about the issue. Gradually, the worker moves to issues that are sufficiently provocative as to yield a range of opinions. An example for an adolescent group might be: "Is drinking alcohol as a teen ever okay?" or "Is it the girl's responsibility to determine birth control decisions?" Once the members assume their positions, the worker asks those in the more extreme positions to explain to the group what has led them to choose their spots. Once the group members hear the responses of their peers, they are given the opportunity to move from their current spots to new positions. Then the worker asks the members to share their reasons for remaining in their positions or making changes.

Population

This exercise may be used by any populations but is particularly recommended for adolescents, because it draws both on the issue of developing independent identity and peer influence.

Therapeutic Values

This activity addresses the influence on the decision-making process in adolescence. It demonstrates in a concrete and dramatic way how some individuals are more responsive than others to the influence of their peers. The activity is nonthreatening but can serve to initiate more substantive discussion. The need for adolescents to give physical expression to their feelings and ideas is fundamental to the therapeutic process, as is the need for them to individualize and form their own sense of identity. The game offers permission for the adolescent to change and move to a new point of view. This movement can be valuable especially since adolescents often feel compelled to maintain rigid positions even when those positions are potentially self-destructive. Change may demand some courage and be confidence building.

Dear Abby, Soap Operas

The worker chooses newspaper or magazine columns to read with the group, or videotapes of soap opera programs to watch with the group that act as catalysts for addressing issues germane to the group and pertinent to the population in general. In the beginning phase, the worker may generate all the material, selecting nonintrusive and nonthreatening letters or tapes. Later on, group members may be encouraged to contribute material for discussion.

Population

This activity is appropriate for any adult population and certain adolescent groups. It is especially useful for group members who have a hard time focusing, problem solving, and verbalizing feelings. Columns from newspapers of many years ago, some of which have been collected in books (see Bibliography), may engage older clients.

Therapeutic Values

This exercise may be used effectively in all stages of group development. In the beginning stage, where trust is low and the need for information is high, members may openly discuss the safely removed drama that reflects certain conflictual portions of their lives, ideals, fantasies, and relationships. The distance of the drama provides a safe arena to address painful issues. Also, in the beginning stage, the content can be used to help members vicariously experience and problem solve around the issues of others and hopefully use this understanding to reflect on their own lives.

In the middle phase of a group, safety and distance are less important to group members than in beginnings due to the increased level of trust, cohesion, and problem solving. In the middle stage, it is possible even more so than in beginnings to use the content of the soap opera or Dear Abby letter to provide grist for the therapeutic mill.

Roll a Role

The worker develops a series of questions appropriate to the population's needs. Questions might relate to sibling issues, parental relationships, or peer conflicts, for example. The questions are put on cards numbered from two to twelve. Several cards should be available for each number. Each group member rolls two dice and selects a card corresponding to the number rolled. The members then take turns acting out solutions to the questions posed on the cards they have selected.

Population

Adolescents and latency-age children, some psychiatric populations, and some developmentally disabled populations

Therapeutic Values

This activity is particularly useful to help group members explore and express feelings regarding a multitude of experiences related to their everyday lives. The worker has a wonderful opportunity to be creative in designing questions geared specifically to the needs of the particular population. Members have the chance to engage in role plays that allow them to express different parts of themselves and to work on problem-solving skills while enhancing their decision-making skills. This exercise emphasizes conflict resolution and is a valuable tool with adolescents, latency-age children, and emotionally disabled adults.

What Would You Do If?

The worker or certain group members write about conflictual situations or feelings: You're in a store, and you're tempted to steal or, You're feeling suspicious, selfish, mean, etc. Individuals or several group members act out the situations and other group members guess what is being portrayed.

Population

Appropriate for children, adolescents, and young adult populations.

Therapeutic Values

In this exercise, group members learn and practice problem-solving skills, which is ego strengthening, and at the same time develop a sense of mastery related to conflict resolution. In the process of exploring the problem and its solution, group members need to work cooperatively and struggle with compromise and impulse control. The activity also provides an opportunity for group members to be creative and to express their feelings openly. The theoretical situations discussed offer a comfortable distance from the vulnerability associated with exposure and leading perhaps more gently to serious discussion.

Tug-of-War

Using a towel for a rope, two people are set against each other. A line is drawn on the floor or ground midway between them. The two group members are adversaries or have been in conflict in the group in the past. The objective is to pull one's opponent over the line.

Population

Latency-age children

Therapeutic Values

This game is particularly useful during the middle phase of group development, which often demands the resolution of conflict between individuals and/or subgroups. The activity helps focus the conflict and the parties involved, dissipates tension and anger, allows for openly competitive feelings, and hopefully thereafter leads to a discussion of feelings and provides a release of tension and energy.

Paper Bag Dramatics

Depending on the population, the worker brings in a variety of objects that function as props: scarves, hats, eyeglasses, tools, utensils, etc. The group members work together using the props to act out scenes, the themes of which arise in an impromptu fashion from group discussion. In the beginning phase, the worker may also supply the theme material.

Population

Appropriate to all populations

Therapeutic Values

In this activity, no matter what the group phase, group members are encouraged to be creative and openly express their feelings. The exercise provides an opportunity for alternate behavior modeling and a safe environment to explore solutions to conflictual issues. The activity develops decision-making skills for group members and is an effective diagnostic tool for the worker. Material chosen should give careful consideration to the developmental and socio-cultural needs of the population served.

Magic Shop

The worker is a storekeeper on a fantasy island (children might participate in creating the "shop" by drawing, pasting, etc. before the exercise begins). Each child enters the shop to buy something intangible, for example, feelings, new parents, the ability to play ball better. The price the child must pay for the purchase is another intangible, for example, feelings of anger or inadequacy that the buyer no longer needs or wants.

Population

Children and adolescents

Therapeutic Values

This activity promotes an atmosphere accepting and encouraging of fantasy. The group members are urged to be creative and explore their feelings in both a verbal and nonverbal manner. The exercise helps the group members problem solve and resolve conflictual situations and feelings that they struggle with in their everyday lives. If the group members help construct the magic shop, as is suggested above, members also benefit from the cooperative skills needed to build the shop. The concept of exchange in the purchasing connects to the idea that all choices have a price and develops a sense of responsibility in decision making.

Making Your Own Doll

This activity requires the worker to provide the children with socks to use to create sock dolls. To eliminate competitive issues, the socks should all be of the same pattern or color and not reflective of any particular race. The worker then invites each child to select a sock. Once this process is completed, the worker places various supplies on the table to be used in designing the sock doll. These should include buttons to fasten by sewing or with glue; patches of different colored cloth or felt, both bright and dark; pipe cleaners; different-colored yarns, possibly for hair; magic markers; glitter; pairs of scissors; and glue. The children then are instructed by the worker to use the supplies to create a sock person, anyone they want it to be.

As they make their dolls, the worker encourages discussion about the project, giving the dolls names and an identity. Questions should focus on where the dolls live, with whom they live, whether they have a family, what the members of this family are like, what they like to do for fun, where they go to school, how they like it, their favorite activities, and so on. Children are also encouraged to question each other about the dolls and to interact in play with their dolls. The worker remains available throughout to assist with any concrete problems the children may have in negotiating the task. The worker may make a doll to model the process for the children.

Population

Children

Therapeutic Values

This project is often an excellent diagnostic tool that functions as a projective test allowing for some expression of the child's internalized self-image. The activity quickly demonstrates for the worker various roles that children may assume within the group, with some children immediately taking on leadership positions and others modeling their dolls after those of the leader's. The doll-making also provides a safe vehicle for the expression of conflictual feelings and reporting of trauma. The activity is an avenue for creativity and imagination. In the playing-out of sometimes emotionally charged feelings and events, the children are able to experience some cathartic release.

When this exercise is used in beginnings, it can become an ongoing part of the group. The dolls may be provided at every meeting along with the supplies to make alterations, should the children choose to make changes. The changes in the dolls likely reflect changes the children experience in relation to the group and to their lives. The doll play may be incorporated as the children wish throughout the course of the group. The ability of the children to choose the doll play or not reinforces their sense of control and empowerment.

Who Am I?

Members in the group are asked to bring some concrete objects to the group that in some way are a reflection of themselves. Suggestions for items might include a favorite or meaningful photograph, a particular item of clothing, a keepsake, an award, or a special letter. All members then are asked to explain the meaning and significance of the objects they have chosen. The worker should encourage further exploration and discussion.

Population

Any population

Therapeutic Values

In the beginning phase, this exercise facilitates introduction of members and some level of intimacy. In some groups, this may begin to bridge cultural differences and sow the beginning seeds of cohesion and mutuality. In middles, the exercise greatly increases the possibility of meaningful sharing and the sense of connectedness. The exercise may be useful for the worker in identifying areas for exploration and work.

The Commercial Game

The group divides into pairs. Partners may be chosen by random selection—choosing names from a hat, for instance. Each member of the pair must act out a commercial advertisement selling the assets of his partner. The worker may want to participate in the process or begin it.

Population

Primarily for children but may be used with some adult populations with difficulties in social skills.

Therapeutic Values

This activity can be used in the beginning or middle phase of group development. In the beginning phase, a group must accumulate knowledge pertinent to each member, and it must develop a sense of trust and safety. When members engage in the cooperative task of creating a commercial that focuses on the assets of another, the task helps the members work together in the process of mutual discovery, thus creating a sense of bonding and trust. For group members, the process serves as a wonderful boost in self-esteem as others acknowledge and appreciate their assets. In the middle phase of a group, where group members struggle toward deeper levels of intimacy and higher levels of risk-taking, this exercise helps group members deepen cohesiveness and stay focused on ego strengths. The activity encourages free-flowing, spontaneous interaction as well as the open expression of feeling.

Activities for Use in Endings

The following activities all help to address issues concerned with separation and individuation, adjustment to loss, evaluation of the group experience, and moving on. Feelings in the ending state of group are complex and powerful. Often the most difficult of emotions related to separation/individuation and loss are re-experienced in primitive intensity. Words alone can fail to convey the emotions effectively. It is necessary to help members deal with accepting change and to allow healthy regression. Activities can permit that appropriate regressive behavior in adults by providing an acceptable physical or concrete vehicle for expression when just speaking about feelings is inadequate.

"Oh What A Time It Was" Activity Group

A reminiscence group can be useful in work with older adults. The worker brings music, photos, or newspaper clippings to the group. Slides, videos, or movies of a particular time period can also be used to help recreate the era the group members shared as younger people. If this activity is in the context of an ongoing group, individual members can also bring in personal photos and items.

The activity consists of the worker introducing the vehicle, e.g., music from the 1930s, and inviting the members to share associations and memories to the music; demonstrations of popular dances may be encouraged. If newspaper articles are used, the worker should invite members to personalize their experiences at the time of that news event.

Population

The exercise is primarily for an elderly population. This activity is appropriate in nursing homes, senior centers, and senior residences. The activity can be adapted for younger populations dealing with transitions.

Therapeutic Values

Reminiscence groups for seniors can utilize multiple vehicles such as music, photos, etc., that generate storytelling and a momentary recreation of the member's early beginnings. The act of reminiscing can allow members to "close" the circle of their lives. Group members reaffirm their struggles and their accomplishments, their joys and their sorrows. This process permits a letting go of the past and a freeing to move forward to the next life task. As a member once remarked after telling her story to the group, "I guess I didn't do so bad, time for the next adventure."

Circle

All members stand up and hold hands. Each member takes a turn to say exactly what he or she is feeling or thinking. Other members are not permitted to respond. The process continues until everyone has spoken. Members are not allowed to drop hands no matter what is said.

Population

Adolescents and adults

Therapeutic Values

This exercise directly addresses the needs to evaluate, review, and recall tasks specific to the end phase of group. Members are required to hold hands throughout the exercise, symbolizing and reinforcing the cohesiveness and acceptance of the group. In this solid and safe atmosphere of togetherness, group members can feel free to express their feelings including those previously unexpressed.

Magic Glasses

The worker decorates a pair of eyeglasses with sparkles, feathers, and similar ornamentation to make them strange and fantastic. All children get a chance to put on the glasses and share with the other group members the magical people or things they see while wearing the glasses. They also are asked to speak about what it has been like for them in the group and how they feel about the group ending.

Population

Children

Therapeutic Values

As with all exercises for children, this activity encourages creative exploration, fantasy, and the use of imagination. The magical glasses provide some distance from the self for the group member, thereby creating an arena of safety where the open expression of feeling is allowed. Children will tend to lose themselves behind the sparkles and feathers and feel permission to take on new roles or regress momentarily to old roles that may enable them to express painful feelings associated with loss and ending. This regression in service of the ego is common with this population and is a healthy therapeutic step toward resolution.

The Web

The worker asks the group members to stand and form a circle. Holding a ball of multicolored yarn, the worker explains the procedure the group will follow. One member starts by holding the end of the string in one hand and the ball of yarn in the other. That member is directed to say something about the group experience, what he or she has gotten from the whole group or a specific member, or what the group has meant to her or him, and so forth. After making the statement, the member tosses the ball of yarn to someone else in the circle while still holding the thread. The next member repeats the process and the next until every member in the circle has spoken. The final result is a web-like structure in the middle of the circle with each member holding a piece of it. The web is bright and multicolored, representing the diversity of the group, and held together by each individual member, representing the cohesiveness of the group.

At this point, the worker then leads a brief discussion on any remaining feelings members would like to share regarding the group and/or the exercise. The discussion concludes with members cutting their ties to the web, symbolizing separation from the group. If they choose, they may keep the threads they are holding (the transitional object). The worker needs to be a fully active participant just as she would be in the ending phase of any group. It is suggested that the worker begin the exercise and role model the expected participation.

Population

Useful for children and adults of any age. Can be used effectively with training groups, experiential classes and seminars, and any type of activity group.

Therapeutic Values

This exercise is highly effective in creating a physical manifestation of a group's life. In the beginning phase, members are building the group, literally one thread at a time. The complexity of middles is symbolized by the multi-colored threads criss-crossing each other and representing diversity of color, style, etc. Throughout the exercise, people are sharing feelings, laughing, and working together exactly as the group has always done. The final cutting of the string symbolizes the final separation from the group by each member and the literal end of the group. This powerful symbolic aspect of the exercise makes it particularly useful in training group workers. The exercise allows for feelings to be expressed and provides a sense of closure.

Although we chose to include this exercise among the activities for use in termination, the activity can be used with variation in beginnings or middles. In beginnings, one might ask group members to make a statement about why they joined the group or to share some information about themselves that they would like others to know. The cutting of the yarn in beginnings might symbolize the completion of introductory tasks and the opening to the future process. In middles, the worker could use the exercise to open up a conflictual issue for greater exploration, asking members to share feelings about the matter when they receive the ball of yarn. Also, in a more general way, workers may ask the members to share their thoughts about where the group is currently and where they hope it may go. In middles, this serves to deepen the intimacy and create cohesiveness. The cutting of the yarn in middles might signify the completion of the self-reflective component and the return to the interactional process.

The Always-Wanted, Never-Got Gift Game

Members sit in a circle with two containers in the center of the circle. These containers may be a variety of things depending upon the population. Each member is given two pieces of paper. On one piece, members are told to write down the favorite gifts they have ever received. On the second piece, they must write down the gift they always wanted but never received. All of the favorite gift papers are placed in one container and the never-received gift papers are placed in the other container. The papers in each container are then mixed. One member, generally the worker to start, draws one slip of paper from each container and reads each paper aloud, commenting on each, one at a time. The worker might say, "What an interesting choice; I wouldn't have thought of that," or some other statement equally innocuous. This comment models responses for the members who will follow.

After the comment, the worker asks the writer of the paper to share what it meant to her, indicating, whether it was a favorite gift, why, and, whether it was a wanted-but-never-received gift, what never receiving it meant. After this exchange, the next member draws two slips and the process is repeated until both containers are emptied. At this point, the worker encourages more discussion and suggests to the group that they may do whatever they like with the slips of paper: keep them, exchange them, or throw them away. All during this process, the worker encourages more sharing of feelings and memories. The group exercise ends when the worker senses that the sharing has concluded.

Population

Appropriate for adolescents and adults of all ages. The activity requires ability to verbalize feelings and to have some life experience.

Therapeutic Values

This exercise encourages the exchange of personal information and the sharing of deep feelings, both of which heighten the level of intimacy in the group. The activity encourages the sharing of hopes and disappointments, losses and regrets—feelings often very difficult for group members to express. This exercise rekindles warm and joyful feelings that have been lost and, most important, offers the opportunity to help repair painful experiences for some members while allowing others the opportunity to express empathy and feel the joy of giving. It is not uncommon for members to openly mourn the gift they never received but desperately wanted from a parent or a deceased spouse and for the group member who drew that gift slip to present the paper to the writer in the final exchange. This exercise creates powerful moments between group members and adds a level of intimacy to the late-beginning phase, the middle phase, and the end phase of groups. The worker may discover that the intimacy of the gift increases as the phase of the group advances. In the termination phase, this exercise can be used, with variation, to enable members to speak about what they felt about the gifts others gave them in the group and the gifts they gave to others in the group. Since this exercise may elicit very painful unresolved issues for group members, particularly in termination, workers must be sure to allow sufficient time for processing.

Go Around

All members stand up and hold hands. They are not permitted to let go. Everyone contributes a sentence about what has happened in the history of the group (a significant event or time for the member).

Population

All populations

Therapeutic Values

This very simple and straightforward activity allows the members of the group to evaluate, reminisce, and complete the circle of the group's life. The activity specifically calls for every person to recall some piece of group history, and an open and accepting atmosphere encourages the free expression of feeling. Additionally this exercise develops a final sense of bonding resulting from a unique shared history and lends closure to the experience.

Memory Game

One person starts explaining, in detail, everything he can remember that happened during a specific time or event in the history of the group. If anyone else thinks that the person who is talking has missed something in relating the story, the new speaker must yell, "hold it!", explain what was missed, and continue with the story. While the group stories are being reconstructed, the worker encourages the expression of feelings associated with the stories.

Population

May be used in any activity groups.

Therapeutic Values

Calling upon group members to discuss in detail a specific group moment addresses the group tasks of reminiscence and evaluation required in the ending phase. This game's design, however, allows for the additional element of reconnecting members to each other during the final stage of the group. The exercise promotes this process by requiring group members to add information that may be left out in the first telling of the story. As each member adds something to the story, the story becomes the "group's story," rather than simply a story of the group. While the group stories are being reconstructed, the worker encourages the expression of feelings associated with the stories.

Credit Where Credit Is Due

The members are gathered in a circle, and each is given a piece of paper and asked to write his or her name boldly at the top. Once this is done, members are asked to pass the paper to the person on their immediate right. Members are then instructed by the worker to write one positive remark about the person whose name is on the paper. (The positiveness of the comment must be emphasized. This is not an exercise intended to elicit criticism.) This comment should be listed on the bottom line of the sheet of paper and then the paper should be folded over such that the comment is covered and no one else may see it. Again, the paper should be passed to the person sitting next in the circle. The process is repeated until all members have added a comment to each list of positive statements. The papers then may be returned to their original owners and unfolded, and the comments read aloud. Group members are encouraged to elaborate on the comments and to share feelings about the comments. When they leave the group, they take their own list of assets.

Population

Any population.

Therapeutic Values

This exercise provides each group member with a positive transitional object as the member leaves the group. It allows members to express positive feelings that may have gone unexpressed earlier in the group and permits group members, who may have had problematic relationships, to give something to each other of a positive nature, in part repairing their differences. This skill of integrating negative and positive feelings is crucial in the development of healthy relationships. Members leave the group with an emphasis on their strengths and capabilities.

Additional Programmatic Material

Aside from the exercises and games listed here, the worker has numerous opportunities to develop programs related to the arts, sports, nature, and tasks of daily living. Groups can work with puppets, films, writing, dramatics, photography, music, dance, art, board games (Scruples and the Thinking, Feeling, Doing Game, for example), trips, parties, cooking, grooming, home-making, traveling (particularly for the physically challenged), speakers, exercise, gardening, self-government, literature discussion, and videotaping. Groups may focus on training, intergenerational or intercultural sharing, recreation, skills development, advocacy, or problem solving.

BIBLIOGRAPHY

Abernethy, A. "The Power of Metaphors for Exploring Cultural Differences in Groups." *Group*, 2000, 26, 219–231.

Abrams, B. "Finding a Common Ground in a Conflict Resolution Group for Boys." *Social Work with Groups*, 2000, 23, 55–60.

Acosta, F. X. "Group Psychotherapy with Spanish-Speaking Patients."In *Mental Health and Hispanic Americans: Clinical Perspectives.* R. Becerra, N. Karno, and J. Escobar, Eds. New York: Grune and Stratton, 1982, pp. 188–197.

Agazarian, Y. M. "Group as a Whole: Systems Theory and Practice." *Group*, 1989, 13(4), 131–154.

Agazarian, Y. M. *Systems-Centered Therapy for Groups.* New York: Guilford Press, 1997.

Agazarian, Y. M. "Systems-centered Group Psychotherapy: A Theory of Living Human Systems and its System-Centered Practice." *Group*, 2012, 36(1), 19–35.

Alonso, A. and Rutan, S. "The Experience of Shame and the Restoration of Self-Respect in Group Psychotherapy." *The International Journal of Group Psychotherapy*, 1988, 38(1), 3–14.

Alonso, A. and Rutan, J. S. "Common Dilemmas in Combined Individual and Group Treatment." *Group*, 1990, 14(1), 5.

Alonso, A. and Rutan, S. "Separation and Individuation in the Group Leader." *International Journal of Group Psychotherapy*, 1996, 46,146–162.

Andrews, J. "Group Work's Place in Social Work: A Historical Analysis." *Journal of Sociology and Social Welfare*, 2001, 28(4), 45–65.

Anstey, M. "Scapegoating in Groups: Some Theoretical Perspectives and a Case of Intervention." *Social Work with Groups*, 1982, 5(3), 51–63.

Arnold, A. *A World Book of Children's Games.* New York: Crowell, 1972.

Baird, B. *The Art of the Puppet.* New York: Macmillan, 1965.

Baker, S. "Coping Skills Training for Adolescents: Apply Cognitive Behavioral Principles to Psychoeducational Groups." *The Journal for Specialists in Group Work*, 2001, 26, 219–227.

Barsky, M. and Mozenter, G. "The Use of Creative Drama in a Children's Group." *International Journal of Group Psychotherapy*, 1976, 26(1), 105–114.

Basecu, S. "Tools of the Trade: The Use of the Self in Psychotherapy." *Group*, 1990, 14(3), 157–165.

Beck, R. and Buchele, B. "In the Belly of the Beast: Traumatic Countertransference." *International Journal of Group Psychotherapy*, 2005, 55, 31–45.

Beckerman, D. and Orvaschel, H. "Group Psychotherapy for Depressed Adolescents: A Critical Review." *The International Journal of Group Psychotherapy*, 1994, 44(4), 463–476.

Beeler, J. and DiProva, V. "Family Adjustment Following Disclosure of Homosexuality by a Member: Themes Discerned in Narrative Accounts." *Journal of Marital and Family Therapy*, 1999, 25, 443–459.

Benjamin, S. E. "Co-Therapy: A Growth Experience for Therapists." *International Journal of Group Psychotherapy*, 1972, 22(2), 199–209.

Benton, G. "The Origins of the Political Joke." In *Humor in Society: Resistance and Control*. C. Powell and G. E. C. Paton, Eds. New York: St. Martin's Press, 1988, pp. 33–55.

Berger, M. "The Impact of the Therapist's Personality on Group Process." *American Journal of Psychoanalysis*, 1974, 34, 213–219.

Berger, M. and Rosenbaum, M. "Notes on Help-Rejecting Complainers." *International Journal of Group Psychotherapy*, 1967, 17(3), 357–370.

Bernard, H. S. and Drob, S. "Premature Termination: A Clinical Study." *Group*, 1989, 13(1), 11.

Berne, E. *Principles of Group Treatment*. New York: Grove Press, 1966.

Bernstein, G. and Klein, R. H. "Countertransference Issues in Group Psychotherapy with HIV Positive and AIDS Patients." *The International Journal of Group Psychotherapy*, 1995, 45(1), 91–100.

Bernstein, S. "Conflict and Group Work." In *Explorations in Group Work*. S. Bernstein, Ed. Boston, MA: Milford House, 1973, pp. 72–106.

Bion, W. R. *Experience in Groups and Other Papers*. New York: Basic Books, 1960.

Block, L. R. "On the Potentiality and Limits of Time: The Single Session Group and the Cancer Patient." *Social Work with Groups*, 1989, 8(2), 81–100.

Bogdanoff, M. and Elbaum, P. L. "Role Lock: Dealing with Monopolizers, Mistrusters, Isolates, Helpful Hannahs and Other Assorted Characters in Group Psychotherapy." *International Journal of Group Psychotherapy*, 1978, 28(2), 247–262.

Bordelon, T. D. "A Qualitative Approach to Developing an Instrument for Assessing MSW Students' Group Work Performance." *Social Work with Groups*, 2006, 29, 75–91.

Bowles, D. D. "Black Humor as Self-Affirmation." *Journal of Multicultural Social Work*, 1994, 3(2), 1–9.

Brandler, S. "Poetry, Group Work, and the Aged." *Journal of Gerontological Social Work*, 1979, 1(4), 295–310.

Brandler, S. "The Senior Center: Informality in the Social Work Function." In *Gerontological Social Work Practice in the Community*. G. Getzel and J. Mellor, Eds. Binghamton, NY: The Haworth Press, 1985, pp. 195–211.

Brandt, L. "A Short-Term Group Therapy Model for Treatment of Adult Female Survivors of Childhood Incest." *Group*, 1989, 13(2), 74–82.

Brayboy, T. "The Black Patient in Group Therapy." *International Journal of Group Psychotherapy*, 1971, 21(3), 288–293.

Breitman, B. "Jewish Identity and Ethnic Ambivalence: The Challenge for Clinical Practice." *Journal of Jewish Communal Service*, 1983, 60(2), 129–137.

Brown, N. "Conceptualizing Process." *International Journal of Group Psychotherapy*, 2003, 53, 225–242.

Bryant, N. "Domestic Violence and Group Treatment for Male Batterers." *Group*, 1994, 18(4), 235–242.

Buckingham, S. and Van Gorp, W. "AIDS Dementia: Essential Knowledge for Social Workers." *Social Work*, 1988, 2, 112–116.

Buckingham, S. and Van Gorp, W. "AIDS-Dementia: Complete Implications for Practice." *Social Casework*, 1988, 69(6), 371–375.

Caffaro, J. V.and Conn-Caffara, A. "Sibling Dynamics and Group Psychotherapy." *International Journal of Group Psychotherapy*, 2003, 53, 135–154.

Camacho, S. "Addressing Conflict Rooted in Diversity: The Role of the Facilitator." *Social Work with Groups*, 2001, 24, 35–152.

Caputo, L. "Dual Diagnosis: AIDS and Addiction." *Social Work*, 1985, 30(4), 361–364.

Chen, M. and Han, Y. "Cross-Cultural Group Counseling with Asians: A Stage Specific Interactive Approach." *The Journal of Specialists in Group Work*, 2006, 26(2), 111–128.

Churchill, S. "A Comparison of Two Models in Social Group Work: The Treatment Model and Reciprocal Model." In *Individual Change through Small Groups*. P. Glasser, R. Sarri, and R. Vinter, Eds. New York: Free Press, 1974.

Cohen, B. D. "On Scapegoating in Therapy Groups: A Social Constructivist and Intersubjective Outlook." *International Journal of Group Psychotherapy*, 2002, 52, 89–110.

Cohen, S. L. "Working with Resistance to Experiencing and Expressing Emotions in Group Therapy." *The International Journal of Group Psychotherapy*, 1997, 47(4), 443–458.

Coleman, E. "Developmental Stages of the Coming out Process." *The Journal of Homosexuality*, 1981–1982, 7(2/3), 31–43.

Congress, E. and Lynn, M. "Group Work Practice in the Community: Navigating the Slippery Slope of Ethical Dilemmas." *Social Work with Groups*, 1997, 20, 61–73.

Coser, L. A. *The Functions of Social Conflict*. Glencoe, IL: Free Press, 1956.

Coyle, G. L. *Group Experience and Democratic Values*. New York: Woman's Press, 1947.

Croxton, T. A. "The Therapeutic Contract in Social Treatment." In *Individual Change Through Small Groups*. P. Glasser and R. Sarri, Eds., 2nd ed. New York: Macmillan, 1985, pp. 169–185.

Currie, M. "Doing Anger Differently: A Group Percussion Therapy for Angry Adolescent Boys." *International Journal of Group Psychotherapy*, 2004, 54, 275–294.

Daley, B. S. and Koppenael, G. S. "The Treatment of Women in Short-Term Women's Groups." In *Forms of Brief Therapy*. S. H. Budman, Ed. New York: Guilford Press, 1981, pp. 343–357.

Daniele, R. and Gordon, R. "Interpersonal Conflict in Group Therapy: An Object Relations Perspective." *Group*, 1996, 20(4), 303–331.

Davis, L. E. "Group Work Practice with Ethnic Minorities of Color." In *Individual Change through Small Groups*. M. Sundel, P. Glasser, and R. Sarri, Eds. New York: Free Press, 1986, pp. 324–344.

Davis, L. F. "Essential Components of Group Work with Black Americans." *Ethnicity in Social Work Practice*. Binghamton, NY: The Haworth Press, 1984, pp. 92–109.

Davis, M. S. *What's So Funny? The Comic Conception of Culture and Society*. Chicago, IL: University of Chicago Press, 1993.

Davis, M., Sharfstein S., and Owens, M. "Separate and Together: All Black Therapy Group in the White Hospital." *American Journal of Orthopsychiatry*, 1974, 44, 19–25.

De Anda, D. and Riddel, V. "Ethnic Identity and Self-Esteem and Interpersonal Relationships among Multi-Ethnic Adolescents." *The Journal of Multicultural Social Work*, 1991, 1(2), 83–98.

Debiak, D. "Attending to Diversity in Group Psychotherapy: An Ethical Imperative." *International Journal of Group Psychotherapy*, 2007, 57(1), 1–12.

DeChant, B., Ed. *Women and Group Psychotherapy Theory and Practice.* New York: Guilford Press, 1997.

Delois, K. and Cohen, M. "A Queer Idea: Using Group Work Principles to Strengthen Learning in a Sexual Minorities Seminar." *Social Work with Groups*, 2000, 23, 53–68.

Dessel, A., Rogge, M., and Garlington, S. "Using Intergroup Dialogue to Promote Social Justice and Change." *Social Work*, 2006, 51, 303–315.

Dickey, L. M. and Loewy, M. I. "Group Work with Transgender Clients." *The Journal for Specialists in Group Work*, 2010, 35(3), 236–245.

Doel, M. "Difficult Behaviors in Groups." *Social Work with Groups*, 2005, 28(1), 3–22.

Dolgoff, R., Lowenberg, F. M., and Harrington, D. *Ethical Decisions for Social Work Practice*, 7th ed. Belmont, CA.: Brooks/Cole, 2005.

Drum, K. "The Essential Power of Group Work." *Social Work with Groups*, 2006, 29(2/3), 27–41.

Dub, F. S. "The Pivotal Group Member: A Study of Treatment-Destructive Resistance in Group Therapy." *The International Journal of Group Psychotherapy*, 1997, 47(3), 333–353.

Duffy, T. "The Check-In and Other Go-rounds in Group Work: Guidelines for Use." *Social Work with Groups*, 1994, 17,163–175.

Duffy, T. "White Gloves and Cracked Vases: How Metaphors Help Group Workers Construct New Perspective and Responses." *Social Work with Groups*, 2000, 24, 89–99.

Duncan, S. C. "On the Group Entity." *The International Journal of Group Psychotherapy*, 1995, 45(1), 37–54.

Dunkel, J. and Hatfield, S. "Countertransference Issues in Working with Persons with AIDS." *Social Work*, 1986, 31, 114–119.

Ehrenberg, D. B. "Self-Disclosure: Therapeutic Tool or Indulgence?" *Contemporary Psychoanalysis*, 1995, 31, 213–228.

Eidelson, R. J. and Eidelson, J. I. "Five Beliefs that Propel Groups Toward Conflict." *American Psychologist*, 2003, 58, 182–192.

Encyclopedia of Social Work, 19th ed. Washington, DC: NASW Press, 1995.

Epstein, L. "Some Reflections on the Therapeutic Use of the Self." *Group*, 1990, 14(3), 151–156.

Epstein, M. *The Trauma of Everyday Life.* New York: The Penguin Press, 2013.

Ettin, M. F., Herman, M., and Kopel, S. "Group Building: Developing Protocols for Psychoeducational Groups." *Group*, 1988, 12(4), 205–226.

Evans, S., Chisholm, P., and Walshe, P. "A Dynamic Psychotherapy Group for the Elderly." *Group Analysis*, 2001, 34, 287–298.

Faulkner, J. E., Ed. *Sociology through Humor.* St. Paul, MN: West, 1987.

Fenchel, G. H. and Flapan, D. "Resistance in Group Psychotherapy." *Group*, 1985, 9(2), 35.

Fieldsteel, N. "The Termination Phase of Combined Therapy." *Group*, 1990, 14(1), 27–32.

Fieldsteel, N. "When the Therapist Says Goodbye." *International Journal of Group Psychotherapy*, 2005, 55, 245–279.

Flores, P. J. *Group Psychotherapy with Addicted Populations: An Integration of Twelve-Step and Psychodynamic Theory*, 2nd ed. Binghamton, NY: Hayworth Press, 1997.

Fluegelman, A., Ed. *The New Games Book*. New York: Doubleday, 1976.

Fluegelman, A., Ed. *More New Games*. New York: Doubleday, 1981.

Friedman, R. M. "Psychodynamic Group Therapy for Male Survivors of Sexual Abuse." *Group*, 1994, 18(4), 225–234.

Frost, J. C. "Support Groups for Medical Caregivers of People with HIV Diseases." *Group*, 1994, 18(3), 141–153.

Frost, J. C. "Countertransference Considerations for the Gay Male when Leading Psychotherapy Groups for Gay Men." *The International Journal of Group Psychotherapy*, 1998, 48(1), 3–24.

Gabriel, M. "Co-Therapy Relationships: Special Issues and Problems in Aids Therapy Groups." *Group*, 1993, 17(1), 33–42.

Galinsky, M. J. and Schopler, J. "Open-Ended Groups: Patterns of Entry and Exit." *Social Work with Groups*, 1988, 8(2), 67–80.

Gans, J. "The Leader's Use of Indirect Communication in Group Therapy." *International Journal of Group Psychotherapy*, 1996, 46, 209–228.

Gans, J. and Counselman, E. "Silence in Group Psychotherapy: A Powerful Communication." *International Journal of Group Psychotherapy*, 1999, 50, 71–86.

Garvin, C. D. *Contemporary Group Work*. Englewood Cliffs, NJ: Prentice-Hall, 1981.

Geller, J. J. "Concerning the Size of Therapy Groups." In *Group Psychotherapy and Group Function*. M. Rosenbaum and M. Berger, Eds. New York: Basic Books, 1963, pp. 413–414.

Gerzy, B. and Sultenfuss, J. "Group Psychotherapy on State Hospital Admission Wards." *The International Journal of Group Psychotherapy*, 1995, 45(1), 1–15.

Getzel, G. "Old People, Poetry and Groups." *Journal of Gerontological Social Work*, 1980, 3(1), 77–85.

Getzel, G. and Mahoney, K. "Confronting Human Finitude: Group Work with People with AIDS." Paper presented at *Tenth Symposium of the Committee for the Advancement of Social Work with Groups*, October 29, 1988.

Gilbert, M. C. and Beidler, A. E. "Using the Narrative Approach in Groups for Chemically Dependent Mothers." *Social Work with Groups*, 2001, 23, 101–115.

Gitterman, A. and Shulman, L., Eds. *Mutual Aid Groups and the Life Cycle*. Itasca, IL: Peacock Publishers, 1986.

Gitterman, A and Shulman, L., Eds. *Mutual Aid Groups, Vulnerable and Resilient Populations and the Life Cycle*. New York: Columbia University Press, 2005.

Glodich, A., Allen, J., Fultz, J., Thompson, G., Arnold-Whitney, C., Varvil, C., et al. "School Based Psychoeducation Groups in Training Designed to Decrease Reenactment." In *Handbook of Community Based Clinical Practice*. A. Lightburn and P. Sessions, Eds. New York: Oxford University, 2005, pp. 349–363.

Gordon, R. "The Two-Minute Check-in at the Beginning of Psychoanalytic Group Therapy session." *Group Analysis*, 2008, 41, 366–372.

Green, T. and Stiers, M. "Multiculturalism and Group Therapy in the United States: A Social Constructionist Perspective." Group, 2002, 26, 233–246.

Gregson, B. The Incredible Indoor Games Book. Belmont, CA: David S. Lake Publishers, 1982.

Grump, P. L. "The 'It' Role in Children's Games." The Group, 1955, 17(3).

Grundy, D. "What Is a Writing Group? Dilemmas of the Leader." International Journal of Group Psychotherapy, 2007, 57, 133–151.

Gumpert, J. and Black, P. "Ethical Issues in Group Work: What are they? How Are They Managed?" Social Work with Groups, 2007, 29, 61–74.

Hahn, W. K. "Resolving Shame in Group Psychotherapy." The International Journal of Group Psychotherapy, 1994, 44(4), 449–461.

Hammer, E. "Use of Metaphor in Individual and Group Therapy: Interpretations Couched in the Poetic Style." International Journal of Psychoanalytic Psychotherapy, 1978–1979, 7(2), 240–253.

Haney, P. "Providing Empowerment to the Person with AIDS." Social Work, 1988, 33(3), 251–253.

Harrison, M. For the Fun of It: Selective Cooperative Games for Children and Adults. Philadelphia: Nonviolence and Children Series, Friends Peace Conference, 1976.

Hepworth, D. H. and Larsen, J. A. Direct Social Work Practice: Theories and Skills. Belmont, CA: Wadsworth Press, 1990.

Hofflet, R. O. How to Lead Informal Singing. New York: Abingdon Press, 1963.

Holmes, L. "Women in Groups and Women's Groups." International Journal of Group Psychotherapy, 2002, 52, 171–188.

Holmes, L. "Gender Dynamics in Group Therapy." Group, 2011, 35(3), 197–206.

Houston, K. and Speakman, N. Wide Games (Activities for Large Groups). Allentown, PA: Outdoor Adventure Enterprises, 1979.

Huth-Bocks, A., Schettini, A., and Shebroe, V. "Group Play Therapy for Preschoolers Exposed to Domestic Violence." Journal of Child and Adolescent Group Therapy, 2011, 11(1), 19–34.

Jacques, J. R. "Working with Spiritual and Religious Themes in Group Therapy." International Journal of Group Psychotherapy, 1998, 48, 69–83.

Jenkins, D. A. "Changing Family Dynamics: A Sibling Comes Out." Journal of GLBT Family Studies, 2008, 4, 1–16.

Jennings, S. Creative Drama in Group Work. London: Winslow Press, 1986.

Kaminsky, M. What's Inside You it Shines out of You. New York: Horizon Press, 1974.

Kaminsky, M. "The Users of Reminiscence: New Ways of Working with Older Adults." Journal of Gerontological Social Work, 1984, 7(1/2), 3–18.

Kanas, N., DiLella, V., and Jones, D. "Process and Content in an Outpatient Schizophrenic Group." Group, 1981, 5(2), 3–10.

Kanas, N., Stewart, P., and Deri, J. "Group Process in Short-Term Outpatient Therapy Groups for Schizophrenics." Group, 1989, 13(2), 67.

Kauff, P. A. "The Termination Process: Its Relationship to the Separation Individuation Phase of Development." International Journal of Group Psychotherapy, 1977, 27(1), 3–18.

Kelly, T. and Berman-Rossi, T. "Advancing Stages of Group Development Theory: The Case of Institutionalized Older Person." Social Work with Groups, 1999, 22, 119–138.

Kendler, H. "Truth and Reconciliation": Workers' fears of conflicts in groups. *Social Work with Groups*, 2002, 25, 25–41.

Kirk, A. B. and Madden, L. "Trauma Related Critical Incident Debriefing for Adolescents." *Child and Adolescent Social Work Journal*, 2003, 20, 123–134.

Kirst-Ashman, K. and Hull, G. *Understanding Generalist Practice*, 5th ed. Pacific Grove, CA: Nelson-Hall Publishers, 2009.

Knauss, L. K. "Ethical Issues in Record Keeping in Group Psychotherapy." *International Journal of Group Psychotherapy*, 2006, 56, 415–430.

Koch, K. *I Never Told Anybody.* New York: Random House, 1977.

Kolodny, R. L. "The Dilemma of Co-Leadership." *Social Work with Groups*, 1980, 3(4), 31–34.

Konopka, G. *Therapeutic Group Work with Children.* Minneapolis, MN: University of Minnesota Press, 1949.

Kraus, R. *Recreation Leaders' Handbook.* New York: McGraw-Hill, 1955.

Kurland, R. "Stages of Group Development." Hunter College School of Social Work, 1975, mimeo.

Kurland, R. "Racial Differences and Human Commonality: The Worker-Client Relationship." *Social Work with Groups*, 2002, 25, 113–118.

Kurland, R. "Planning: The Neglected Component of Group Development." *Social Work with Groups*, 2005, 28, 9–16.

Kurland, R. "Debunking the 'Blood Theory' of Social Work with Groups: Workers are Made and Not Born." *Social Work with Groups*, 2007, 30(1), 11–24.

Kurland, R. and Salmon, R. "Not Just One of the Gang: Group Workers and Their Roles as an Authority." *Social Work with Groups*, 1993, 16, 153–169.

Kurland, R., and Salmon, R. "Purpose: Misunderstood and Misused Keystone of Group Work Practice." *Social Work with Groups*, 1998, 21, 5–17.

Kurland, R., Getzel, G., and Salmon, R. "Sowing Groups in Infertile Fields," In *Innovations in Social Group Work: Feedback from Practice to Theory.* M. Parries, Ed. Binghamton, NY: The Haworth Press, 1986, pp. 57–74.

La Sala, M. C. "Lesbians, Gay Men, and Their Parents: Family Therapy for the Coming out Crisis." *Family Process*, 2000, 39, 67–79.

Langs, R. *The Technique of Psychoanalytic Psychotherapy, Vol. 1.* New York: Jason Aronson, 1973.

Levine, B. *Group Psychotherapy: Practice and Development.* Englewood Cliffs, NJ: Prentice-Hall, 1979.

Lietz, C. "Strengths-Based Group Practice: Three Case Studies." *Social Work with Groups*, 2007, 30(2), 73–88.

Lopez, D. and Getzel, G. "Survival Strategies for Volunteers Working with Persons with AIDS." *Social Casework*, 1987, 68(1), 47–53.

Luepnitz, D. *The Family Interpreted: Feminist Theory in Clinical Practice.* New York: Basic Books, 1988.

McGee, T. F. and Schulman, B. N. "The Nature of the Co-Therapy Relationship." *International Journal of Group Psychotherapy*, 1970, 20, 25–36.

Macgowan, M. "Increasing Engagement in Groups: A Measurement Based Approach." *Social Work with Groups*, 2003, 26, 5–28.

McNicoll, P. "A Group Worker Responds to a Mission-Based Model for Social Work." *Social Work with Groups*, 2008, 31(1), 25–28.

Malekoff, A. *Group Work with Suburbia's Children*. Binghamton, NY: Haworth Press, 1991.

Malekoff, A. *Group Work with Adolescents: Principles and Practice*. New York: Guilford Press, 2007.

Manigione, L., Forti, R., and Iacuzzi, C. "Ethics and Endings in Group Psychotherapy: Saying Good-bye and Saying it Well." *International Journal of Group Psychotherapy*, 2007, 57, 25–40.

Markus, H. E., and Abernethy, A. D. "Joining with Resistance: Addressing Reluctance to Engage in Group Therapy Training." *International Journal of Psychotherapy*, 2001, 51, 191–205.

Mason, S. and Vazquez, D. "Making Positive Changes: A Psychoeducation Group for Parents with HIV/AIDS." *Social Work with Groups*, 2007, 30, 27–40.

Mazza, N. and Price, B. "When Time Counts: Poetry and Music in Short-Term Group Treatment." *Social Work with Groups*, 1985, 8(2), 53–66.

Middleman, R. *The Non-Verbal Method in Working with Groups: The Use of Activities in Teaching, Counseling, and Therapy*. Hebron, CT: Practitioner's Press, 1980.

Millan, F. and Ivory, L. I. "Group Therapy with the Multiply Oppressed: Treating Latino, HIV-infected, Injecting Drug Users." *Group*, 1994, 18(3), 154–166.

Mishna, F. and Muskat, B. "Social Group Work for Young Offenders with Learning Disabilities." *Social Work with Groups*, 2001, 24, 11–31.

Monahan, J. R. "Developing and Facilitating Aids Bereavement Support Groups." *Group*, 1994, 18(3), 177–185.

Mones, P. "Verbal Communication Level and Anxiety in Psychotherapeutic Groups." *Journal of Counseling Psychology*, 1974, 21(3), 399–403.

Monette, P. *Becoming a Man: Half a Life Story*. New York: Harcourt Brace Jovanovich Publishing, 1992.

Mulkay, M. *On Humor: Its Nature and its Place in Modern Society*. New York: Basil Blackwell, 1988.

Musselman, V. *The Day Camp Program Book: An Activity Manual for Counselors*. New York: Association Press, 1947.

Normand, W., Iglesian, J., and Payn, S. "Brief Group Therapy to Facilitate Utilization of Mental Health Services by Spanish Speaking Patients." *American Journal of Orthopsychiatry*, 1974, 44(4), January 37–42.

Northen, H. and Kurland, R. *Social Work with Groups*, 3rd ed. New York: Columbia University Press, 2001.

Nosko, A. "Adventures in Co-leadership in Social Group Work Practice." *Social Work with Groups*, 2002, 25, 175–183.

Nosko, A. and Wallace, R. "Female/male Co-Leadership in Groups." *Social Work with Groups*, 1997, 20, 2–16.

Orlick, T. *The Cooperative Spoils and Game Book: Challenge without Competition*. New York: Pantheon Books, 1978.

Ormont, L. *The Group Therapy Experience: From Theory to Practice*. New York: St. Martin's Press, 1992.

Ormont, L. "The Leader's Role in Resolving Resistance to Intimacy in Group Setting." In *The Technique of Group Treatment: The Collected Papers of Louis R. Ormont*. L. Furgeri, Ed. Madison, CT: Psychosocial Press, 1993, pp. 85–100.

Ormont, L. "Cultivating the Observing Ego in the Group Setting." *The International Journal of Group Psychotherapy*, 1994, 45(4), 489–506.

Ormont, L. "The Craft of Bridging." In *The Technique of Group Treatment: The Collected Papers of Louis R. Ormont.* L. Furgeri, Ed. Madison, CT: Psychosocial Press, 2001, pp. 263–277.

Ormont, L. "The Leader's Role in Dealing with Aggression in Groups." In *The Technique of Group Treatment: The Collected Papers of Louis R. Ormont.* L. Furgeri, Ed. Madison, CT: Psychosocial Press, 2002, pp. 299–320.

Papell, C. and Rothman, B. "Social Group Work Models: Possession and Heritage." *Journal of Education for Social Work*, 1960, 2, 67–77.

Papiasvili, A. and Severino, S. "Senior Citizens' Group: The Supervisory Process (A Case of Parallel Processes)." *Group*, 1986, 10(4), 211–217.

Pharr, S. *Homophobia: A Weapon of Sexism.* Little Rock, AR: Chardon Press, 1988.

Pinto R. "HIV Prevention for Adolescent groups: A Six Step Approach." *Social Work with Groups*, 2000, 23, 81–100.

Pollio, D. E. "Use of Humor in Crisis Intervention." *Families and Society*, 1995, 76(6), 376–384.

Pollio, D. E. "The Evidence Based Group Worker." *Social Work with Groups*, 2002, 25, 57–70.

Pressman, B. and Sheps, A. "Treating Wife Abuse: An Integrated Model." *The International Journal of Group Psychotherapy*, 1994, 44(4), 477–499.

Regehr, C. and Hill, J. "Evaluating the Efficacy of Crisis Debriefing Groups." *Social Work with Groups*, 2002, 23, 69–79.

Retholz, T. "The Single Session Group: An Innovative Approach to the Waiting Room." *Social Work with Groups*, 1985, 8(2), 143–146.

Rice, A. H. "Evaluating Brief Structured Group Treatment of Depression." *Research on Social Work Practice*, 2001, 9, 148–171.

Rice, D., Fey, W., and Kepecs, J. "Therapists' Experience and Style as Factors in Co-Therapy." *Family Process*, 1971, 11(1), 1–12.

Rittner, B. and Smyth, N. J. "Time-limited Cognitive-behavior Group Interventions with Suicidal Adolescents." *Social Work with Groups*, 1999, 22, 55–75.

Rogers, C. R. *A Way of Being.* Boston, MA: Houghton Mifflin, 1980.

Rohnke, K. *Silver Bullets: A Guide to Initiative Problems, Adventure Games, Stunts and Trust Activities.* Hamilton, MA: Project Adventure, 1984.

Roman, C. A. "It is Not Always Easy to Sit on Your Mouth." *Social Work with Groups*, 2002, 25(1/2), 61–64.

Roman, C. A "Group Worker's Personal Grief and Its Impact on Processing a Group's Termination." *Social Work with Groups*, 2006, 29(2/3), 235–242.

Rose, S. "Coping Skill Training in Groups." *International Journal of Group Psychotherapy*, 1989, 39(1), 59.

Rosenbaum, M., Ed. *Handbook of Short-Term Therapy Groups.* New York: McGraw-Hill, 1983.

Rosenthal, L. "New Member 'Infanticide' in Group Psychotherapy." *International Journal of Group Psychotherapy*, 1992, 42, 277–286.

Rosenthal, L. "Castouts and Dropouts: Premature Termination in Group Analysis." *Modern Psychoanalysis*, 2005, 30, 40–53.

Rutan, J. S., Alonso, A., and Molin, R. "Handling the Absence of Group Leaders: To Meet or Not to Meet." *International Journal of Group Psychotherapy*, 1984, 34(2), 273–287.

Sapia, J. "Using Groups for Preventing Eating Disorders among College Women." *The Journal for Specialists in Group Work*, 2001, 26, 256–266.

Scheidlinger, S. "On the Concept of the Mother Group." *International Journal of Group Psychotherapy*, 1974, 24(4), 417–428.

Scheidlinger, S. "On Scapegoating in Group Psychotherapy." *International Journal of Group Psychotherapy*, 1982, 32(2), 131–143.

Schiffer, M. *Children's Group Therapy.* New York: Free Press, 1984.

Schneider, R. "Group Bereavement Support for Spouses Who are Grieving the Loss of a Partner to Cancer." *Social Work with Groups*, 2006, 29(2/3), 259–278.

Schoel, J., Prouty, D., and Radcliffe, P. *Islands of Healing—A Guide to Adventure-Based Counseling.* Hamilton, MA: Project Adventure, 1988.

Schopler, J. and Galinsky, M. "Can Open-ended Groups Move Beyond Beginnings?" *Small Group Research*, 1990, 21, 435–449.

Schulman, L. "Learning to Talk About Taboo Subjects: A Lifelong Professional Challenge." *Social Work with Groups*, 2002, 25, 139–150.

Secemsky, V. "Managing Conflict: The Development of Comfort among Social Workers." *Social Work with Groups*, 1999, 21, 35–48.

Shapiro, E. and Ginzberg, R. "Parting Gifts: Termination Rituals in Group Therapy." *International Journal of Group Psychotherapy*, 2002, 52, 319–336.

Shaw, S. B. "A Modern Psychoanalytic Approach to Caregiver Support Groups." *Group*, 1997, 21(2), 159–174.

Shechtmann, Z. "Prevention Groups for Angry and Aggressive Children." *The Journal of Specialists in Group Work*, 2001, 26, 228–236.

Shen, I. "Talking with Adolescents About Race and Ethnicity: What a Group Worker Needs." *Social Work with Groups*, 2003, 26, 61–75.

Shilts, R. *And the Band Played On.* New York: St. Martin's Press, 1987.

Shulman, L. "Scapegoats, Group Workers, and Pre-emptive Intervention." *Social Work*, 1967, 12(2), 37–43.

Silverstein, J. L. "Acting-Out in Group Therapy: Avoiding Authority Struggles." *International Journal of Group Psychotherapy*, 1997, 1(January), 31–45.

Simon, J. "The Group Therapist's Absence and Substitute Leader." *International Journal of Group Psychotherapy*, 1992, 42, 289–291.

Simonton, S. and Sherman, A. "An Integrated Model of Group Treatment for Cancer Patients." *International Journal of Group Psychotherapy*, 2000, 50, 487–505.

Siporin, M. "Have You Heard the One About Social Work Humor?" *Social Casework*, 1984, 65(8), 459–464.

Smith, C. A. *From Wonder to Wisdom: Using Stories to Help Children Grow.* New York: New American Library, 1989.

Smith, L. C. and Shin, R. Q. "Social Privilege, Social Justice and Group Counseling: An Inquiry." *Journal for Specialists in Group Work*, 2008, 33, 351–366.

Smith, L. and Vannicelli, M. "Co-Leader Termination in an Out-Patient Alcohol Treatment Group." *Group*, 1985, 9(3), 49.

Sobel, J. *Everybody Wins: Noncompetitive Games for Young Children.* New York: Walker, 1983.

Spolin, V. *Theater Games for the Classroom: A Teacher's Handbook.* Evanston, IL: Northwestern University Press, 1986.

Springer, S., Pomroy, R. V., and Johnson, T. "A Group Intervention for Children of Incarcerated Parents: Initial Pitfalls and Subsequent Solutions." *Groupwork*, 1999, 11(1), 54–70.

Steinberg, D. M. "She's Doing All the Talking So What's In It for Me? (The Use of Time in Groups)." *Social Work with Groups*, 2006, 28, 173–185.

Thomas, H. and Caplan, T. "Spinning the Group Process Wheel: Effective Facilitation Techniques for Motivating Involuntary Client Groups." *Social Work with Groups*, 1999, 21, 3–21.

Tsui, P. and Schultz, G. L. "Ethnic Factors in Group Process: Cultural Dynamics in Multi-Ethnic Therapy Groups." *American Journal of Orthopsychiatry*, 1988, 58(1), 136–142.

Tuckman, A. and Finkselstein, H. "Simultaneous Roles: When Group Co-therapists Also Share a Supervisory Relationship." *The Clinical Supervisor*, 1999, 18, 185–201.

Ulman, K. "The Ghost in the Group Room: Countertransferential Pressures Associated with Conjoint Individual and Group Psychotherapy." *International Journal of Group Psychotherapy*, 2002, 52, 387–407.

Van Duesen, K. M. and Carr, J. L. "Group Work at a University: A Psychoeducational Sexual Assault Group for Women." *Social Work with Groups*, 2004, 27, 51–54.

Van Wormer, K. and Boes, M. "Humor in the Emergency Room: A Social Work Perspective." *Health & Social Work*, 1997, 22(2), 87–92.

Vannicelli, M. "Leader Dilemmas and Countertransference Considerations in Group Psychotherapy with Substance Abusers." *International Journal of Group Psychotherapy*, 2001, 51, 89–99.

Vichnis, R. "Passing the Baton: Principles and Implications for Transferring the Leadership of a Group." *Social Work with Groups*, 1999, 22, 130–157.

Virshup, E. "Latency Group Art Therapy: Teaching Socialization Skills through Art." *Child Welfare*, 1980, 54(9), 624–644.

Waldman, E. "Co-Leadership as a Method of Training: A Student's Point of View." *Social Work with Groups*, 1980, 3(1), 51–58.

Wallas, L. *Stories for the Third Ear: Using Hypnotic Fables in Psychotherapy.* New York: W. W. Norton, 1985.

Washington, O. M. and Moxley, D. P. "The Use of Prayer in Group Work with African American Women Recovering from Chemical Dependency." *Families in Society*, 2001, 82, 49–59.

Washington, O. G. and Moxley, D. P. "Promoting Group Practice to Empower Low-income Minority Women Coping with Chemical Dependency." *American Journal of Orthopsychiatry*, 2003, 73, 109–116.

Weinberg, H. "Group Process and Group Phenomenon on the Internet." *International Journal of Group Psychotherapy*, 2001, 51, 361–379.

Weinberg, H. "The Culture of Group and Groups from Different Cultures." *Group Analysis*, 2003, 36, 253–258.

Whittaker, J. K. "Differential Use of Program Activities in Child Treatment Groups." *Child Welfare*, 1976, 55(7), 459–467.

Williams, M. "Limitations, Phantasies, and Security Operations of Beginning Group Therapists." *International Journal of Group Psychotherapy*, 1966, 16(2), 15–62.

Wright, F. "Men, Shame, and Group Psychotherapy." *Group*, 1994, 18(4), 212–224.

Wright, F. "The Use of the Self in Group Leadership: A Relational Perspective." *International Journal of Group Psychotherapy*, 2000, 50, 181–199.

Yalom, I. D. *Inpatient Group Psychotherapy*. New York: Basic Books, 1983.

Yalom, I. D. *The Theory and Practice of Group Psychotherapy*, 3rd ed. New York: Basic Books, 1985.

Yalom, I. D. and Rand, K. "Compatibility and Cohesiveness in Therapy Groups." *Archives of General Psychiatry*, 1966, 13, 267–276.

Zampitella, C. "Adult Surviving Siblings: The Disenfranchised Grievers." *Group*, 2011, 35(4), 333–347.

Zaslav, M. and Kalb, R. D. "Medicine as Metaphor and Medium in Group Psychotherapy with Psychiatric Patients." *International Journal of Group Psychotherapy*, 1989, 39(4), 457–469.

INDEX